From Three Worlds

New Ukrainian Writing

Edited by
ED HOGAN

With Guest Editors
ASKOLD MELNYCZUK
MICHAEL NAYDAN
MYKOLA RIABCHUK
OKSANA ZABUZHKO

12

glas   Moscow & Birmingham

ZEPHYR PRESS
Boston, Massachusetts

Editors:
NATASHA PEROVA
ARCH TAIT

Editors for this issue:
ED HOGAN, ASKOLD MELNYCZUK,
MICHAEL NAYDAN, MYKOLA RIABCHUK,
OKSANA ZABUZHKO

This special issue is #12 in the series of *Glas: New Russian Writing.*

Design & production: Ed Hogan, with Giles Anderson, Anjali
   Gupta, Helena Lisovich, Kathleen O'Malley, Anna Panszczyk
Front cover: "Requiem" by Ivan Marchuk, 1993
Back cover: From a series, "The Rustling of Broken Stalks,"
   by Mykola Kumanovsky, late 1980s

GLAS Publishers (Russia)
Moscow 119517, P.O. Box 47, Russia • Tel./Fax: (095) 441-9157
E-mail: perova@glas.msk.su

GLAS Publishers (U.K.)
Department of Russian Literature, University of Birmingham,
Birmingham B15 2TT, U.K. • Tel./Fax: (121) 414-6047
E-mail: a.l.tait@bham.ac.uk

North American Sales & Editorial Office:
Zephyr Press, 13 Robinson Street, Somerville, MA 02145, U.S.A.
Tel: (617) 628-9726; fax: (617) 776-8246
E-mail: edhogan@world.std.com

ISBN 0-939010-52-6 (pbk)
ISBN 0-939010-53-4 (cl)
Library of Congress Catalog Card No. 96-61121

GLAS is indexed by the Modern Language Association (MLA).

The editors and publishers gratefully acknowledge the support of:
the National Endowment for the Arts, the Woskob Fund for Ukrainian Studies at
Pennsylvania State University, and the Dr. Iwan and Dr. Myroslawa Iwanciw
Fund for Ukrainian Studies at Pennsylvania State University.

NOTES: Words or phrases marked with an asterisk (*) have explanatory notes, which are found at the end of the stories. For the sake of clarity, "A Crowning Experience" by Kostiantyn Moskalets has footnotes.

We employ "Kiev" in this publication as the spelling of the capital city of Ukraine, since it is the one familiar to most readers. However, it should be noted that the present official spelling is "Kyiv," which is based upon transliteration from the Ukrainian language. This usage has become established in the years following the independence of Ukraine in 1991.

In the poetry, an asterisk at the bottom of a page indicates that there is no stanza break. By contrast, an asterisk at the bottom of a page of prose indicates a section break.

IN THE SUMMER OF 1993, I found myself on a train traveling from Budapest across the Carpathian Mountains and the broad plains of Ukraine to Kiev. At that moment, my knowledge of Ukrainian literature was almost nonexistent, but this was soon to change.

A few weeks before, Askold Melnyczuk, poet, novelist, and editor of *Agni Review,* had invited me to hear writer Volodymyr Dibrova give a reading at the summer language program of Harvard University's Ukrainian Research Institute. Although the reading was in a language I did not know, the response to Dibrova's tale about young Ukrainians struggling against collective farm boredom was so warm and enthusiastic that I gained a sudden perception of a national literature virtually unknown to English-speaking readers. I had the year before been appointed U.S. consulting editor to the Moscow-based independent journal, *Glas: New Russian Writing.* Then and there I conceived a proposal for a special issue showcasing contemporary Ukrainian writing.

Zephyr Press and *Glas* are proud to copublish *From Three Worlds: New Writing from Ukraine,* which makes available in English for the first time many of the best current exponents of a literature we do not know for one simple reason: under Communists and tsars alike, Ukrainian culture has been an endangered species. For most of the past 250 years, publication of books in Ukrainian has been severely limited or forbidden, as has university-level teaching in the Ukrainian language. Many educated Ukrainians paid the supreme price. In sweeping purges of 1930–32, a large part of the intelligentsia was arrested, sentenced to hard labor or executed in the first step of Stalin's campaign to reduce Ukraine — "this land of ours that is not ours," in the words of poet Taras Shevchenko — to submission. It is fair to say that Ukraine felt the heavy hand of the Red Terror first. By the end of the Thirties, "periodic waves of arrests and executions had virtually annihilated the intellectual and artistic cadres of Ukraine," writes Roman Szporluk in his *Ukraine: A Brief History.*

In Ukraine as elsewhere in the U.S.S.R., the penalties for being a disapproved writer slowly moderated after the mid-1950's. Many of the writers in this collection participated in a vigorous literary underground, but could not publish officially until the end of the 1980's.

To the degree *From Three Worlds* succeeds in its goal of introducing contemporary Ukrainian writing, it is absolutely dependent upon the contributions of the four Guest Editors. Our selection of authors relied, in the first place, on the nominations of Kiev-based editor and critic Mykola Riabchuk and poet Oksana Zabuzhko. Askold Melnyczuk and Michael Naydan, chairman of the Slavic Department at Pennsylvania State University and indefatigable translator of Ukrainian as well as Russian authors, made further suggestions, affording us the opportunity of considering quite a wide body of work.

To my surprise, the fiction in particular suggests a stronger affinity with American writing than with that of Russian contemporaries. If this is true, perhaps it is because the Ukrainians seem more concerned with the style and the story than their more discursive and philosophical Russian brethren.

The translations were for the most part prepared by native speakers working with accomplished American writers, mediated by the editors. It made for a complex collaboration, but since no comparable publication is available at this writing, we felt the work demanded nothing less.

We thank all of our translators. Without their dedication and inspiration, these stories and poems would be mere dry bones. Solomea Pavlychko, author, critic and editorial director of Osnovy Publishers, has been a key participant from the beginning. Askold Melnyczuk and Michael Naydan in particular have provided aid and comfort in more ways than I can name. I would also like to express our appreciation to the following for their assistance in bringing this project to fruition: Andriy Bondar, Robert De Lossa and the Ukrainian Research Institute at Harvard University, Roman Procyk and the Ukrainian Studies Fund, Basil Fedun, Marianna Lisovich, Edward and Olena Melnyczuk, Dzvinia Orlowsky, and Mary Ann Szporluk.

We dedicate *From Three Worlds* to artist, writer, and translator Volodymyr Hruszkewycz (1943–95).

Ed Hogan
8/15/96

ACKNOWLEDGEMENTS

"Requiem" by Ivan Marchuk (front cover) and other works
by the artist on pages 19 & 20, are reproduced by permission.
Painting from a series, *The Rustling of Broken Stalks,* by
Mykola Kumanovsky (back cover) and other works by the artist
on pages 31–34, 119–120 & 137 are reproduced by permission.
Four bookplate etchings by Kumanovsky are used by
kind permission of George and Nina Woskob.
Photographs on pages 10, 76–87, 174–180, 225, and 265 are
by Tania D'Avignon, and are reproduced
by permission. All rights reserved.
"Clytemnestra" by Oksana Zabuzhko, translated by Lisa Sapinkopf,
is reprinted by permission of *Agni* Magazine.
"A Definition of Poetry" by Oksana Zabuzhko, translated by
Michael M. Naydan, is reprinted by permission of *Agni* Magazine.
"With a Bird," "One Syllable Missing," and "Remembrance" by
Vasyl Holoborodko, translated by Myrosia Stefaniuk, were first
published in *Icarus with Butterfly Wings* (Toronto: Exile Editions,
1991); they are reprinted by permission of the translator.

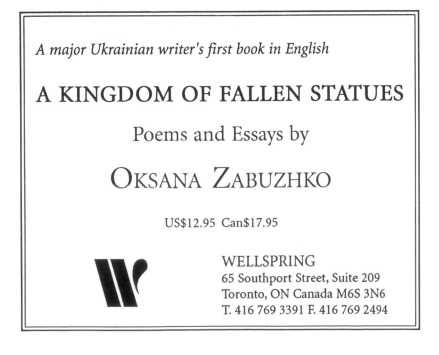

A major Ukrainian writer's first book in English

A KINGDOM OF FALLEN STATUES

Poems and Essays by

OKSANA ZABUZHKO

US$12.95 Can$17.95

WELLSPRING
65 Southport Street, Suite 209
Toronto, ON Canada M6S 3N6
T. 416 769 3391 F. 416 769 2494

Solomea
PAVLYCHKO

Facing Freedom: The New Ukrainian Literature

Translated by Askold Melnyczuk

I n the decade since Gorbachev's *perestroika*, the new Ukrainian literature has enjoyed an atmosphere of freedom it hasn't known for centuries. Many writers, however, experienced that freedom well before the country declared independence in 1991. Indeed, it was largely the inner freedom felt by writers and the intelligentsia that led to independence.

The evolving literary culture has no clear contours. A spate of esthetic possibilities flooded the mainstream simultaneously and those writers not lost in the rapids suddenly found themselves afloat on what Jefferson called "the boisterous seas of liberty." When they were finally cast ashore, they were like survivors of several shipwrecks who rush to greet each other only to discover that they barely share a language. These newly surfaced writers emerged from radically different circumstances. What could they have in common, these former dissidents and ex-Communists, the psychically scarred and the prodigies of privilege? Two things, anyway. All had stories to tell and, for the first time, all had the chance to compete for an audience.

The previous decade had been ugly. The Seventies were years of vicious repression and political pressure. Few risked open protest. At the same time, an artistic underground was gestating. Its ideas were grounded in Eastern philosophies stressing the autonomy of the individual, of an identity separate from society.

A philosophical and formal orientalism remains an essential characteristic of Oleh Lysheha, who in the mid-Seventies was involved in an attempt by young intellectuals from Lviv to publish the unofficial journal *Skrynia (The Chest)*. Another group, whose best known members were Mykola Vorobyov and Vasyl Holoborodko, passed poems among a small circle in Kiev. Then there were the so-called "metaphorists": the most original writers here were Vasyl Herasymiuk, Ihor Rymaruk, and Ivan Malkovych. Finally, the youngest generation fixated on the shattering of taboos in the spheres of language, theme, and form. The most skillful riders of this wave — Yuri Andrukhovych, Viktor Neborak, and Oleksandr Irvanets — announced their existence openly, calling their group Bu-Ba-Bu (which stands for Burlesque-Bluster-Buffoonery). The movements tended to overshadow writers who belonged to no school and subscribed to no ideology. Many of these loners happened to be women; Natalka Bilotserkivets, Liudmyla Taran and Oksana Zabuzhko are the most prominent. But there were also men, including Oleksandr Hrytsenko and Attyla Mohylny.

Moreover, publication of the forbidden classics of Ukrainian literature from the last centuries compelled virtually every writer to reconsider their place on the continuum of letters.

The eclecticism of the scene was reflected in the first, informal literary journals that appeared in the mid-Eighties. These were most often typewritten in many carbons, rendering some of them nearly illegible. And yet they were passed from hand to hand and widely discussed. Two places in Kiev where it was possible to meet the writers themselves were the apartment of Mykola Riabchuk, a critic, poet, prose writer, editor, publisher, and above all the catalyst for a new generation; and in the office of Ihor Rymaruk, who remains the poetry editor for the "Dnipro" publishing house. Informal literary readings first took place in the rooms and studios of individual writers and artists, among a narrow circle of friends, spreading gradually and semi-officially to various public lecture halls and finally ending up at the Writers' Union. The events electrified both writers and audiences, who understood that they were participating in a political and esthetic metamorphosis. It later became clear that these two not necessarily concentric revolutions had occurred simultaneously; both had great significance and helped free the culture from all manner of conventions, restrictions, and recipes.

Young writers held evening readings of erotic poetry — that it was suddenly possible to write about sex intoxicated them. This had, after all, been a forbidden subject since the Twenties. Moreover, one could write about the military, the brutality and violence of the Soviet regime, and about Lenin-Stalin-Trotsky and other related figures. Finally, writers needed to formulate some version of their national history. Was Ukraine an occupied territory, or had communism been a stabilizing agent binding together a heterogeneous population? What was Ukraine really like? What relationship did it bear to the country refigured by folk stories, or by the intelligentsia in the diaspora? And what was "my" role as a Ukrainian writer to be in the new society? What is "my" true literary heritage? The questions of inheritance and traditions inspired countless arguments.

In the "new" texts, words and sentences and syntax were broken (some of this had occurred in the Twenties, but as it had later been proscribed by the state, it felt entirely new). Raw obscenity and street idioms never before used in Ukrainian fiction or poetry, began appearing in print with some regularity. Western literatures had known similar euphorias over the breaking of taboos: first in the Thirties, and later in the Sixties. These days Henry Miller shocks no one; he merely annoys the feminists. However, the vulgate did open doors for new wave prose writers such as Bohdan Zholdak and Volodymyr Dibrova, as well as for a few poets, including Oleksandr Irvanets.

Another crucial change in attitude had to do with where a writer sought approval and empowerment. Heretofore, a writer remained unrecognized unless his or her book was published in Russia or until he or she was mentioned by an important Moscow literary critic. Suddenly Ukrainian writers lost interest in this game. Although the West remained indifferent to their work, a benediction from the East seemed irrelevant. Ukrainian literature began curing itself of an old and deep sense of provincialism, marginality, and inadequacy. She (literature) was no longer interested in the refined and specialized languages of the worker, the professor, or the collective farm director. Models of intellectual and esthetic orientation were shattering and writers began looking for approval from within.

Eclecticism still reigns: formalism, free verse, rap-influenced recitation all thrive side by side. The principal transformation in poetry, as well as in prose, had to do not with form but with diction. In the last years, urban sounds, anxieties, cynicism, and crude humor have won admission to the palace — no, make that the pub — of art.

Older critics tended to view these developments as little more than posturing and bravado. They simply couldn't see beyond Rymaruk's long hair or Pashkovsky's military boots, which really were imposing. (Alas, he no longer wears them.) The "hooligans" meanwhile mocked the language of politically engaged art at every turn while at the same time attending anti-Soviet demonstrations and gatherings outside Parliament, and supporting the students who held a hunger strike in October of 1990.

In 1991, Ukrainian independence, the most important event in the country's history in this century, freed writers enormously. As long as they remained stateless, they were more or less stuck with endlessly shoring up the foundation on which a literature might be built. All earlier attempts over the last hundred years at creating "art for the sake of art" had failed. Now, at last, writers can move beyond their role as missionaries proselytizing on behalf of the Ukrainian language. Today, for the first time, they have a choice. Those who wish to may work in politics, education, or as propagandists, using their gifts for ideological purposes. Others may rally under beauty's banner or, on the contrary, strive to shock with deliberate ugliness.

Neonationalists are not impressed by this liberation. They continue to claim that the new state, its spirituality, and its literature, do not accommodate them. They reject the influences of the West, declare religious belief the first sign of creative force, and aim at building "a true state" and a "real" national literature. It's not hard to understand their concern: Ukraine has not turned into the land of their dreams and the Ukrainianaphones remain an oppressed minority in most eastern Ukrainian cities.

Independence has, however, had even less happy consequences: it has created a crisis in publishing which is felt by every writer in the country. Ukraine does not have a single paper mill within its borders. Until 1992, the country had no independent publishers. The last books of Zholdak, Vynnychuk, Dibrova, Rymaruk, Herasymiuk and others were published in 1991. Only a handful of books appeared in 1992, and 1993 was the least fruitful year in the entire century for the publication of literature.

Government publishing houses went bankrupt and subscriptions to literary journals dropped sharply. The few remaining magazines are grossly behind schedule. As a rule, new periodicals put out no more than two or three issues before going bust. Freedom opened the floodgates on Western writing, above all on work from America and chiefly in Russian translation, which has overwhelmed the Ukrainian book market. Contemporary Ukrainian literature is hardly published. The things that do appear do not deserve to be called books as they are printed on awful paper in broken type with ragged covers.

Yet one journal, *Suchasnist (The Contemporary Scene)*, publishes new novels which are studied and debated by everyone who reads Ukrainian. Under other circumstances these works might become bestsellers, though at the moment they rarely appear as separate books. The literati are once again reduced to passing around typescripts.

The "new literature" is various, argumentative, and self-contradictory. The above mentioned Bu-Ba-Bu have survived a decade and now keep to themselves, remaining aloof even from their admirers, who tend to be "unserious," liberal, urban, cosmopolitan. For these readers, literary activity is a game in which the author plays hide and seek with the audience. The writers are formalists for whom the structural aspects of art dominate ideology and content.

Their antithesis are the "serious" artists, the neonationalists, the village stylists, as well as the professional pilgrims and mystics. The issue of "Ukrainianness" plays a key role in their theories, and they regularly refer to more than one generation of "fathers" and ancestors against whom they wish to be measured. In 1993 one such circle formed a group known as "The New Literature." Their ideologue, Yevhen Pashkovsky, had, by age 32, published four novels. His prose is far more original and interesting than his group's ideology, which smacks of pathos, pomposity, and partisanship. Pashkovsky, like his antipode Andrukhovych, is also a formalist. He is a writer of remarkable prose rhythms. For a while he was considered a genuine innovator; however, he remains essentially a moralist and would probably subscribe to the *sententia* published in an issue of the journal *Osnova:* "There are more important things in life than writing."

Until recently all discussions about socialist realism and dissident literature were conducted under the shadows cast by the walls of entirely unliterary and very real prisons. The most interesting works of the decade preceding *perestroika* are various writers' letters from prison and exile. Meanwhile, the more literary work of political dissidents, with minor exceptions, already feels dated.

Dissident writers were limited by their political programs. Those who abandoned polemics for fantasy and science fiction, new age philosophy, or esoteric poetry had an easier time creating the New, and emancipating themselves — and literature — from established canons: romanticism, populism, traditional verse forms or the conventions of the realistic novel.

It's difficult for some to accept that the days of "official" dissidence are over. They long to fight, to oppose the ruling elite. And the elite provides ample ground for opposition. However, it pays little attention to writers, leaving them bereft of the external pressure to which they'd grown so accustomed.

At the same time, all must face a gruesome legacy: the fate of

Ukrainian writers from the past. They lie buried inside a grave a century deep. During the seventy-year long existence of the USSR hundreds of Ukrainian writers were either murdered or died in prison. The first of these, Hryhory Chuprynka, was shot by the Bolsheviks in 1921. The last, Vasyl Stus, died in 1985 in a Siberian labor camp.

Aside from the actual physical plants of the numerous "correctional facilities" which threatened an entire society, there was a larger prison without walls spread across the entire country. The state ran a monstrous house of repression, and writers were merely its most dangerous denizens. Even some of the best known, most servile, officially celebrated party loyalists lived under the constant surveillance of the KGB.

And while recent history is already treated as a bad dream, it continues to paralyze the psyches of writers, knotting their thoughts and their hands. Almost all are trying to explain and understand a haunted past which gives them no peace. Without coming to terms with this, it's not possible to evaluate the current scene. That is why the past continues to impose itself on contemporary literature, which mainly describes the way things were rather than how they are.

Among the young, the past has given birth to feelings of guilt, inferiority, and fear. The newest literature wants first to condemn and then to forget it. In Yevhen Pashkovsky's essay, "Literature as Crime," he blames all those who accepted Soviet reality, and especially those who contributed to the creation of it. But he fails to see the danger in fostering a literature of retribution.

Retribution is in fact the business of the hero of Yuri Andrukhovych's novel *The Moskoviada*. His autobiographical hero is filled with hate for the empire and its capital, Moscow, although he is drawn there and spends most of his time in its vicinity. Hating it, he also hates himself, his weakness, his inner emptiness. Ukrainian prose has never had a hero this empty and alienated. But what is his view on the future? Does he intend to inhabit this loathing for his past and for himself forever? Or will analysis and confession liberate him from his complexes? I suspect the latter impulse will win; Ukrainian culture is growing increasingly critical not only of its traditionally hostile surroundings but also of itself.

Living inside the ruins of a prison produces one final, widespread mode of discourse: that of violence and cruelty. This began with stories about the army, which for a time appeared to be the central theme of a generation. The brutality of military life is consonant with the harshness of post-Soviet life in general. It is a life without love, saturated in reciprocal violence, where men rape women and women men, where prostitution, betrayal, and sexual cynicism are the norm in human relations.

The most interesting voices are those which are free of the "prison house complex," which aren't turned to the past, and don't rehearse the old myths or worship in the ancient temples, but instead breathe in the present. These belong mainly to a few women. They are more universal, without the note of rage animating their male colleagues. Most still rely on the patriarchal tradition in which they "sing" about the joys of motherhood, their love for their men, or the "tragic fate of Ukraine and Ukrainian women," producing various "laments." This offers male critics an excuse to unfairly group all women writers on the periphery of the traditionally masculine culture.

It's harder for them to deal with those who don't fit this stereo-type, as, for example, Oksana Zabuzhko. Hers is the surest female, and feminist, voice to sound in Ukrainian culture in a decade. Intel-lectual, smart, and logical in her prose, in her poetry she speaks as a woman of feeling, even passion. Zabuzhko is concerned with feelings, and not with the tortured sex obsessing the prose of the most brilliant male writers, who seem as yet unprepared for feelings. In their work, sex is primarily a necessary distraction, as well as an occasion for linguistic byplay. For her sharpness, sincerity, and intensity of poetic feeling, Oksana Zabuzhko may be compared to Sylvia Plath, whom she has, incidentally, translated into Ukrainian.

"Youth is over," said Andrukhovych nostalgically on the tenth anniversary of Bu-Ba-Bu. The new Ukrainian literature enjoyed a turbulent and ultimately lucky adolescence. What necessity it discovers as time moves on remains anyone's guess.

Born in 1936 in Moskalivka, western Ukraine, IVAN MARCHUK now resides in New York City. He graduated in 1965 from the Lviv Institute of Applied and Decorative Art, where his teacher was Roman Selsky, the greatest figure of Western Ukrainian artistic modernism, who had in turn been a student of Fernand Léger in Paris during the 1920's. Marchuk's work was exhibited in Moscow, Kiev and other Soviet cities from 1960 to 1989, including a 1979 show in the Malaya Grusinskaya Art Exhibition, the principal site for showing dissident art in Moscow. Only in 1990 was he officially recognized by the Soviet artistic establishment. More recently, his art has been exhibited in museums and galleries in the U.S., Canada, and Australia, including the Museum of Ukrainian Art, New York City; Multicultural Center, Cambridge, Mass.; Chaika Gallery, Detroit; the Ukrainian Cultural Center, Philadelphia; Five Ways Gallery, Sydney, Australia; and the Ukrainian Art Gallery in Toronto. His work has been noted by art critics in the American press, including Vladimir Voina in the *Boston Herald*, who wrote: "...Marchuk's paintings expressed the desire for independence, the pain and anger, the pride and hope of [his] people."

Front cover: "Requiem," 1993
19: "Melody," 1994
20: "Musicians," 1993

Volodymyr
DIBROVA

Beatles Songs

*Translated by James Brasfield
& Peter Ho Davies*

I Saw Her Standing There

One, two, three, four!...

In my fourth year of high school, I was friends with a boy named Okeksandr. Even then he could play great guitar. He taught himself two numbers for the school concert — "Twist-oo-gay" and "Gonzalez" — and recorded them on those thick old X-ray films you could make at the DIY record studio over on Red Army Street, not far from the public baths. You could record pop songs there — "Black Cat," "Haly-galy," "Love is a Never Ending Ring" — or just the sound of your own voice.

For instance:

"Dear Lyubov Omelianivno! Best Wishes on International Women's Day from Class 4B."

"Twist-oo-gay" and "Gonzalez" were at the bottom of the list. Next to where it said — "Folk songs. Amer."

Oleksandr and I translated the words of "Gonzalez" together:

Yo bete kuntome
Sheety Gonzalez
Oway om kindagroovy brue
Stob olof jo trinrin
Vizzat phoossy nay foo.

A guy at the studio promised he'd record some "beetles" or "beetniks" for us the next time we were there. Even our papers were full of them, how they smashed furniture and paraded about with toilet seats round their necks.

We'd agreed to go down to the studio together the next day but I was late. I was kicking my heels, waiting for the tram. At last it poked its nose round the corner, crept out of the side-street and rumbled down toward me. It was still twenty yards away when something went off under its wheels with a bright burst of sparks. The rails were streaked and a stench of sulfur filled the air. Some kids must have tossed matches under the tram.

I was about to jump on anyway when this interfering guy grabbed me by the collar and hauled me off to the police station, where a sergeant and a plain clothes cop threatened me with prison if I didn't write down exactly what had happened.

When I finally got out it was too late to make it to the studio so I went straight to Oleksandr's. He showed me the new X-ray film he'd picked up and switched on his old turntable. He'd got a new needle for it, specially. As soon as it touched the record those X-rayed ribs and bones began to crackle. We heard the sound of eggs breaking, frying. The record went round and round, picking up speed.

Gnash, grind went all our hissing enemies.

Moan, groan, hummed all our tongueless martyrs.

Then all of a sudden, it came at last, calling out—*One, two, three, four!*—the cheeky cry of freedom.

The Ballad of John and Yoko

The way things are going
They're gonna crucify me.

It's no big deal. Just another day of married life.

– Stop drinking, – she says.

– Why'd we come to this wedding in the first place? I want to know. Twenty-five rubles down the toilet.

I get up and dance with the bridesmaid. She's a real cracker, giving off sparks. It's good I didn't take my jacket off, she could burn a hole right though her frock and my cumberbund. Angela, her name is. A student. I want her number.

– Sit down and get a grip of yourself.

– Of what?

– People are looking.

– Like who?

– You're disgusting!

– What's wrong now?

– You call that dancing?

– You what?

– I'm warning you. I'll leave!

– Well, just don't forget to give me the coat check on your way out, or I'll freeze.

– Bastard!

– Listen, Valiunchyk, haven't we already been through this?

– I hate you!

What can you do with a jealous wife, eh? But she knows who's the boss. She knows who brings home the bacon. Five hundred rubles a month, minimum. But I'm not a machine. I enjoy a good time as much as the next guy.

– Stop drinking!

– Just a sip. There's only a little left at the bottom.

– It was full. You've swigged it!

– It's only Albanian brandy. You ought to try some. Go on. Just wet your whistle.

– Fuck off!

That bubbly neon goddess, Angela, is flashing looks at me. Hang on, you little vixen, just let them play something slow. Her strapping husband is giving me a look. What's up, comrade? It was only a dance.

A weathered ex-major is busy sounding off about how the air and the water aren't what they used to be. All along the Dnieper, before the dams were built, the river glittered with fish. Not like those muddy rivers the Siberians are always going on about. He's making it up as he goes along, but he's all right. He's related to someone on the groom's side. He says he has a tent, a boat, three spinning rods and an old jalopy. A nature nut. Anyway, halfway through the sermon he lost it and belched. I guess we're all human.

Across the hall there's a party of foreigners. Looks like another wedding.

– Now, do you mean azote or *ozone?* Can you be a little more precise?

A young woman, a professor by the look of her, is getting into it with the major. He's claiming there's a unique species of weeping willow, unknown outside our neck of the woods, growing on the banks of the Desna. According to him this willow charges the air, fills it with sweet fragrances, purifies the water, heals wounds, prevents heart attacks and exhales azote. The major fishes along the Desna

every summer; he reckons he knows it like the back of his hand.
– But what exactly do you mean: azote or *ozone?*
– Don't interrupt!
– I'm a professional biochemist, I'd just like to know your sources.
– You little nerd!

The groom's parents drag him off behind a bunch of tulips to keep him out of trouble until the party's over.

Back across the hall — applause. A dark man with a bushy moustache (probably a Yugoslav) is giving the newly-weds a clay decanter, the kind you can find in any souvenir shop. They're speaking English. Next to the Yugoslav there's this gorgeous blonde. Swedish or American, I'd bet. She gives me a look. I wink back. She grins. Her teeth are as straight and white as a toothpaste ad. I've got to ask her for a dance. How do they say it in English? Pardon...? No, eekskuse me...? You dansin...? How do they just say, "Let's dance"?
– You're mixing them again!
– What?
– Beer, wine, vodka...
– Valia, love, why don't you just have a little tipple?
– D'you think I can't tell what your thinking?
– Oh, for heaven's sake. Why don't you just go home? Watch the box. You'll catch the end of Part III of your show.

She tells me tomorrow she's going to get a lawyer and file for divorce. I tell her all right, just don't forget the coat-check. Better still, fetch me my coat.

She bites her lip and stalks off. All around us people are smiling. Who'd have thought it would come to this after ten years together? Think about it: I make all the money, I give her everything she wants. Why the hell can't I let my hair down sometimes? Just because a part of me, deep down inside, longs for a little beauty, wherever I might find it, does that make me an animal?

Valia brings my coat and tosses it in my lap. I listen to her high heels clicking away across the floor. Her face is twisted, lips trembling, little eyes full of hurt and hope. No! You just can't chain a man down. So she's undemanding. So she's caring. So what? All right, she does make me fresh dumplings from scratch, doesn't use that frozen, packaged stuff you can't even cut with a knife. She's a good cook, I'll give her that. The kids are never ill. But you can't stop a man wanting to slip the ball and chain sometimes.

Angela's brute of a husband is going on at her, poking his fork in my direction. The idiot's on the verge of calling me out. Oh, I'm sick of these do's! Weddings, New Years, birthdays — there's always some jealous husband spoiling for a fight. What if I went abroad? Zaitsev, that good for nothing, picked up an American wife, didn't he? He's an engineer like me, we worked in the same office. Off to America he went with her and while he's looking for a job he decides to redecorate their house. It's easy over there. They've got millions of wallpaper patterns and the glue! One stroke of your brush, and the paper sticks forever. He did four rooms and two kitchens in three days, no sweat. His father-in-law walks in, takes one look and his jaw hits the floor. That kind of work costs an arm and a leg over there.

When the band come back and begin to play I make my move on the blonde with the teeth. Straight and white as a sabre-tooth tiger.

– Eekscuse mee, – I says, – dansin?

– Try it in Russian, pal, – she tells me.

We get to know each other. My hunch was right: it is a wedding party. A French engineer building a big factory on the outskirts for some multinational is marrying his interpreter. Among the guests are an American couple, some Dutch, Germans with their kids and the Yugoslav. And the only looker is the local blonde. That minx is the maid of honour. Her name's Valichka, too, by the way. She's just moved into a one-room apartment somewhere outside the city but she doesn't have a telephone yet. The lines probably won't reach her till the year 2000.

She eyes the Dutchman, then the Yugoslav, but she won't dance with me.

– So, what's it like over there? – I asked Zaitsev, when he came home on a surprise visit.

– Like a dream.

– Why did you leave, then?

– Ah, there was no one to have a pint with. No one to just hang around and chat with.

– See, – I says to this Valia. – Better think twice before you swish that blonde mane away from me. But she still won't give me her address.

Back across the hall, Angela's husband is standing behind my chair, so I have a chat with the gloomy major, who's happy to tell me about his stint in the Far East, on the Kamchatka Peninsula. It was hell over there. They weren't allowed home for fifteen years. The officers spent their leaves at spas drinking pure alcohol and playing cards for forty-five days straight. Now he's retired, with a small pension. He has his tent, a boat, three spinning rods and the old jalopy. He says he goes fishing near Suvyd, on the Desna, says it's the best place, bar none. You can't beat it. And you never will. That's *how* good it is.

Angela's fat-faced husband sits down next to me and grabs my elbow.

– You and me. Outside, – he says.

The guests are gathering to congratulate the newly-weds and I manage to slip away in the crowd to the other side of the hall. I should have kneed the fat bastard in the balls. You just squat there and think it over, I should have told him. Then we'll step outside.

But I fetch my coat and let it go. At the door someone slaps me on the back and gives me a hug. It's the well-oiled major again. He's taken with me and wants to tell me all about how he and his wife went off to Sochi,* years ago. It was his first leave and their suitcases were stuffed with rubles.

– You can't imagine, – he says, shaking his head, – how much one ruble could buy before monetary reform.

Over his shoulder I see the jealous brute's mates running after me. I give the sentimental old major a shove and get out of the line of fire quick as I can.

It's late and there are no buses. The snow crunching under my feet sounds like change falling through a hole in my pocket, like loose heavy chains, rattling at each step.

Tomorrow morning I'm supposed to photograph two mums with their kids. Then a wedding. Both on color film. I'd better not forget my big blue bag. Chances are I'll be able to bring home lots of leftovers after the party.

Last night she threatened suicide again. How, I asked her, how exactly are you planning to do it? She cried. What a pain. Bored, stupid and hopeless.

On the other hand, when you've been burnt, the best you can hope for is to have someone close lay on hands. Not necessarily down there. No, anywhere'll do. Anywhere at all.

Published in Ukrainian in *Pisni Beatles (Beatles Songs)*, Kiev: Progress Publishers, 1990)

Notes:

Sochi — a resort on the Black Sea

A Portfolio of Bookplates
Mykola Kumanovsky

Despite being the target of constant KGB surveillance and even physical assault, MYKOLA KUMANOVSKY has been one of Ukraine's most prolific artists. Born in 1951 in the village of Sataniv in the Khmelnytsky region of Ukraine, he studied art at the Lviv School of Art and Lviv Institute of Applied and Decorative Art in the 1970s. After classes his education continued in the cultural underground of the city's cafes where the Ukrainian intelligentsia met to exchange ideas during the repressive Brezhnev regime. It was in the tricultural (Ukrainian-Polish-Jewish) city of Lviv that he discovered Western art and was influenced by Breughel, Bosch, and Magritte. Following college graduation, he moved to the provincial city of Lutsk, where he worked in abject poverty and suffered continuing KGB harassment. As an artist he can be seen as a neo-symbolist engaged in transcending the mere objectification of reality to convey a deep inner spirituality through color, light and the linear nature of his painting. His main influence is surrealism, which he connects with Breughel, from whom he has borrowed the images of bells, birds, and fish as elements of his own iconography. One can also see a meditative Eastern consciousness, for instance, in the loose Confucian garb worn by the Cossack standing over the Tartar warrior in the back cover illustration. He reaches back as well to Ukrainian spiritualism, especially the Ukrainian Baroque of the 16th–18th centuries. Some of his most acclaimed work includes some thirty illustrations to the Ukrainian translation of Samuel Beckett's *Watt*. Since Ukrainian independence was achieved in 1991, Kumanovsky has been successful selling many of his paintings to Western art connoisseurs. He has had one-man shows in Philadelphia, New York, and Newark, N.J.

Back cover: From the series,
The Rustling of Broken Stalks, late 1980s
31–34: Bookplates (etchings), 1980
119: "The Hand of God," 1994
120: "Bottled Shut, He's as Silent as a Fish," 1994
137: "An Enchanted Rabbit Stealing a Loaf
of Bread and the Moon," 1994

Kostiantyn
MOSKALETS

A Crowning Experience

Translated by Assya Humesky with Jessica Treadway

She's amazed by this slumbering summery show
subtitled throughout by raindrops and daisies
in which her hair is like a sorrowful banner
that flutters at night upon a green wind.

She must make a beginning, so there can be an end.
She must return from the silent prison
beneath the evening birds' timorous wreath
beneath the withered leaves' wavering crown.

Hryhorii Chubai

1. Night at a military outpost

"We must flee into the mountains," she said to the sergeant. He gave her a wicked smile, spat to one side, and went off to make another phone call. The night was black with a violet tinge, and the lanterns within were blinding white. Perhaps it was beautiful, but Ottla was too tired to know. She sat down near the chestnut tree and dozed off, lulled by the rustling leaves. "Combat infantry equipment" — the words, heard somewhere, whirled in her head — "yes, the combat infantry equipment and the seventh detachment, yes disciplinary penalties and a tight situation, a situation close to somebody, yes there is no room for them to hide…" They were firing somewhere in the mountains; the sergeant reappeared, listened to the shots, and yawned; the radio near the barracks was transmitting an opera by Donizetti; altogether it was a very disquieting night. The sergeant looked at the chestnut tree and thought that he could bang Ottla, take her and have his way with her; but he was afraid of catching a disease, besides which, the phone rang. "Finally, that bitch," the sergeant thought, and he ran inside. The bitch informed him that there was no gas and that the bus would not come until early morning, and then she inquired if by chance a young girl of about sixteen or seventeen had turned up, a girl with long golden hair, come on now, do you catch on, her name is Ottla, and she is the daughter of General D., and last night she ran away from home, and now half the garrison is searching for her again — ? "There is someone here," the sergeant said, "she was begging to be taken over there, such a fool, I sent her off, the bitch, I'll go and ask what her name is." He put down the receiver and ran to the chestnut tree. "What's your name, bi..." She screamed, opening her eyes. "Ottla," the sergeant said.

"What," she said.

"Ottla, go to the telephone, your father's waiting for you there," he said, and she got up and went to the checkpoint, but there was no one there and she looked at the sergeant with suspicion. He smiled sheepishly but wickedly and handed her the receiver. "Hello, Ottla here," she said, and she listened for a long time to what she was being told, and then she said, "All right, I'll wait, tell papa not to worry, I am handing it over," and she gave the receiver back to the sergeant. He also listened for a long time and very attentively, then said in a strange voice, "yessir," put down the receiver and sat at the desk avoiding looking in Ottla's direction. "Good thing I didn't bang her," the sergeant thought, "just think of it, a general's daughter, the bitch, if I had taken her, why, they would have shot me and hanged me, no, there is someone up there in heaven after all, no matter what they told us in school and in political indoctrination classes," and he looked at Ottla with hatred, but she had already made herself comfortable on the cot with her back turned away from him and was fast asleep. The sergeant took his overcoat, covered the girl with it, and left; now it was he who sat under the chestnut tree listening to the leaves rustle, catching bits of the latest news coming from the barrack, straining to hear if the telephone was ringing, and still not believing his incredible good luck that he didn't take her, although actually he didn't even want to very much, didn't really want to, that phone rang just in time, and she, the bitch, turned out to be the general's daughter, the daughter of D. himself.

Meanwhile, Ottla, the bitch, daughter of D. himself, was dreaming of the sunny Sotopka pier, and swarms of swans in the cold Baltic water turning upside down with their funny feet sticking up, and several battle ships moored on the horizon; and they were firing noiselessly and simultaneously at a gigantic dragon which was slowly nearing the pier. "He is going to eat me up," Ottla dreamed, but she wasn't afraid, only very curious and delighted; they kept firing from the ships, shells were exploding quite near her and near the dragon, but he nimbly dove beneath the water, and she was not afraid of shells because her dad was General D. "Dad" — what a funny word. She had quite recently heard it somewhere, but where? Ottla looked around and saw Rainer Maria Rilke with Lou Andreas-Salome. "So that's how it is," she thought. "I must ask them about something — they know absolutely everything, and because of *her* even Nietzsche became crazy." "Tell me, is it June now?" she asked, turning to them without further ado; "Yes, June, it's June," nodded Rainer and Lou. "Then why is it so cold?" Ottla asked, trying to check the tremble growing inside her. "Because we are now in the year one thousand eight hundred ninety eight, little girl," Lou explained to her kindly. "That is not true!" Ottla shouted; in reality, it was simply that the overcoat had slipped off onto the floor, and Ottla woke up.

She listened to the voices coming from outside. Yes, it was Papa talking to the sergeant. The air outside the window was pinkish green; June, she'd been caught again, well, the devil take it, maybe she herself had wished for it.

"And then they stopped firing?"

"Yes, Sir, General, Sir."

"Hmmm… that's all right, though it's strange. Did you bang her at least?"

"No, Sir, General, Sir."

"Hmmm… That's strange also. What a fool you are. You should have banged her. So she'd know next time…"

"Yes, Sir, General, Sir."

"Hmmm… it seems you're not such a fool after all. All right, tell the company commander that you are now a master sergeant. Or better yet, I will write him a little note…"

"Yes, Sir, General, Sir."

General D. took a map board from his car and began writing the note, paying no attention to the sleepy Ottla who emerged from the check point.

"You could have strummed a little more softly. You're hollering so loudly the whole border can hear you," she said.

"We'll talk about this later, in private," the general said. "Sit in the back."

"But I want to sit in the front."

"And I told you: in the back. But then you're going to get it anyway."

"I don't give a damn," Ottla said and sat in the back.

The general handed the note to the sergeant and slapped him on the back, and the armored car disappeared behind the hill.

It smelled of dust and young sagebrush. There was not a cloud in the clear blue summer sky. A lark sang and water ran from the tap; Ottla had forgotten to turn it off. The sergeant craved sleep madly; he took off his tunic and began to douse himself with water cold as an ice floe, as snow, as hoarfrost, as hail, as stones falling from the sky, as the look of General D., as the look of his own eyes red from sleeplessness reflected in the mirror, turned green with age, long and incomprehensible as life; cold as water from the faucet. For a while it helped, his head grew warmer inside, time became a little shorter. His eyes didn't smart any more, but his relief still hadn't arrived.

The master sergeant didn't know yet that his entire relief had gotten squealing drunk and given the company commander a trashing — the very same *rotnyi-rvotnyi** to whom General D. wrote the note; the drunk relief raised a mutiny flag over the barrack and died in horrible agony because the antifreeze turned out to be of inferior quality, of malignant quality, that antifreeze turned out to be no good for the relief for whom the newly appointed master sergeant was waiting, he who did not bang, did not take, did not even win Ottla that night; he did not win either the night or Ottla, who ran away from home for the third time, for the fourth time, and for the fifth and sixth time, perhaps even for the seventh time — who knew? She herself lost track of her escapes. "With her, it's like her period," General D. had commented recently, and it was a good thing Ottla didn't hear it. Otherwise she would have shown him the periods of the moon, and those of the sun, the earth, the sky, the water, and under the water.

2. Ottla's Room

"Mares — women, neither fat nor slim with long legs and plump behinds a wonderful physique a high but not wide forehead their embrace is passionate and their kisses are firm and strong their walk is very very fast and they love red flowers — poppies dahlias roses — and

---

*A rhyming pun: *rotnyi* means "company commander"; *rvotnyi* means "vomit," as in the adjective *rvotne* ("emetic": tending to produce vomiting).

clothes red as poppies dahlias roses and when a mare is excited awakened stimulated then it is almost impossible unrealistic illusory hallucinatory to quench her craving who knows exactly how to quench her insane inhuman marish passion for lovemaking she strikes and pinches her partner during intercourse she bites and scratches gnaws and tears him apart into tiny pieces the size of the petals of a poppy dahlia or rose," Ottla read. She laid aside the magazine and sank into a reverie. Almost everything was true except for the red flowers and clothing — those were just the very colors she hated. Could anything in the world compare to yellow chrysanthemums or… or…. Ottla searched around the room with her eyes; her knapsack was still lying laced up under the television set. Ottla jumped off the sofa and untied the sack, and among the jeans, blouses, stockings, bras and panties she found her yellow skirt, her favorite in the world, terribly wrinkled but clean. It was in this skirt that she danced with Colonel R., and only some imbecile could have given preference to a red skirt which, incidentally, Ottla also owned; but at this moment for some reason it slipped her mind, and instead she tried in vain to remember where she had put her iron. The iron wasn't there; enraged Ottla ran out to the stairs ready to yell furiously, "Marta!" but she lost her speech and her arms and her long legs the moment she saw that outside her door stood a desk, and next to the desk was a chair, and on the chair sat a lieutenant — the most horrible thing in all nature — an unfamiliar, unknown, stray lieutenant, probably one of *them*, surely of *them*, for where else except among *them* could you find a lieutenant with glasses? "Well, Papa," Ottla thought at last, "this I will not forgive you." The gift of speech returned to her, and Ottla immediately made use of it.

"Listen, Four Eyes, what exactly are you doing here?" Ottla asked, sitting on top of the desk.

Four Eyes deliberated for a moment. Then he said, in an unexpectedly high-pitched voice, freezing Ottla's insides to the core: "I am carrying out my patriotic duty."

"Here?" Ottla asked in amazement.

"Patriotic duty may be and should be carried out everywhere," Four Eyes declared.

"How many broads have you banged so far?" Ottla was curious to know.

"None."

"Nothing strange about that. If you want, I'll be your first?" she whispered, placing her hot hand on his cold one.

"No, I don't. Thanks."

"Why? It's so delightful... Perhaps you're afraid? Don't be afraid, my little gosling..."

"I am not afraid of anyone in the world. I am afraid of only one thing: not to carry out my patriotic duty in an appropriate manner and within the assigned time or deadline."

"Aha, I get it," said Ottla, removing her hand, "he couldn't get anyone for this job but a castrated imbecile. Well, okay, do your patriotic duty while I go look for my iron. I'll show you how to make cold scrambled eggs."

"Go back to your room; it is prohibited for you to leave!"

"I'd like to shit on your prohibitions," Ottla said as she started down the stairs.

"If you don't come back, I'll be forced to fire at your lower extremities," a voice behind her warned.

"Ho, ho, ho," Ottla laughed in a demonic bass, and at that instant a shot rang out; a bullet whistled past her left ear.

Ottla turned pale as death and looked back. The lieutenant was standing behind the desk, aiming at her face.

"So that's what you are," Ottla said quietly, "you shithead, degenerate, sodomite, homo, eunuch, lieutenant..."

And she fainted.

Already, from below, came the pounding boots of two soldiers of the guard. They lifted Ottla carefully and carried her into the room. The lieutenant entered behind them, gathered the yellow skirt from the sofa, and hung it over the armchair. They lowered Ottla onto the sofa. She opened her eyes, saw above her a face with glasses, and vomited right into it.

The entire third floor belonged to General D.; the first and second were occupied by the district headquarters. Ottla's room was formerly her mama's; when Mama died, the general made the baby's room into his office, and moved Ottla here. The windows in this room faced east, and as she woke Ottla delighted in the morning rays as they reflected off Mama's books. The books stood in an antique oak bookcase, pressing tightly against one another as if trying to protect themselves against the incomprehensible fate of living in a general's home. Flaubert and Musil, Proust and Kafka, Shakespeare and Rilke, Hölderlin and Virginia Woolf. Ottla read all of them after Mama's death, not understanding much, more guessing than understanding, and frequently not getting anything at all — still, she perhaps guessed and imagined a hundred times more than the authors themselves had had in mind.

Most of all, she loved Proust. Sometimes it seemed to her that it was her own mother who had written that epic when she was still quite young, as young as Ottla was now, and only hid behind a male pseudonym, like George Sand; Mama hid from General D. behind the pseudonym "Marcel Proust" because he would have killed her if he had learned that she wrote so much, and all of it in French.

In the corner there was a television set, and along the wall a sofa; then the room took a sharp turn and there, in a deep niche, was the holy of holies — Ottla's bed, a wardrobe with her dresses, and a floor lamp which she used for reading at night, especially during a thunderstorm or when the rebels moved very close to the city. Once a rocket hit the neighboring building where the city court was located, and it caught fire; Ottla ran out onto the balcony in only her nightgown, and watched for a long time as the court files containing cases against the guilty — but more often against the innocent — burned. How the soldiers ran about putting out the fire — and she didn't sleep from then till morning, aroused by the fire and by the sudden realization that there was a chance for her to escape this place forever, or at least to become a woman.

The room smelled of her perfume and the ceiling was very high. Ottla spent hours sitting before mother's three mirrors, experiencing for the first time the taste of lipstick and the wavy elasticity of her eyelashes, thick and luxuriant as if made of the fur of some rare animal; the thrilling purity of her smooth skin under armpits shaven for the first time; a kind of heavenly freshness exuding from there and from here and also from over there, tormenting with its softness and urgency, caressing cruelty and unfulfillment. For the hundredth time, Ottla ran a comb through her golden silky very long hair; she drank coffee, talked on the phone, listened to music and again turned to the mirrors, exhausted by her reflection which was eternally one and the

same, eternally incomprehensible, and eternally appealing. At random
she would take a book off the shelf, open it, and read:

The Venetian sun will rise with its gold
in my hair; a wondrous realization
of all alchemy. The splendor of my eyebrows
—you can see them arching like bridges.

they soar high above the silent threat
of my eyes, and the secret current
of lagoons is their link, so that the sea
with its high and low tides splashes,
ever changeable, ever in motion.

Whoever has seen me envies my dog
whom my bejeweled hand now strokes
after a moment's rest, and no fiery flame
can char that hand, nor anything hurt it;
and the young lads of proud and ancient families
perish from the touch of my lips
as if they had taken poison.

R.M. Rilke, "The Courtesan"*

Ottla thought about Colonel R. She had danced with him re-
cently several times; he, too, belonged to a very old, locally esteemed
family; he was a childless widower, and was somehow genuine in his
new colonel's uniform, and very powerful. Ottla, feeling her eyes fill
with tears, threw herself to the floor face-down on the rug, biting her
lips and telling herself not to cry — otherwise, Dear Ottla, all your
preening in front of mirrors will go for naught and there's only half an
hour before evening, he will come to pick you up; after all, he prom-
ised. So she caressed the rug, the soft, kind rug, and only sniffled but
did not cry, not a tear.

It was in this same room that Ottla had vomited into the hateful
lieutenant's glasses. The whole room stood by, ready to defend her in

---

*Die Kurtesan" and subsequent Rilke lyrics, translated by Assya Humesky
from the Ukrainian translation by Bohdan Kravtsiv (*Rechi i obrazy* [*Things and
Images*], Nuremberg, 1947).

case this idiot should try anything; the chandelier came on guard, ready at any moment to fall on his empty straw head with shit for brains; the rug stirred, ready to coil like a python and strangle the rotten Four Eyes in a smothering embrace; and Yukio Mishima opened the door of the bookcase, ready to jump out at any moment and plunge his honorable samurai sword into the lieutenant's base back; but the loathsome lieutenant smelled danger all around him, and without even a whisper left the hostile room. The soldiers hesitantly marked time by the sofa. The flap of Ottla's housecoat had turned up, and they couldn't take their eyes off her bare suntanned thigh, firm and resilient; the soldiers became little frogs and the thigh a python... One more minute and they would have leapt into the open maw, but Ottla sensed it, groaned, and said, "Go to hell and call Marta here, tell her to bring some water, tell her to bring a lot of water, a bucket-full."

"Yessir, yessir." The little frogs nodded their heads, saluting her inappropriately, backing toward the door, still not believing their salvation.

They left and shut the door tightly. Ottla remained alone with her room. "See," she said in a whisper to the bookcase, "see what's going on?" She felt like crying, but she had a splitting headache. Ottla looked at her yellow skirt and began to cry, after all.

3. The Lieutenant

Lieutenant Kh. went to the bathroom, where it took him a long time to wash himself and clean his tunic. Returning to the military post, he telephoned General D.

"General, Sir, the target has made the first attempt."

"What are you blabbering about?" said the general, not understanding.

"The first attempt was made by the target, General, Sir."

"What, in cunt's name, target? Who is he?"

"She is the target who made the first attempt, General, Sir."

"Are you drunk?" The general was getting angry.

"May I inform you, General, Sir, that I am always sober."

"So what? That means you're a fool. It's nothing to boast about. Who are you, in that case?"

"General, Sir, I am Lieutenant Kh., who is maintaining surveillance on target O., which made the first attempt, which is a she, whom you ordered this morning that I, Lieutenant Kh., guard against crossing the boundaries of the district headquarters."

"You could go nuts," the general said, gulping down a small glass of vodka. "You totally confused me. So you are Lieutenant Kh.?"

"Yes, Sir, General, Sir."

"And what do you want from me?"

"According to your order, General, Sir, I report that target O. made the first attempt at leaving the premises of the district headquarters."

"Oh, you mean Ottla?" the general realized, downing another glass of vodka.

"Yes, Sir, General, Sir."

"So, what is it all about?"

"ShewantedtogooutGeneralSir."

"She wanted to go out?" repeated the general, gulping down a third glass of vodka.

"Yes, Sir, General, Sir." Lieutenant Kh. pulled out a handkerchief and wiped sweat off his brow.

"So, it wanted to go out, to flee. Wanted. Tedwan. Antwed. To flee. Leeto. 'Put your affairs off till *lito*…'* The victor. Neborak. Ottla — *od tla do tla*. If they do not bring me that cow for execution then there will be great reordering on the front of labor achievements and the wild strawberry patches will forever be overgrown with marijuana…"

Lieutenant Kh. listened respectfully.

General D. gulped down a fourth glass of vodka.

"Hello!" the general said.

"I am listening, General, Sir."

"Is this the long distance operator?"

"ThisisLieutenantKhGeneralSir."

"What lieutenant? Why are you bothering me since early morning? This nonsense is all I need. I don't understand anything." General D. shrugged his shoulders and poured a fifth glass down his

---

*Lito (pronounced *"lee-taw"*) is Ukrainian for "summer." The line which follows is a quote from a poem by Viktor Neborak. Then, Ottla's name gives rise to word play meaning "from the background to the ground."

throat. "What do you want from me? An apartment? There are no more apartments, they are all gone. A car? There are no more cars, all are gone. O dear cattle, where do they get such cows, and I am barefoot and have to walk on cow manure that's still warm... Listen, are you perhaps the lieutenant that I assigned this morning to guard Ottla?" the general asked, and he drank a sixth glass of vodka.

"Yes, Sir!" Lieutenant Kh. almost rejoiced.

"Oh, that's how it is. So, how is she? She didn't try to get out, did she?"

"Yes, she tried to get out, General, Sir. I was forced to shoot. She became frightened and lost consciousness or, to make it short, she fainted. We carried her back. She regained consciousness and vomited on me. Now she is lying quietly."

"Good," said General D. "She'll try the balcony, and they're already waiting for her below. He-he. Hi-hi. Ha-ha. Ho-ho. Hu-hu not ho-ho? Continue surveillance, hero. In case something happens, call me. I'll present you for a promotion. Do you know my telephone number?"

"Yes, Sir, I do, General, Sir. General, Sir, she tried to seduce me."

"She sure made a good choice," the general said, as he put down the receiver and emptied a seventh glass.

Lieutenant Kh. looked at Marta standing before his desk, a bucket of water in her hands.

"What do you want?" the lieutenant asked.

"May I go to Ottla, she called for me..."

"Go," the lieutenant permitted. "But no funny stuff."

Marta entered the room. A moment later, both she and Ottla were bellowing a duet. Lieutenant Kh. made a face and wanted to spit, but he had to swallow back because Colonel R. was coming up the stairs. The lieutenant got up, saluted, and wanted to say something, but Colonel R. gave him such a look that Kh. swallowed again.

"Who was firing?" Colonel R. asked.

"I, Colonel, Sir."

"Why?"

The lieutenant was hamstrung by his underwear, and his hamstrings trembled. For Lieutenant Kh. knew perfectly well that the colonel and Ottla were having an affair, that everyone was expecting news of their engagement, and that if it hadn't been for Ottla's latest escape, this engagement could have become an accomplished fact. The thought of the escape, which was not to the colonel's advantage either, gave Lieutenant Kh. some courage.

"I was acting on orders from General D., Colonel, Sir."

Colonel R. knocked on Ottla's door. Marta, all in tears, looked out. She had just finished cleaning up.

"Oh, it's you," Marta said, "wait just a minute," and she disappeared behind the door, then emerged holding a bucket. She nodded as a sign of agreement, as a sign of permission to enter, as a sign.

When the colonel disappeared into the room, the lieutenant made another call to General D.

"Target number two has arrived. No. 2, No. 2, No. 2," Lieutenant Kh. said softly.

"Damn it!" General D. got it right away and poured down the seventeenth glass of vodka. "Is he mad?"

"Like a dog."

"Hey, hey! Hey! Hey-hey-hey!" the general yelled into the receiver, and gulped the eighteenth glass of vodka. "Swatchout how you select your swords! Sfilter the smarket! Swhat skind of scomparison is sthis? Safter sall he sis still a scolonel." SGeneral SD. sgulped sthe snineteenth sglass of svodka, "sno mores ands nos lesss, not ssome kinds of shittys lieutenants. Scomparison! Perhaps you will soon report in verse? Watch them and in case of something — well... I will be there right away, fuck your mother and th-th-theirs!!!"

General D. drank the twentieth glass of vodka and flew out of his office.

At that same moment the door to Ottla's room was flung open and Colonel R. flew out. He swung his arm with all his strength and punched Lieutenant Kh. right in the mug. The glasses struck the wall and broke. Blood gushed from his muzzle, from his split lip. Ottla was already standing on the stairs, looking with hatred at the nearsighted lieutenant, who was holding a hankie with one hand, pressing it to his nose, and with the other, mechanically, searching for his glasses — first on the desk, then groping on the floor.

"Let's go, darling," said Colonel R.

Ottla looked into his eyes and smiled. They laughed out loud and started down the stairs. The colonel took Ottla's arm and she pressed tightly against him.

The bullet flew between the Colonel's right ear and Ottla's left ear and hit smack into the wide forehead of General D., who was panting as he climbed toward them. For an instant nobody knew what had happened.

4. The Funeral

The summer rain came down in torrents. Crowds of people stood under umbrellas near the district headquarters, waiting for the body to be carried out. No one could have imagined a more senseless death; some of the citizens were inclined to think that it was the work of partisans; a few hinted at a conspiracy among the higher-ups. "You will see, it will be Colonel R. and no one else who will take the place of the poor General..." The provocateurs from the secret service to which Lieutenant Kh. also belonged were spreading rumors about the almighty hand of the Vatican — it was obvious in this case that the Vatican was not involved, and that this story was nothing but nonsense. For the moment, everyone forgot that Ottla's mother was a foreigner — which was what they could never forgive the general, even after she died: "That's his punishment for not taking one of ours"; "If it hadn't been for those foreigners, the rebels would never have captured the mountain pass — the foreigners send them money, support Menelaus, and create public opinion across the ocean"; "It's because of the foreigners that Menelaus mounted an uprising." While he was alive General D. was indifferent to this kind of talk, and now he was all the more so. He lay with his forehead bandaged in a luxurious casket, of prewar design, dressed in a new uniform, his war decorations glittering sadly on small satin pillows — thirty-five orders and one-hundred-forty-eight medals. Disregarding the rain, virtually the entire city which he had defended for the seventeen years of Ottla's life came to pay its respects and to see him off on his last journey with appropriate ceremony. A massive amnesty was declared in connection with the funeral, and yesterday's slaves with shaven heads stood by the headquarters in a separate group, pressing tightly to their chests wreaths with mourning ribbons which bore such inscriptions as "To the brave General from the grateful criminals," "We have repented," "General, we are with you," and "You are with us, General." It was an amazing spectacle — the idiotically tragic death transformed the souls of murderers, robbers and rapists, and a host of small-time black marketeers as the morning *Timezeit* reported. The same correspondents managed to count all the wreaths brought by the grieving citizens — they declared there were exactly seventeen thousand, symbolic of the General's seventeen years of self-immolating service to the motherland ("the ugly mother,"* as she was affectionately called by the common people)... How are we, how are we, how are we, to survive this terrible, unjust, frightful-frightful loss?

Funeral marches resound. It's time to say good-bye, time for relatives and close ones, close ones and relatives, damn them, those damn relatives and these crazy close ones, but Ottla's not there. Isn't she a close one? Isn't she a relative? Who else but Ottla is closer and more related, the most related and the closest — but where is she, for mad mother's sake? Perhaps something is wrong with her? Yes, there is something wrong with her, very wrong, in the worst way, and since she is the most related, the closest, she feels the very worst, it couldn't be worse. There is a doctor at her side. They'll have to close the lid on the casket without Ottla. *Never again in her life...* The screws squeal sadly, the lid fits tightly — awning, eyelid — lid, all the same.[†] Colonels and generals, majors and lieutenant colonels, first lieutenants and captains; second lieutenants and lieutenants; sergeant majors and ensigns, sergeants and master sergeants, junior sergeants and sergeants, privates and privates first class, civilians and privates, all pick up the coffin and place it on their shoulders and backs bent by grief and sorrow, on their collarbones and shoulders, on their shoulders and their necks, on their backbones and their waists, on their sacra and vertebrae, on their shoulderblades and the napes of their necks in order to proceed ever so slowly-slowly-s-l-o-w-l-y toward the exit.

Outside, they set the coffin on a gun carriage, covered with a battle flag, and the procession slowly winds its way in the direction of the Vovchy Cemetery. A combined brass band plays with great skill. Over thousands of heads resound chamber[‡] compositions. Tens and

---

*A pun: *rodina* in Russian means "motherland," while *urodina* means "ugly monster."

[†]Double entendre: "the lid" *(kryshka)* in colloquial speech means "the end, death."

[‡]Word play: the Ukrainian *kamera* means "chamber" or "prison cell."

hundreds of thousands of people plod behind their defender and compatriot, the papa of their city. The ground beneath their feet flows with muddy water, lightning flashes, blessed times are coming, there's thunder...* "You see, even nature grieves for our Papa," the grade school teacher intones between sniffles. The children are drenched to their underwear, but suffer bravely. See, even nature grieves for our Papa. They want to become just as iron-willed as their general was, equally valiant heroes and heroines. With heroin it's a bit more complicated, but today, on the occasion of these extraordinary events, they are even selling it without prescription, albeit for double the price. Yes, the deceased general allowed the sale of heroin and LSD-25 openly; prescriptions were issued monthly along with coupons for bread, sugar, salt, and soap — but what was he to do, the poor wretch, when the city had been under siege by the partisans for seventeen years, and only rarely would a bird fly up and reach into the middle† of the territory controlled by them, let alone the helicopters. As for the transport planes, you might as well forget about them right now and never ever mention them again. No one succeeds in breaking through the antiaircraft guns and rocket cordons of the partisans, those cursed, disgusting, stupid, debauched, unwashed partisans who thirst to capture our dear city and to stop the sale of alcohol and tobacco, not to mention heroin and LSD-25; who thirst to close down all the brothels with their supple boys and girls, aged five to eighty; and who in their disgustingly sober partisan dreams envision church services in Orthodox and Catholic churches everywhere. Incidentally, thanks to D. not a single one remains in our most dear city, not a single she and not a single he, all Catholics, Protestants and Orthodox were herded one night into the cathedral, the precious cathedral, and they flew off, flew upward; and still they dream of families, doomocracy,‡ the hell with it all — they all flew off together and stopped shitting on each other, today we have sweet peace; besides,

---

*The last two phrases are a quote from Ivan Franko's well-known poem "Hrymyt": "Thunder! A blessed time is approaching." The poet speaks metaphorically about a revolution.

†This line is a quote from Gogol's famous description of the mighty river Dnieper: "It's a rare bird that will reach the middle of the Dnieper."

‡Word play: *demokratiya* (democracy) plus *domkrat* (car jack) produces *domkratiya*.

who hasn't read their proclamations? That's right, no one's read them, why in the name of the devil should we read them? Family — that's when you screw one and only one woman in the course of your entire life; while in our dearest city in the course of one day you can screw all the women and men so long as your health holds up. Our forces catch those saboteurs again and again, they shoot down their planes and helicopters, they burn the saboteurs in the squares next to those pissed-on* places where their shitty Orthodox and Catholic churches once stood, they crucify them on crosses — and they couldn't care less, those accursed ones still creep up on us, toward us, and now there is no more General D. to fight them off, he has served his time, that's what G.C. Tranquilizator wrote in the evening edition of *Timezeit.*

The farewell salute was given with live ammunition and fired in the direction of the partisan mountains. Later, it was said that in one evening, three times as many partisans were killed as during the entire previous year, but that was not quite true; the partisans got wind of General D.'s death in time, and retreated to previously prepared positions. Besides which, befuddled by grief and the increased doses of heroin, the gunners incorrectly estimated their trajectories, and the majority of the shells fell on their own barracks and on the check point. The master sergeant who had been promoted by General D. was among the first to perish, as he sewed the new epaulettes onto his tunic...

The border guard decided that a landing party of partisans had sneaked into the rear, so, turning their rocket launchers 180 degrees, they gave them a mighty response, as a result of which innumerable citizens and citizenesses perished at the grave of their general.

It was an unprecedented slaughter; again, it had to be blamed on the partisans, who had lost every trace of humanity, so the next day all the newspapers came out with headlines framed in black saying, "A Beastly Retribution at a Peaceful Funeral," "This is Their True Face," "Rebels and Foreigners Decided to Destroy Not Only General D.," and "Shame on Christians and Their Lackeys!" Even the international observers, who had long since given up on the city and on

---

*Pun: *obitsiani* (promised), *obistsiani* (pissed over)

everything that took place there became alarmed and sought out the partisan leaders in the mountains in order to find out who really was responsible for the affair, and when they did find out, they shrugged it off with practiced disgust. The partisan leaflets which exposed the real culprits of the massacre were met with disbelief by everyone in the city. It wasn't the first time that the partisans tried to shift responsibility for their horrible crimes.

Such was the funeral of General D. When the newspapers of recent days were brought to Lieutenant Kh. in the military jail where he was being held, he had only to glance at the headlines to begin shaking all over, as if he were already sitting in the electric chair; it seemed that any minute smoke would rise from his nose and ears. At that moment, he knew that even an electric chair would not be considered enough for such a... such a... for such a lieutenant as he. And that's why he simply expired, just like that.

5. The Suitcase

Kneeling throughout the night, not daring to rise
she called to him begging darkly
a sensitive girl, "Over there — a serpent, look!
He is standing guard, I wonder why!"

R.M. Rilke, "Saint George"

Of course, if Ottla had been at the funeral she, too, would have perished. But she had insisted to Colonel R. and General S., who conducted the ceremony, that she would never set foot there and that they must leave her alone. So they left her alone, and she locked herself in her room and cried a little, and dozed off for two or three hours; then she took her tape player, put on the headphones, and played Uriah Heep at full volume; because of this she could hear neither the sounds of the orchestra, nor the farewell salvo, nor the border guards' firing, nor Marta's knocking on the door, when she came running scared to death to tell her to run to the bomb shelter. Marta had concluded that Ottla, overcome with grief for her papa, had hanged herself, and she took off for the shelter alone. It was getting dark and Ottla lit a candle — she did it instinctively, unaware that there was no power anyway, and that there wouldn't be any for two more weeks; she felt the floor shaking under her feet, but she thought it was an earthquake or the salvo, or finally, that she didn't give a damn about anything in the world including tremors so long as Uriah Heep was playing, so long as the candle was burning, so long as she turned the pages of the album with reproductions of old Italian masters of the blessed Trecento — here, Vitale de Bologna had painted Ottla as a golden-haired queen with a crown on her head, and Lieutenant Kh. was an ugly monstrous dragon into whose gaping jaws Colonel R. was driving a tremendously long spear. Ottla looked closer at the horseman and sighed with disappointment. No, St. George did not resemble Colonel R. in the least. What a shame; but the dragon without glasses was the spitting image of Lieutenant Kh. Yet the horseman did resemble someone. He also had blazing golden hair. Perhaps it was Mama? No, it was a horseman, not a horsewoman. Ottla put the album aside and turned off the cassette player. She heard a noise; someone was walking rapidly up the stairs, heel tapping nervously. Ottla guessed that it was Marta and went to open the door.

"My God," Marta screamed from the doorway, "just what are you doing to me, why am I being punished like this? They are shooting on all sides, there are explosions everywhere — perhaps an uprising has started, or maybe the partisans have forced their way into the city. I thought I wouldn't see you alive again, just... just..."

Marta began to howl.

"Marta, dear, quiet down," Ottla said. "What explosions, what shots? It's simply the festive salute — that is, not festive but funereal. Don't you understand, you silly?"

Ottla listened; somewhere in the distance, ambulance sirens wailed.

"A fine salute, if you ask me," Marta sniffled, "half the staff barely escaped from there and you say 'a salute.' Some salute, sure thing — it was your damned rebels who caused this catastrophe. Why didn't you open up for me, why? Did you want to do something to yourself?"

"For God's sake, Marta, do you really think that I am such an idiot? I just took a nap, then listened to music, I listened to music full blast and didn't hear anything... There was a thunderstorm, and the floor was shaking under my feet and I couldn't imagine..."

"You were listening to music?" Marta was horrified, and she

wiped the tears with the palm of her hand. "You were listening to music at the time your poor papa was being buried—and at full blast, at that? Ottla, you have lost your mind; you have lost your mind, Ottla, by God, how you indulge yourself—first, you don't go to the cemetery, don't even come to say goodbye to the *body*, and at the very moment when they are lowering the casket into the grave, you listen to *music*? Perhaps you knew that the rebels would fire at the funeral? Perhaps it was you who told them about it?"

"Shut up, you fool!" Ottla yelled. "Shut your trap, otherwise I don't know what I will do to you! They were listening to *music* over there, too! What right do you have to lecture me, you yokel! So you think that I purposely saved my hide and exposed those wretches to the rockets?"

Ottla sprang at Marta and like lightning slapped her face over and over, then collapsed onto the sofa and began to wail. Marta began to wail too. For five or six minutes there was continuous wailing, a complete madhouse. Then Marta screamed:

"That's not at all what I meant to say, it just *came out* that way because I was anxious, because I thought that you were no longer alive in this world, but you are, and I was so happy, but you clobber me as if I were some goddamn lieutenant, and I am not Lieutenant Kh. to you, I am not Lieutenant Kh., I am not Lieutenant…"

"Stop the hysterics," Ottla cried in turn. "I know you aren't Lieutenant Kh., thank God, I haven't gone completely crazy yet, although I should have gone crazy because how else could I endure all this, when you—you!—say that I—I!—set up those miserable johns to be shelled, although they should all have been destroyed to the last man a long time ago, but I didn't send them there, I was listening to music, and you say that I was listening to music at a time when… but how was I supposed to know, well just tell me, tell me, tell me, if you are so smart! Just think—I hit her maybe once, maybe, unintentionally—so what, and here we go, we've got a tragedy: but remember how you terrorized me when I admitted that I tried those pills, and you beat me, and the bruises didn't fade for a week, but they all scarf down those pills, and stick themselves with needles, and mainline, but you don't go and beat them, well forgive me, forgive, Marta dear!"

Marta ran up to the sofa and gave Ottla a big hug, and they both began to cry all over again, but those were the last tears, the storm was receding beyond the city, the last claps of thunder were barely audible; it smelled of gilly-flower and acacia, of a fresh and clean evening after rain. The candle burned low, and wounded children agonized in the throes of death, and suddenly everything became quiet, silence came and hung over them all, and silence was in their midst, and this was in the summer... "Sergeant Marta report for duty," the staff orderly announced from below.

"Go," Ottla said and kissed Marta on the cheek. "Go and find out everything the best you can and tell me later, I will be waiting. The key to his room, do you have it? Give it to me. Give, give, I'll give it back to you. I have to look, there may be something about Mother in there..."

Marta, without saying a word, removed the key to the general's study from a bunch of keys she carried and handed it to Ottla. This was a crime. But these days, everything was like that. Besides, it didn't matter, anyway.

"Lock the door," Marta said, and she ran down the stairs.

Ottla listened. Still the same old silence. She must go, while there's an opportunity, she must go, even though her teeth are chattering and her hands tremble, and there's a tiny quiver in her knees; she must go, even though her heart shrinks with fear and her lips are turning purple...

Ottla jumped out into the corridor and listened once more, then ran back into her former room, stuck the key into the keyhole, turned it — all this by feel — and hit the light switch. There was no light. Ottla cursed and ran back to her room, grabbed another candle, lit it from the first one which was about to go out, and, shielding the flame with her hand, walked briskly to General D.'s study.

Thank God, the window was covered by drapes. Ottla tugged at the drawers in the General's desk — all of them were locked except one, the lowest one; she found a pistol there with three cartridge clips. Ottla dropped the pistol along with the cartridge clips into the deep pocket of her robe, shut the drawer, and opened the doors to the wardrobe containing the General's uniforms; two civilian suits hung there as well. Ottla set the candle on the desk and began searching through the pockets. Aha, here are the passports... one was the general's, the second was also the general's, the third — the general's, goddamn... your passports; hey! — citizen of Switzerland — not bad,

Papa! — every one of them, of course, with a fake surname; actually, the devil only knows which ones are genuine and which ones are fake — there! Ottla found her passport, and another one, also hers, whose existence she had never suspected, although she'd dreamt such a thing often. Mother of God, am I also a Swiss citizen?! Some kind of "*...bein.*" This could drive you nuts. For a moment her breathing stopped and a strange feeling tightened her throat, something akin to pity and gratitude to the General — to *Papa*! But there was no time to waste. Ottla gritted her teeth and, bending down, felt under the wardrobe with her hand. She pulled out a briefcase. Wonder what's in it? What if it's locked? Ottla placed the briefcase on the desk and pressed on the locks — it opened! She peeked inside and whistled involuntarily: dollars in packs of hundreds! Who needs the movies, what are movies when such a briefcase exists! And here are some papers, probably with military secrets. Ottla threw her passports into the briefcase, snapped it shut, and took a breath.

In principle, it was time to split. But... but... there was still the sofa bed. Ottla ran up to the open sofa, lifted one half, and looked inside. Some folders, boxes, cases — and suddenly the blood rushed to her head — there was her mother's slim suitcase, the one Ottla had tried to remember vaguely all her life but could not recall, and she was tormented, trying to convince herself that it was only a dream: her ailing mother stroking little Ottla's hair and saying, "When you grow up, take this suitcase and read what's in it, just don't forget O-3563, repeat, repeat once more O — Ottla, three-five-six-three, my little girl, my darling daughter..."

Ottla took the metal suitcase and the briefcase and brought them to her room, shoved them under the bed, and put the pistol with the cartridges under the pillow. Then she returned to the study, picked up the candle, looked around — is everything all right? No, not everything; the general's passports were still lying on the desk. Then she had an *idea*; she stuck the passports into one of the uniforms, in the curtains, in some of the papers scattered on the floor and on the sofa, and in turn set each on fire, holding the delicate flame of the candle to it. Then she went out into the hall, locked the door, entered her room, pulled on jeans, sweater, and sneakers, and went through the back door to Marta's room.

"Marta, here is the key, go to headquarters and stick around so everyone can see you. I set the study on fire; soon they'll smell it and rush to put it out. In the meantime, I will be sitting in the bar, over there where they are holding the wake, and later I will escape for good, for real. Alibi, Marta dear, you need a foolproof alibi," Ottla whispered into Marta's ear.

The latter drew away and, with eyes full of terror, backed away from her.

"You've gone completely off your rocker," Marta whispered, "they'll shoot us, at least me, that's for sure."

"Yes, but that's not important. What are you gaping at? Quick, off to headquarters!"

Ottla went down to the officers in the basement, ordered a gin and tonic, then took a seat next to Major T. and, accepting his ardent condolences, asked him to tell her about the shooting at the funeral.

"Good thing you were not there, child," said Major T. "I haven't seen such a meat grinder anywhere, and I have seen many meat grinders. That scum has become totally shameless. Christians! Do not kill! And there were children there, too. By God, if it hadn't been for Colonel Z. from the armored transport, if he hadn't honorably brought me to this secluded bar to honorably commemorate your papa... it's a good thing you weren't there. That's one more worry I could do without, but feminine intuition and beauty, that's something..."

Major T. was noticeably soused, and the rest of the officers as well: oppression reigned in the hall which was full of those who had witnessed incredible, indescribable scenes: oppression climbed in clouds of tobacco and every other kind of smoke over the heads of the valorous herd which had lost its shepherd; all were soused and oppressed, oppressed and soused, oppressed and sad, sad and unhappy, unhappy and again soused and the other way around. Some came up to Ottla to express their deepest sympathy. Ottla accepted their sympathy with all its depth, accepted the oppression and drunkenness, sadness and unhappiness, and tensely waited for the fire sirens to begin wailing. Expressions of sympathy were getting deeper, more ardent and sincere. Candles flickered, gas lamps smoked, tension was rising, and the hour was getting very late.

6. The Escape

Ottla pressed on like crazy. It was a long time since General D.'s armored car had reached such speed, and it grew dizzy from lack of practice. The provincial towns looked pale in the morning mist; the sun was rising directly over the road. "Time for a break," said Ottla, slowing down in order to light a cigarette. She was becoming nauseated by cigarettes and the exhausting pace, but she still feared pursuit and still did not know how she would manage to overcome the last, most unassailable outpost. She had bypassed the two previous outposts by taking old forgotten routes which Colonel R. had shown her once during an unforgettable — o-oh, oh, Ottla yawned — trip to the mountains to pick some lavender. Such tiny flowers, but their smell can make you lose your mind; Ottla remembered a song a Muscovite woman sang about them once when she was still little. She couldn't understand anything about that song with the exception of a single word, "lavender"; then came var-var-var and again "lavender," but her angry blood could burn that lavender, and that Muscovite, and that last, most unassailable outpost — but Ottla kept on accelerating, biting her lower lip and trying to squeeze tears out of her eyes so they wouldn't get heavy, but the tears wouldn't come. The old abandoned routes confounded the armored monster that was accustomed to soft and refined highway. Ottla felt sleepier with every passing moment and finally she could stand it no longer; she turned into a grove, turned off the motor, and instantly sank into a deep, downy sleep in the wide back seat; bird songs flew in through the open window, it smelled of summer and freedom. Ottla slept so deeply and happily that she did not hear the helicopter carrying Colonel R. fly twice over the road. They were searching for her, and searching quite thoroughly.

A little more than four miles remained before the final outpost, beyond which rose the mountains that were in rebel territory; in that direction, beyond the crossing, lay the border. They shouldn't delay her at the border, but at the outpost, who knows? The border was Ottla's last hope. She would leave the car to the rebels, then she would board a ship, and bye-bye "ugly-Motherland," or whatever else they call her. But the outpost was guarded with utter ruthlessness — the most loyal, the choicest pricks served there — and Ottla was awakened three hours later by thoughts of the pricks and by a ray of sunlight on her cheek. A large butterfly fluttered inside the car: it was pale blue, very elegant. Ottla opened the door, shooed the creature to freedom, then pulled out the thermos with coffee which Lisa had prepared last night, and sandwiches made by Marta after the fire. She began breakfasting and thinking, thinking, thinking, breakfasting and thinking, but only silly fantasies came into her head, such as that General D.'s car ought to have wings, that the devil was responsible for her being born in this imbecile country, and the like. "Nothing to be done," Ottla sighed, screwing on the thermos cover.

She climbed out of the car, spread the rest of the sandwiches on a napkin for the birds, did some half-hearted morning exercises, and glanced with hatred at the car, her only possible salvation. She should have brought Marta along; at least they could have taken turns at the wheel at night. Ottla felt that she'd had enough sleep, but her head was somehow empty and heavy, somehow not just so, somehow not Ottla's; she remembered the suitcase, pulled it out of the car and, settling down on the grass, pressed the code numbers. O-3563, "Ottla, three-five-six-three, my darling daughter..." The lock clicked. Ottla hesitated for an instant, then opened the suitcase.

A photograph lay on top. In the photograph was a very young, smiling Mama in a Japanese kimono, and embracing her was — a still very young captain. Ottla looked closer at the captain and felt the hair on her head slowly but steadily rise.

There could be no doubt — Mama was being embraced by Menelaus, the commander-in-chief of the rebel armies, the bitter enemy of General D.

At that moment Ottla understood every-every-everything. She was convinced that she had already seen that photograph, and more than once. She knew what was written on the back. She even remembered the handwriting — although at *that* time, she had not yet known how to read. But Mama knew how to read. And this is what was written on the back:

"My dear Helen, I am praying and will be praying for you and for our little daughter Ottla. Let God look at the three of us and rejoice in his successful handiwork. I kiss-kiss-kiss my beloved little girl. Menelaus."

Then there were the letters. Getting acquainted, meetings, love, engagement, marriage, parting, Ottla's birth, a long hiatus, the letters

ever shorter and on ever poorer paper. The last one read:
"*Take care of Ottla. And forgive me, if you can. I will return, you do know that. I will be victorious and then I will return. No matter what, my beloved. Menelaus.*" Ottla raised her eyes. The sun was shining and the birds were singing, and young leaves cast a dense shadow on the color photo: the colorful kimono, the full dress tunic. So that's who the rider with the blazing golden hair, painted in that distant Trecento, reminded her of: oh, better if I'd been born back there and then. A butterfly fluttered about — the same one, pale blue. She felt the urge to drive somewhere. But drive where, with her mama dead and her papa Menelaus?

7. Ottla meditates

I am Ottla. I=I, Ottla=Ottla, I=Ottla. Helen+Menelaus=love. Helen+Menelaus=Ottla. Ottla=love. Love=I. I am. I=am. I+am=Ottla=love. Am=love. I am Ottla=I am love. I am love? I=Love=am. I=love. I=Ottla?
Am I? Am. I? I. I=Ottla? Helen+Menelaus=love? I=love? ???
I=Ottla=she. She=*she*. *She*=shi. Shi=army. Stability. For a manly human — happiness. There'll be no shame. Is she human? She's become manly. Become manly? A hermaphrodite? Hermaphrodite=she? Hermaphrodite=he+she. He — Menelaus+she — Helen=Ottla. Ottla=hermaphrodite? *Nein!!!* Riders on the storm. Riders on the storm. People are strange. Who do you love? Colonel R.: Hello, I love you. Touch me. Light my fire. Love me two times..."* "If that disgusting Christianity had not conquered through murder and blood; if the joys of our paradise were not reduced to the insolent blissful vision of an unknown something, something which cannot be understood or fathomed; if our hell was made up of something other than fiery bottomless pits, monstrous devils, wailing and gnashing of teeth; if our paintings could be of something other than brutal scenes of people being flayed, of hanging, of baking, of frying, of hideous slaughter; if all our saints weren't wrapped to the tip of their noses; if our chaste and virtuous rules did not forbid exposed

---

*Names of songs and lyrics by Jim Morrison of the Doors.

shoulders, thighs, women's breasts, total nudity; if the spirit of the mortification of the flesh had not dried up those breasts, had not made those thighs flabby, those shoulders emaciated and awkward; if our artists and poets were not shackled by those terrifying words 'blasphemy' and 'profanation'; if the Virgin Mary had been the mother of delight or if beautiful eyes, beautiful breasts, shapely thighs had drawn the Holy Spirit to the Mother of God, if that had been recorded in the book of her life; if the archangel Gabriel had been praised in it for his beautiful shoulders; if Magdalen had had some kind of love affair with Christ; if at the wedding at Canna, Christ, a bit tipsy, something of a dissident, had fondled one of the bridesmaid's breasts and Saint John's behind, not quite certain whether he would remain faithful to the apostle whose chin was barely covered with fuzz…" Ottla forgot the rest of this excerpt they had had to memorize a year ago, and she had received an "A" for it. *Let God look at the three of us and rejoice in his successful handiwork.* Yeah, some success. I wonder, where is Mama now? "Mama is in paradise," Marta said once. How does Marta know? She knows, because she is a believer. And I, am I a believer? If I am a believer, then General D. is in hell. It's I who is in hell, not General D. Papa. *Tato.* Patao., Patho. That's what it is, "patho." Well then, go back to Niklasstrasse and don't strain your brain. The Colonel is already waiting. *I will return, you do know that. I will be victorious and then I will return.* I wonder, did Papa know whose I really am? Why was he so afraid of my running away? Could it be he thought I was his? And Mama? It seems that she deceived both D. and Menelaus. But why didn't Menelaus kidnap us? Most rebels kidnapped or ransomed their families, everybody knew that. Did Mama sleep with the General? How would I know? And is that any of my business? And where will I go now? To Switzerland. To Niklasstrasse. To Menelaus' troops. To a nunnery. To a brothel. Or to… to fuck. To pray. To kill. To be killed. To be. But I am. God, help me. A little more, just a drop — and I will understand. Forgive me that I memorized that cretinous excerpt by heart. It would have been better if I had flunked. To start a family. Or to find an interesting job — to become a journalist. Telejournalist. To translate. Proust. To translate Proust and Maritain, and not Diderot or Limonov. To breed fish. To be in movies. To make movies. To sing. To dance. To pursue culture.
    But what for?

To stumble into paradise. To stumble into hell. In paradise you will be with Mama. In hell you will be with Papa. In the mountains you will be with Menelaus. You will be = I will be. But I am. I = am. I = I. I = Ottla. Ottla = Helen + Menelaus. Helen + Menelaus = love. Ottla = love. But must it equate? Why? Because it must. Because am = to be. Everyone knows that anyway. To hell with everyone. And with their knowledge. No one is I. I am. I am Ottla. Ottla is not love. Insofar as she is not love, she is not. But I am. But why?

Ottla spat and began gathering the letters scattered around the clearing. She placed them into the suitcase and threw it under the back seat. The sun was still quite high. The Venetian sun will rise with its gold... She closed all the windows and doors. Wrapped herself in armor. Took the wheel. Started the motor. Looking back over her shoulder she forced herself to back up, something she had never tried before.

And now, no longer looking back, she rushed full speed toward the outpost.

8. Approaching

Instantly a helicopter appeared above the road. Colonel R. gave a sigh of relief. "Ah, your mother was a whore," Ottla thought as she shifted into fifth gear. Colonel R. turned pale. "She's going to crash, the whore," Colonel R. thought, and catching up with the car he began to descend. "Up your ass," thought Ottla. If he lands in front of me I will smash full speed into him. The colonel sensed her determination and began to ascend. An armored truck stood in Ottla's way; on top of it, soldiers sat and smoked. "Move the armored truck," the colonel said on the walkie-talkie. They moved the armored truck. Two minutes later, hurricane Ottla roared by them. The soldiers were stunned. They had never before seen anything like it. And they never will. "Ottla," said Colonel R. "Ottla," responded the speaker on Ottla's right, making her start. The car skidded a little. "Ottla, they won't let you through. They are following different orders. I cannot help you at all. Stop. We'll think together. Ottla, remember everything that happened. Ottla, you will die. Stop, Ottla." Ottla stepped on the gas and no longer trembled. The helicopter, as if doomed, followed behind.

"Well, look what they have come up with," Colonel R. spoke up again a while later.

The outpost gate was wide open. A white road, absolutely deserted, with no potholes or pebbles, rose up into the mountains and disappeared beyond the crossing. This was called freedom.

But in front of the gate stood soldiers, deployed in two rows. There were twelve soldiers. They blocked the white road to freedom. This was much more frightening than the armored car — some of them were smiling scornfully. Ottla was flying. "Disperse," Colonel R. said feebly on the walkie-talkie. Down below, the warrant officer straightened the walkie-talkie on his chest, but did not respond. No one made a move. "She'll stop," the colonel thought, and turned his eyes away from the road.

Ottla looked carefully ahead of her. For a moment it seemed to her that soon she would wake up. Only twice in her life had she raced so quickly. But this was more frightening than speed. She could no longer tear her hands away from the steering wheel nor her foot from the accelerator, to brake, to turn to the right or to the left, to stop, to make a U-turn, to back up. Such things no longer existed. She was paralyzed. The way one becomes paralyzed in a dream, and then immediately wakes up. What paralyzed her was not freedom, which could be seen beyond the heads of the eighteen-year-old youths in the form of an empty white highway that headed into the hills... freedom didn't paralyze, but fear in the face of speed, or more truly, fear in the face of fear, brought on by speed or by this, that, those who were behind her and who stood in her way. Ottla always loved to race, but then she controlled the speed, and now the speed controlled her — her head, neck, shoulders, arms, breasts, stomach, groin, vagina, hymen — for Ottla was still untouched — uterus, anal opening, long, beautiful slender legs, and the nails on Ottla's hands and feet were controlled by the speed; she did not hear how the bones cracked, how a terrible scream echoed in unison; how blood, sperm, urine, feces and blood sprayed in fountains from the crushed bodies, how skulls split open, eyes popped out and brains spilled onto the wonderful grey concrete, jelly, snot, bloody mush, the automatic fire following after; "what have you, what have you done, Ottla — a — a — a!" the speaker clamored in an empty car, in which there was no more Ottla, but only speed, speed sat behind the steering wheel and stepped on the gas, and saw how a rocket flew up from just over the mountain and understood that the helicopter had exploded in the summer sky behind her, because it was still summer after all, God's own

summer; after that the speed began to diminish, the wheels began making
ever fewer revolutions, there were everfewer revolutions, there were ever
fewer wheels, the record changed voices and in a full-bodied bass began the
finale. "A — A — A — VE, MARI — I — I — A," and stopped.

The car stopped. Ottla mechanically groped for the door handle,
opened it, and stepped out. Her head was very empty. Something
oozed out of it. Ottla felt that with every minute there was less and
less Ottla in her head and more and more emptiness. She took a few
steps, stumbled and fell to the grass. The grass was very green. Here
there was no speed. Bees simply flew. The sun shone. The air was
fragrant. Finally, Ottla began to breathe, deeply deeply, slowly slowly,
softly softly. She understood that she was waking, after all. But she did
not open her eyes. She heard isolated words that in the end had noth-
ing at all in common. They were like bees — they flew up, flew away,
and at no time was it ever the same bee. They simply descended, took
Ottla's nectar, then rose abruptly, flying away into the blinding black-
green sea which smelled of currants. Everything was so simple: in the
middle of the sea, there lived a Beekeeper in a boat. His bees lived in
the beehive. And now Ottla flew to him and brought her honey. The
Beekeeper looked closely at her and did not smile. But Ottla did not
see this. She simply crawled on his hand. She lay face up and looked
into the incredibly blue sky. The bees do not see their grey-eyed Bee-
keeper. They do not recognize his face. They see the blue sky, smell
the clean smell of the earth and of currants. Tears come to their eyes
— to those same eyes which will never see their Beekeeper — and then
the sky disappears. Rains pour down — abundant, flower-bearing
rains. A flood rages and the apple trees bloom. You have just killed
three boys. And *you* want to live. And you want to *live?* And you want
to live? And they did too. And then, perhaps, they didn't. They could
have scattered, if they wanted to. Could have killed their commanding
officer, who gave them such orders and who also wants to live. And so
on. At any rate. They are long since in the Kingdom of Heaven, and
you are still here. Until you, too, are killed. Or until you become old
and die of this. Of what? Of that which all old people die — of life,
which you crave now. God, what a beautiful butterfly! God, how
magnificent this butterfly of yours is! What do You say? *Eupithecia*
nabokovi McDunnough.* Aha, it turns out that the Beekeeper speaks
Latin and English at the same time. Not bad!

He summoned them for the final repast
and (like a shot aimed at a bird in the garden)
his single word frightened their hands away from the
    loaves of bread
from all sides they seek an escape.
But he is like the twilight all around and everywhere.

R.M. Rilke, "The Last Supper"

Ottla whispered through her rough, burning lips and — fell asleep? awoke?

1992
Village of Matviyivka,
Chernihiv province

Published in Ukrainian in *Suchasnist* No. 10, 1990

***Eupithecia nabokovi* McDunnough — Novelist Vladimir Nabokov (1899–1977) was an avid collector of butterflies from an early age. During his years in emigration, he was employed from 1941–48 as a researcher at the Harvard University Museum of Comparative Zoology. Several butterfly species have been named after him, including "Nabokov's Pug," *Eupithecia nabokovi* McDunnough, "which I boxed one night in 1943 on a picture window of James Laughlin's Alta Lodge in Utah." Nabokov, *Speak, Memory* (New York: Vintage Books, 1989), chapter 6.

Evhenia
KONONENKO

Three Worlds

Translated by Michael M. Naydan with M.T. Sharif

G randma hadn't been able to get up for several years. Toward evening when mother helped her with her essential toilet, the boy would move to the hallway where there was an exquisite wide windowsill. He brought his books and a bench from the kitchen and sat down to write, the windowsill serving as his desk. "Let the boy do his work." The neighbors of the communal apartment put their fingers to their lips. Behind him the kitchen buzzed with three stoves and the only sink; doors slammed in the endless hallways.

These sounds gradually became necessary for reflection. He made the most stunning discoveries of youth at his windowsill. He read his favorite books and completed his school assignments conscientiously. He was glad to get away from the irregularly shaped room with its low window that looked out onto a steep, inner courtyard. From the hallway an astonishing panorama of the city opened up to him. As a little boy he had crawled with his friends onto the roofs of buildings. But nowhere else were the colors of spring or fall so intense and nowhere else did the cupolas of the churches shine so brightly. Nowhere else did the Dnieper so mysteriously commingle with the blood of this young Kievan, who in this city had only a weary mother, a luckless grandmother, both incapable of relating to him, and an irregularly shaped room in the former apartment of a lawyer with either a Jewish or German surname, a trace of which remained with the letter "ъ"* on the entrance door. The lawyer, who had died long ago, used to wander along the hallways of his old residence, and a well-trained ear could still differentiate between the echo of his steps and the shuffling and tapping of the current residents.

Sometimes Marianna came. Her mother would shout from behind the doors: "Leave the boy alone! Let him do his lessons!" But Marianna would sit down at the edge of the windowsill and enthusiastically examine his books. She herself never did any homework; she ate standing up in the kitchen next to the stove and ambled around in her school uniform till evening. Marianna was very pretty — graceful, slim, with a pure, sweet face, and sensuous, golden hair that she never braided. He loved to stare at Marianna when she wasn't looking at him. "Pretty, very pretty, this is essential in a communal kitchen!" he thought. He wasn't in love with Marianna and was proud of this fact. He didn't end up hooked by her sumptuous pony tails and her tiny youthful breasts. Marianna simply contributed a sense of comfort to him while he sat at his desk. Sometimes, when he didn't have others to speak to, he taught Marianna the suppositions he formulated at his perch. "Do you understand, there are three realms in the human world?"

Every classification shuts out the wide world, he knew this even then, but all the same, this vertical division of the world of people inexplicably engaged him.

"The Third World... The geography teacher used to tell us about it. Or was it the history teacher?"

"No, this isn't it at all... This isn't what I'm speaking about... Three worlds... The lower world, the middle one, and there, above, the higher. All of us live in the second, middle world. We stand in lines, or, even if we don't... We drive in overflowing traffic... We do something for our daily bread. Sometimes we go to visit people with biscuit cake."

"Uncle Yura yesterday brought us 'Kiev' cakes! We were lucky! Nearly without standing in line! They were selling them on the corner of Zhytomyr Street. Can you imagine?"

"Even if we get 'Kiev' cake, all the same, this is the middle world, not the higher. Below us is the lower world... There, people sleep on dirty mattresses in cellars. They can't play cards. There are prisons, investigators, isolation cells, the routine of being struck on the mouth with blows, black eyes..."

He grew silent, because he remembered that uncle Yura had recently given a black eye to Marianna's mother.

"All of this, of course, occurs in the middle world, but there, below, you understand, all this is a hundred times more horrible. The laws are terrible and people aren't even people!"

Someone once placed a letter in their mail box which read something like the following: "You scum, put five hundred rubles under the stone or else I'll tear out your uterus." His frightened mother had run to the policeman.

"That's not for you, that's for Valka from apartment 30," the officer reassured her.

This incident proved to him the coexistence of the horrifying lower world with the gray and monotonic middle one, but he was engaged most of all by the world of normal people.

"There also exists a third, higher realm where Shakespeare is read! In the original! Without a dictionary! People gather to read poetry and listen to music, not to get drunk, even though they may have a glass of whiskey. Do you understand? One can grasp something about existence…"

"What's there to understand? When there's money, everything's good. There'll be books and music. Black marketeers offered my mother 120 rubles for Bulgakov*. Where can you get that kind of money? That's the cost of a polyester suit! Do you know how much they ask for a nice record player?"

Marianna's answers didn't irritate him. What could you expect from a hopeless inhabitant of the middle world? Unpleasant conditions could thrust this kind of person into the lower world, but no stroke of luck would ever allow her to poke through the upper boundary, beyond which eternity began.

Most of all he loved to sit at the desk windowsill at the end of spring, when he no longer had to drag extension cords across the long hallway for the lamp. In the lilac sky the first star flared. The current of the Dnieper turned blue, like the veins in your throat. And when the fruit trees blossomed, the view was maddening. He would open the window, without fearing the furious drafts of the large uncomfortable apartment, and sometimes pale pink petals flew in. Then it seemed to him, just a bit farther, and he'd escape the nets of the middle world into the third realm. There would be someone for him to speak to, and a place to meditate alone. Eternal books could be read, and eternal questions debated. Next to him would sit a pretty girl, like Marianna and just as intelligent and as good as she was.

"Young man, why don't you do your homework in my room? I have a nice writing desk, I almost never sit at it."

He shuddered. For the first time someone had addressed him with the formal "you." The speaker was Mykola Markianovych, owner of the room with the fake leather door. The room had once served as the lawyer's study and was so large that Mykola Markianovych and his deceased wife managed to parcel out a small vestibule for themselves and, by decree of the regional council, to install their own bathroom. As a result Mykola Markianovych didn't use the communal facilities. This meant he didn't take part in cleaning them either, which roused anger in the communal kitchen. Nevertheless, Mykola Markianovych had to boil his tea pot or ineptly cook his kasha on a stove he shared with the throaty Zinka. In the kitchen they called Mykola Markianovych "professor," although, as it became clear, he had never achieved that rank, even though he taught at the university for many years.

"Professor, your kasha's boiled over again!" Zinka screamed with particular rapture. This was the janitress's triumph. If she saw his mother throwing out the trash in the wrong can, Zinka would hiss, "And a school teacher, no less!"

Mykola Markianovych submissively wiped off the stove with the dish cloth, burning his hands on the hot grating.

"Professor, you've taken the wrong rag! How many times have we told you — the rag for the stove is hanging on a nail, and this one's for the dishes!" Zinka refused to calm down.

"Why don't you use my room, young man?" Mykola Markianovych repeated.

And so he ended up behind the fake leather doors. Mother didn't allow him to bother the old man very often, but now and then he would sit at Mykola Markianovych's desk, in front of a bronze set with an ink well, next to a lamp, whose stand was the figure of a beautiful woman. Mykola Markianovych sat in the armchair with a book or a newspaper; sometimes they talked… Stacks of books rose to the ceiling of the ancient room. The paintings and photographs on the wall reminded the boy of an altar. He felt like praying in that room, even though there weren't any icons in it.

But sometimes Mykola Markianovych didn't hear the knocks at his door. It would have been awkward to knock louder, so instead the boy would return to his window, where he could think, read and write. And Marianna didn't even get in the way.

"Well, how is it? Is it beautiful in the professor's place?"

"Very. Do you understand, Marianna, that it's the third realm. That highest one. Right here, quite near us."

"Your professor spent some time in a prison camp. Did you know that?"

He knew. He knew that the worlds intertwined, and that in the abysses of the lower world could be found people from the higher one. In his copybook he noted: "Belonging to the higher realm makes it possible to remain a human being in the horrifying lower world. But how do you make your way to the third realm from the bloodless quagmire of gray, everyday life?"

"I know, Marianna. By the way, he studied Farsi there. He was in prison with a Middle East specialist."

"What's Farsi? Are they some kind of Kung-Fu exercise?"

"Perhaps they are exercises in the struggle for life..."

When he entered the university, they were allocated an apartment in Raiduzhny Heights*. Grandma died around that time.

"You wouldn't have been given a three-room apartment anyway," the inspector of the housing office placated them.

Life continued but in a different way. Only rarely did he drop by Mykola Markianovych's. When he did, he also revisited his windowsill, gazed out over Kiev and caught up on the latest news of the communal apartment. Marianna's mother had divorced uncle Yura so they could take over the irregularly shaped room. Marianna was preparing to marry a huge blockhead who felt her up in the hallway, without even noticing how beautiful she was.

After several years the time came for him to get married. When he returned from his honeymoon trip, he found out that Mykola Markianovych had died. That was it. The old people were leaving. New ones weren't replacing them. He would never be for anyone what Mykola Markianovych was for him. He would never point out to anyone the path to the third realm. Never again would he drop by his previous residence, or look out at the city through that window. Lord, how sad he felt! His sadness hurt his young wife. And her pain hurt him.

Life went on, and life's paths led him no longer to Mykola Markianovych's lavish apartment. A little boy was born. He had to rush home from work. But, one fine spring day, when leaves took flight, he resolved to take his one and a half year old son to see his old building. This was an adventurous idea. He changed the child's first diaper by the metro exit, a second diaper on Volodymyr's Hill. This was the last one his wife had given him. The child, unaccustomed to long trips, began to whine. The dazed father nervously calculated whether he had enough money to take a taxi home.

He took the child into his arms and made it to the promised site. He sat down on a bench, letting the boy walk around, and lit up a cigarette. He raised his head and found Mykola Markianovych's

French window. In the corner there was a single window that marked his former desk.

"Hello! Is this your kid?" A corpulent, ugly woman sat down next to him. "You don't recognize me? I had to have a third kid to snatch up the professor's apartment. Now there are just two families there. Did you hear me? They sent Zinka to the salt mines. The Khomenkos took over her rooms. We're dividing up the kitchen. We'll just take the front, and they'll take the back. We'll have a separate apartment, just like you. We'll be living in the third realm! I remember how you studied your lessons in the hallway. Three worlds... I remember! We covered that window with boards, to make shelves for canned goods. Come in for a visit!"

Published in Ukrainian in *Suchasnist* No. 4, 1994

Notes:

The letter "ъ" (the hard sign in the Russian language) indicates that the name plate was a pre-revolutionary one. The letter was removed from the end of words as part of orthographic reforms adopted after the 1917 revolution.

Bulgakov — Mikhail Bulgakov's novel *The Master and Margarita*, which was banned in the Soviet Union until the mid-1960's

Raiduzhny Heights — *Raiduzhnyii* means "rainbow."

A Portfolio of Photographs
Tania D'Avignon

Pages 76–87 & 198–205

Yevhen
PASHKOVSKY

Five Loaves and Two Fishes

Translated by Volodymyr Hruszkewycz
English style-editing by Ed Hogan

Every evening Baba Maria took her grandson Pavlo's thick workbook to the shrine in the corner of the room, lit the votive light beneath the icon and, opening the Bible, taught herself to write, tracing each letter onto the blank page. The reflections from the icon gilded her age-freckled hands, the moon blazed wildly above the orchard, its rim chipped by an apple tree – and she remembered her childhood: the path from the earthen stoop to the stable warmed by the cherry redness of fallen leaves, the white horsehair on a nail by the door, two horseshoes, the little sac of bile to treat the cattle for horsefly bites, *there came in those days prophets from Jerusalem to Antioch. And one rose among them by the name of Ahab and through the Spirit prophesied that there would come a great famine throughout the whole world, as was once in the time of Claudius.* In the fall military transports snaked through the village, everyone knew that this did not bode well, as they took our horses, collectivized the land, plowed up the graveyard so that we had to break the corpses' knees with a blow to lay them properly into their coffins. The orphaned land remembered the creaking of wagons, the thunder of a drum and the moaning of a harmonica, we put out the lamp, lay down to sleep, the poorest peasants raced headlong down the road, with cornflower wreaths they bedecked the heads of the supply detail, who chased off horseflies with their Red Army caps, with bayonets affixed on perforated tubes they spread dung behind the barns; spread the white rot in the cellar bin, the caked straw in the loft, from then on they slapped our boots with their bayonets, to knock loose any grains that might have lodged in the soles and sank their claws into the landowner in the name of the Revolution; the faded flag tangled whitely around its staff on the porch of the town hall, and they promised to mount a radio loudspeaker on a post*. Now it was the domestic fowls' turn, in just a few days they had slaughtered all the roosters, and the white feathers swirled fiercely in the wind like a snowstorm, stuck to the sweaty napes of the mangy horses, to the officers' tunics, to the black grease on the wheel axles. *And I looked, – and behold a pale horse. And he who sat upon him was named Death, and Hell followed with him. And power was given unto them over the fourth part of the earth to kill with sword, and famine, and plague, and with the beasts of the earth.*

Father kept six horses, my brothers presided over the ceremonies at local weddings with Cossack* gusto, Marko decorated his weapons with crimson tassles, riveted them all over with copper coins, it made the heart shiver, just let the young bride clap her hands, and the young colts would prance from foot to foot in a tipsy circle, children blew on clay whistles in the pear tree, the lilac streamers which hung overhead tickled the villagers' faces and were intertwined with a jasmine shrub beyond the long wedding table. The soldiers took Father, rode the horses into the ground, tied my brothers' arms behind their backs, "You'll live off the fat of the land in the new settlement, kulak* viper," only one whip was left free on the harrows in the cattle shed. – With no one to feed them, Mother set out for Western Ukraine, ground rye, tended other people's children and gathered grain in a little sack for her own bluelipped ones, kernel by kernel, dried crust by dried crust, she couldn't raise a spoon to her mouth without crying, the little ones hung on my sister's neck. Mother would faint from despair and pray that there be no famine; grandpa and grandma grew ill on the journey, so they just threw them off the railroad car, Father ended up in the mines. Later, a letter came from a friend of his: "Styopa's lungs were riddled with mine dust, your falcon bore his suffering, he was buried without a priest." *And each of them was given white clothing, and told to rest a little longer, until the number should be complete of all their fellow servants and their brothers, who would be slain, as they themselves had been.* My brothers sent word from prison in Berdychev, "We are scattered in separate cells, God willing, we'll survive our sentence, we'll yet sit together around the table under the ash tree and drink a toast, and sing." Even though she drove herself to exhaustion, Mother covered the sores on her feet with cobwebs, and reached the quarters of builder Belsky in Berdychev, who worked among the prisoners on the road construction gang. She gave him a parcel with two onions, two Easter eggs, a piece of bacon as thick as a finger wrapped in a scrap of linen, a bean pie smeared with garlic. "Not a chance," said the builder, "plague has spread through the prison." At night the laddersided wagon thudded heavily in passing, Mother hid behind a chokeberry bush in the cemetery, by dawn she had kissed each lump of dirt on the fresh mound again and again, falling asleep on her knees and dreaming of the letters written her in lilac ink by the deceased. Nobody could be bothered with the dying: complain all you want, pound your head against the walls, only the sad remembrance of the morning remained in the evening, when they would drag them to this place by the heels after the interrogations, Mother shook the sticky clay from her knees and limped home, after all she still had two daughters to look after.

In the fall the headmaster's groom, Petro Savchenko, climbed the maple to the church roof and chopped the cross down with an axe, wiping his rust-covered hands on the legs of his army pants, then panicked when it came time to climb down, his arms hung stiff as wood, no way could he reach the branch, the crowd's stares jarred him from below, and that's how the villagers remembered him: neck twisted, ear pressed to the faded patch of the epaulette on his shoulder, fingers scratching against the rusty sun of the cupola, spraying red rust into the people's eyes, for that evening he had guzzled too much moonshine, he burned up, the women in their despair were afraid to save him. Some time later they spied a bare-foot kobzar* in the church vestibule, who ate wild pears and taught them how to store pickled cabbage leaves, wild berries, green tomatoes for the winter, showed them how to grind wild hemp, pigweed and cornhusks in a mortar. He bent his head forward, with his hand shook the flecks of rust from his grey locks, sown there from the cupola by the wind, picked an overripe cucumber from Moskalenko's garden, hadn't even taken a bite, when the enraged brigadier fell on him with a yoke crossbar, across the back, across the back, and into the devil's thornbush, the blood flowing from his eyes smeared his face, he crawled out of the village and a terrible shadow under a red sky descended on the sycamores, silent and leafless on the riverbank, they found him past the bridge with no handrail, foam licked his unruly head, a green leech was fastened to his neck. *No more shall the light of the lamp appear in you, no more the voices of the bridegroom and the bride be heard in you! For your traders were once the merchant princes of the world, for with your sorcery you deceived all the nations. For the blood of the prophets and of the saints was found in it, and the blood of all who had been slain on earth.* Our mother went humbly begging. Wretched Mykola, the neighbor's boy, said, "Auntie, give me just one pickled apple." "Where from, precious, there, see, my children are growing listless, their swollen legs runny." "Auntie, listen, I dragged myself down to the treeline, hanged myself on a fir tree, which didn't frighten me, suffered the needles in my chest, my head, it seemed, ached from the fumes of imagined food odors." It was quiet, so quiet, occasionally a bucket clinked against a well joist, on the bare bell-tower an owl moaned, maddened by the stench of corpses, the living once more succumbed to despair, as happened on Holy Thursday, and shielding our candles with our hands, we slowly stumbled out of the church, gathered and thought, we have one last resort, and behind one anguish two evils lay in ambush. *And the devil said to him: "If you are the Son of God, tell this rock to turn into bread."*

Mother tied Halia and me to a table leg, she put stewed licorice into a cup, tucked a loaf of sourdough bread into each of our blouses, and said, I'll go to town, exchange the gold cross for food, we were silent, not a breath escaped our lips, when filthy Moskalenko barged into the hall, threw Mother down, tore off her cross, her wedding ring rang against the floor, he bared his teeth: "Run and complain to the new powers, run, they love heathens." Mother hugged us to her bloodied breast, God forbid that we should venture out the door, savages were stealing little children, and she both feared and hoped we might drift off to sleep and die on our own, she went with her bag then along the fence, that's the last we saw of her. *You, give them to eat. But they answered: We have no more than five loaves of bread and two fishes.* It was quiet, oh so quiet, but before, whenever our mother burst into song, the boys in the next village would begin to dance. Sister was the first to fall asleep forever under the coarse linen, for me the table still held the aroma of wheat flour on the rolling pin in Grandmother's hands, with which she rolled out the dough for pies, the aroma of smoked sausage with Christmas horseradish, of potato cakes in a bowl with fried onions and crackling, of beet soup spilled onto the oaken boards. I dreamed about a mustached peasant: he spat on the stone, gave the scythe a good sharpening, knocked his pipe out against the scythe handle, preparing to mow the river, milky in the fog, to crop the brooklime in the river shallows, the ripples running before a heavenly breath, that splashing woke me, and I saw: a granite darkness of clouds hanging over the windows, some sort of scratching struck my ear, as if heaven and earth, turned to stone by the cruelty, were grinding the rest of the living. There was a commotion under the table, I looked, two glowing coals flashed, the rat leaped back, backing away, its tail between its legs, Halia's fingers, thrust into her hair, embraced her head in a crown of thorns, her eyes glazed over, her leg crossed under her stomach turned bone white at the calf, I didn't have the strength to chew through the knot, I scraped the ground, the clayey earth spread like burning grease through intestines, the earth trampled by the dead carried both life and death equally, hairs stuck to my lips, the sand cracked painfully and smelled of poppies, the rat streaked by into the opening under the stove and its eyes glowed there with the horrible embers of a family's ruin. Groping along the wall I managed to limp to the door, abruptly jarring the cradle with my elbow, setting it rocking beneath the rafters, in its creaking death sang a lullaby, a stork trod through the mud, dressed in red, wearing red boots*. Behind the chest I found a wax candle which had brightened the faces of the whole family last Easter, and I crawled outside furtively, the worms that surfaced after the rain unceasingly devoured the softened ground and the air smelled of pitch from the thresher, where last year we had slaughtered a pig. *And I saw a new heaven and a new earth, for the first heaven and the first earth had vanished, and there was no longer any sea.*

I nibbled on the candle, a steam engine hooted at the station; in the valley, small birds hiding from a hawk shook dust from the pussy willows, a fox stalked the legions of mice among the shrubs of marsh growth, nothing harbingered fall, nor winter, nor spring, time split apart, only the wall of corn lamented against the window and black leaves buried the river, pleading, "How long must we do penance before the fish." The invisible right hand of God scattered here a swarm of starlings onto shrivelled plums, and there some sated rooks onto the road*. *And I looked, and I heard an eagle calling with a loud cry as it flew in mid-heaven: "Woe, woe, woe to the inhabitants of the earth at the sound of the remaining trumpets which the next three angels must now blow!"* Near the station I gnawed some more on the candle, bit through it and spat out the wick, bitter at the sooty end, with the back of my hand I rubbed the wax from my teeth. The railway shed smelled of cow-dung, light filtered through a crack in the door onto the hands of an old man who was eating a bit of crumbled bacon fat off his knife, onto a woman with a kerchief wound around her knee and two toddlers in her arms. "*Sausage makers* came to our village," she said, "my husband defended himself with a pitchfork, and there he moldered. I managed to force my way through a window and escape into the meadow, tearing headlong through the woods. I heard something panting at my back, the wolf almost on top of me, I kicked with my feet, it tore at my skirt, the threads blackened on its teeth, my arms turned to cotton, the children began crying, the wolf backed off into the shrubbery, this beast was more humane, oh Lord…" The old man threw down the salted piece of skin, later I became fearfully thirsty, the old man told his tale: "I had dragged myself over to the town, the village had gone belly up, and nobody to give it a Christian burial, I thought to beg a piece of bacon from someone in the town, so that today a memorial could be sung and a cross be decked with an embroidered linen, but it was just a dab of bacon, so they wouldn't seal the grave, evil spirits, had we only known to flee in the spring, but you've grown arthritic, old man, and everything is readied for you in the other world." The old man urged against begging for alms near the marketplace where, behind a paned window, two big louts with white smocks over their uniforms leaned with their elbows on the counter, the shelves bent under hardened lumps of sugar, under loaves sprinkled with caraway seeds, now and then people took gold from their bundles and while one merchant weighed ornaments, another pulled herring by their tails from a small keg, flies swarmed to the broth on the floor. The attic smelled of onions and mouse droppings, until midnight, while the bricks still retained heat, I warmed myself against the chimney, on the barrack steps a puppy chewed at fleas and an old man in glasses hunched over a table in the basement soldered and sealed the holes in the pots, with a handful of straw he rubbed the sooty glass, every day the number of lanterns on the shelves increased and nobody asked for them. In the middle of the night I took a candle from my waistcoat pocket, smelled it, and put a bit of the household light on my teeth: the wax smelled of autumn apples, drove the shudders from my body. Once again the chimney sighed with heavy indifference, once again the rascal wind rattled the topmost branches of the acacias, and once again the little mice scampered for bits of onion in the moonlit nooks, and there wasn't even a good cat to chase them off! Somewhere from beyond the town came the crack of shot after shot, the army defeated the defenses put up by the hungry villagers, and by morning a fire burned in the mine, smoke seeped from the earth piled around the mine shaft, like the bitterness of ashes in a cold stove, in the pre-dawn light coal dust drifted over dried wormwood, over an upturned pull-cart with its wheels in the air, over people who, shrugging their shoulders in the chill and huddling against a rain squall under waterproof awnings, hurried to work at the sound of the siren. Occasionally the flare of a match scratched by stone-scarred hands illuminated the muddy rainwater that ran down the peaks of their caps, it's here that Father rests, here is his unsung grave, I thought to myself, wanting to resurrect fear through sorrow, so sweet death would remember me, no use, the black rains hammered down, a bobtailed puppy wedged itself under the roof overhang and whimpered, expecting a kick, the old man continued to prepare the lanterns, covering the floor around the table with them, it seemed that people purposely rid themselves of the sad quiet light, which was showered with rust and sputtered in the empty pot when the tradesman shook it by his ear.

My candle, grown dim from the dust cloud, was barely a reminder of home: a light sprinkle of rime on the doorway sealed with twists of straw, Mother bringing in a vat of lye out of the freezing cold, salt crackling in the crimson oven, and here an old lady out on the street untying a bundle and plucking at a loaf of bread, somehow we'll endure until the harvest, not sown by anyone, this sort of wheat springs up in the fields, I'll crush the ears of grain in the wash tubs, such a smell of groats will fill the room, it would be a sin not to live to see salvation. The old lady went over to the well, drank some water, leaning, leaning, when suddenly, bump, she cracked her head against the tub, next day they took away her body. After a while I lost my taste for herring, I would scrounge in the ditch behind the merchant's, pound the heads and tails on a rock, it was garbage and then you couldn't drink enough water, your stomach would bloat, to this day I cannot pray away the fear that sent goosebumps through me when I took the bundle from the old lady's dead hands, grasping, as if pulling me to her, blood gushed from my nose, I heard someone hammering, the merchants had plastered their faces to the windowpanes, laughing, they took me to an orphanage, there I chewed up the remains of the candle. *Lord, terrible is Thy punishment. May your loins be girded, and the lamps in your hands lighted.* These days my grandson Pavlo is a bit dull-witted, afraid of everything, rouses from a broken sleep, every Sunday his mother fixes him a sack of food for school, his father used to deliver mineral fertilizer to an airplane, now angina is killing him, the earth swaddles the evil and the just, the sated and the saints. – And a voice came to me last night: *You will soon die, and an azure dove in a golden shower shall embrace the book with the seven seals with a sweep of its wings, extinguish the lamp and bear to the celestial altar the testimony of the eve of the Great Judgement.*

Published in Ukrianian in *Svitovyd* No. 2, 1994

Notes:

"…and they promised to mount a radio loudspeaker on a post" — These loudspeakers in village squares were both a status symbol and a tool for government propaganda.

Cossack (Kozak) — from Turkic *kazak*, or freeman; frontiersmen, adventurers, runaway serfs who formed a martial society in the Ukrainian steppe. Beginning in the 15th century, they banded together for mutual protection. Over time, the Cossacks developed a democratic military organization which, in the middle of the 17th century, gave rise to a massive anti-Polish uprising, and led to the birth of the early modern Ukrainian state called the Cossack Hetmanate.

kulak — The term applied to all but the poorest peasants by the Soviet authorities as they sought to collectivize agriculture. Kulaks were exiled, sent to labor camps, or killed in the 1930's.

kobzar — Kobzars were blind minstrels who wandered from town to town and who played a lute-like instrument, the kobza.

"A stork trod through the mud, dressed in red, wearing red boots" — There is a Ukrainian lullaby about a stork tromping through the mud in "red boots," referring to his bright red stork legs. Here, however, there is bitter irony in the lullaby for a dead child, for the reference in this case is to Red Army soldiers.

"The invisible hand of God scattered starlings and rooks" — Starlings are garbage pickers, while black rooks, in folklore, are harbingers of death.

Valery
SHEVCHUK

The Moon's Cuckoo
from the Swallow's Nest

Translated by Myrosia Stefaniuk
English style-editing by Debra Spark

Yulka was small, only five centimeters taller than short Natalka, with squat hips on stumpy legs but with breasts so surprisingly large that they burst out of her clothes. Her face was as round and flat as the moon and a tiny nipple nose rose like a beak from the center of it. Her grey lips were undistinguishable from the rest of her face, and her eyes, topped by a fine furrow of brows, were round, grey and astonished. Her wispy hair, of the same grey color, was clasped back with a rubber band. She appeared one day from one of the villages near Zhytomir, obtained the prescribed documents, and established herself at one of the toxic factories. She lived for a while in a communal dorm and then got a room on the outskirts of town, a room so small that it could hold only a bed, a small table and a chair. The room had two windows but no separate entrance. The landlady who sold it to her said Yulka could walk through her room for now, but as she spoke, she narrowed her eyes so that even a blind man could see this would only be a temporary arrangement. Yulka wasn't dumb; she realized that the former mistress of her room would not tolerate this inconvenience for long, but the landlady wanted to sell, Yulka wanted to buy and that settled the matter. Yulka became the owner of a room in a building on a hillside in which there were nine such cubby-hole dwellings. So far, there were only eight TV antennas on the roof, and each room had a shabby built-on entrance, some with little stairways or porches, all of them fastened to the building like swallows' nests.

"After you settle in some, you can build an entrance through one of the windows," the former owner of Yulka's room said benevolently, narrowing her eyes again. This was almost an ultimatum, but Yulka silently agreed to it because she knew perfectly well that it wouldn't be enough merely to buy the room. If she wanted to live in her own home instead of those horrid communal quarters, eventually she would have to invest time and money in her new place, and this would be no small problem for her. Yulka had already spent all her savings on the room, and it was unlikely that she could put anything away from her earnings at the toxic factory.

And that was why during her free time, she opened the window, pushed up the chair (that she had bought with the bed and table, along with the room from the landlady), and set her exquisite bosoms — that practically burst out of her blouse — on the windowsill. She sat this way — motionless, dozing or daydreaming — and stared at the willows along the river, or at the portion of the street that was visible from her sill. Or maybe she wasn't looking at anything or anyone, for as she sat, her face became indifferent, like a greying moon that had perched on a windowsill to rest for a while. Yulka was so still and aloof that every man who happened to pass by, inadvertently turned his face toward her. Some merely threw her a glance, others flashed toothy grins, but no one stopped or attempted to talk to her, although everyone's eyes took in her voluptuous breasts. Yulka reacted not at all to these gazes; it was as if she didn't see anyone. Or maybe it just seemed that way, for who can guess what a woman thinks, or what she sees or doesn't see.

[Yulka continues to perch daily on her windowsill. At length, a man named Shurka Kuksa notices her... and her breasts. He becomes instantly determined to have her, both because he is so smitten with her breasts and because he is, for the moment, between lovers. He has recently left his mistress, who had been pressuring him to marry her. And while Shurka Kuksa is a man who can't do without a woman, he is also a man with no interest in marriage.

Shurka Kuksa propositions Yulka. She scorns him at first but when he claims that he's the kind that can do anything, Yulka agrees to consider his advances, but only if he installs a door where her window now is. This strikes Shurka Kuksa as ridiculous. He's never been much of a worker, and, he proudly admits to himself, he is used to getting women at no cost.

Still, Shurka Kuksa is, quite literally, moonstruck. He can't get Yulka off his mind as the light of the moon pours down on him. He decides to go to the Podil* to look for a door. He thinks he'll take one from a dilapidated building there, but the place has already been stripped, so he ends up stealing a door from the "White House," a communal building (not unlike the Swallow's Nest where Yulka lives) that houses one of Shurka Kuksa's former mistresses. Shurka brings the door to Yulka and, expecting his reward, gropes Yulka's breast. Yulka doesn't react to his touch and refuses him any more access to her until he installs the door.

The next day Yulka leaves the "Nameless backstreet" where she lives and goes to work. Shurka spends the day installing the door. As he does, he gets nosy questions from the "goat-woman," the former occupant of Yulka's room who is now Yulka's landlady. (Yulka's landlady looks like a goat, but indeed every woman at the Swallow's Nest seems to resemble a barnyard animal.) The women of the building watch while he works. Ludka, the local busybody — and a virgin who lives alone — also watches. At the end of the day, Shurka buys some home-brew from the landlady, gets a bit drunk on it, and falls asleep in Yulka's room. He dreams that all the women from the Swallow's Nest dance around him naked in their animal likenesses, and sing a lullaby to him in their animal voices. In the dream, Ludka is the only one who is not naked and does not resemble an animal. She comforts Shurka because "he's stupid and neglected," and the poor wretch, who has known only misunderstanding and abuse, is moved to tears. Then, in a semi-sleep state, he sees:

"...*the moon's daughter walking down the Nameless backstreet...a narrow dirt path winding through a barren valley without shrubs, trees or grass. She walked along it slowly on stumpy legs, tired, filled with poisons inhaled at the toxic factory, her face deadened and indifferent, her grey eyes overflowing with those same poisons.*"

It is Yulka, who has returned from work. Shurka asks for his "payment" but Yulka refuses him, because her door needs a lock and because he is drunk. She tells him, emphatically, "I can't stand drunks." He leaps at her, pawing her, but she kicks and screams and sends him on his way. The next day, he returns and installs the lock. Yulka makes him dinner and promises him payment if he returns after eleven, the time when the entire Swallow's Nest rocks with the rhythms of men making love to their wives.

Sober and sprayed with eau de cologne, Shurka returns that night. On the way, he feels some unease about the busybody Ludka, who he assumes is following him. But he continues on to the Swallow's Nest, where he finds Yulka — hot to the touch — and makes passionate love to her.

Meanwhile, Ludka, who is, indeed, following Shurka, feels a bit apprehensive about spying on him, because earlier in the evening her friend was telling her about extra-terrestrials who steal virgins. She suspects that the "mysterious and strange street character, Rudko," the man who has been staring at her so intensely as if "some fine thread had already linked them some time earlier," may, in fact, be an extra-terrestrial. Her concerns fade away as she follows Shurka, but her sadness returns as she spies on Shurka at the Swallow's Nest. She feels she is the only one who is left out of the love that is taking place all around her. And she raises her arms to the cold, star-studded sky and cries out

"... *to that invisible nothingness which is everything and sees everything and knows everything and controls everything. Let it show itself—that force which has the body of hope and the eyes of love; let it pour its eternal pitcher of radiant milk down on her as well...so that she would not be a lone reed with despair for its seed, so that she too would have purpose in this world.*"

Then she sees Rudko, that strange and mysterious man "who sought out the lonely and the pure, and endowed them with a mystery," walking toward her. He stands there, "flooded by the moon's radiance," then leans over her as she lies prone in the cool womb of the earth, strokes her hair, wipes her tears and assures her gently that everything will be fine.

Several days later, and with everyone at the Swallow's Nest watching, some wooden boards are unloaded in front of Yulka's house. Yulka informs her landlady that she's going to install a gas stove and cylinder in her room, since she can't use the landlady's kitchen forever. Yulka claims to have received an allotment of boards from work, but the boards are so old and worn that nobody believes her. They tell her she has to take them out of the yard and Yulka starts to drag the boards up the hill, stacking them below her window. —*M.S.*]

Meanwhile, Shurka Kuksa decided to wander over to the Nameless backstreet in hopes of reaching an agreement with Yulka about his next night visit, but in the nick of time he noticed that she was dragging boards, so he hid among the willows, telling the smashed bucket that lay there, "She's hot but very expensive. If I'm not careful, I'll become her personal slave."

Shurka Kuksa spoke this out loud, and then lay back on the grass, gazed at the bright sky, listened to the larks, and succumbed to sweet idleness, crowning his pleasure by sucking on the sap of a stem.

Yulka lugged the boards, secretly expecting Shurka to catch her in the act, because she had a feeling that he wouldn't abandon her after their first time together, and when he returned, she could just turn the job over to him, albeit at the price of another one night stand. And then, Yulka thought, she would make a deal with him about building an addition.

With this one operation, Yulka wanted to catch several rabbits. Rabbit number one: construction of an addition for a gas stove. Rabbit number two: getting this done without any special losses, even though she had nothing in particular to lose. And finally, rabbit number three: Shurka Kuksa wasn't married — Yulka had found this out for certain — so she hoped to use these projects to get a firm hold on him. There was Lord knows how much work still to be done in that Swallow's Nest in which she had invested all her money. If Shurka Kuksa worked on the nest, he'd get used to it, because, in a way, it would be his then, too. So in that respect, Shurka Kuksa had guessed correctly: Yulka did want to make him a live-in slave.

But Shurka was a child of a system that proclaimed: "Better that everyone (except officials) be poor than that half be poor and half be rich," and so he preferred to lie idle on the grass rather than to carry Yulka's boards, even if this meant sacrificing a night's pleasure. He regretted this a little but consoled himself simply; he closed his eyes, letting the sun's rays sweetly caress his eyelids, and in his imagination replayed everything that had happened to him in the Swallow's Nest. It was all sweet and delightful, and he dozed contentedly while Yulka labored. She was boiling mad at him now; the bum had failed to turn up.

As soon as she finished the work, he woke. He continued to rest while Yulka cleaned up, ate, and washed the dishes, her anger cooling. Then, when she had settled in her single window, he sighed, picked himself up and headed toward the Nameless backstreet. Being a man, he couldn't stay away from Yulka when he still had hopes that he might pluck a flower from her field.

When he spotted her round face in the window and those flowing bosoms on the sill, he paused, leaned back against the fence, and called out to her, "Oh! You're back from work already!"

"As you can see!" Yulka snipped curtly.

"I sure put in nice doors for you," Shurka Kuksa said tongue-in-cheek. "Like a picture."

"Doors are doors," Yulka replied straightforwardly, referring to the actual doors and not his silly innuendo.

"What are these boards under your window for?"

"I want to put in an addition," she said, more gently.

"Listen," Shurka Kuksa began directly, "maybe you'll invite me for a visit today too?"

Her round astonished eyes poured gray opalescence over him like cold water.

"Why not," she said. "If you make an addition for me."

Shurka got upset. This was really too much. "Do you know what it costs to have an addition made?"

"I'm not forcing you," Yulka said calmly. "You asked, and I answered."

"To make an addition you have to be a carpenter."

"Well, yes," Yulka said. "You did put in a door."

"Doors are simple. I can't build an addition."

"Suit yourself," Yulka replied and turned away from him to look at the riverscape, or maybe at the moon, which was already visible even though the sky was bright and there was plenty of light all around. The moon, carved in the bright sky, looked a bit astonished, almost like Yulka's eyes, and for some strange reason, Shurka Kuksa felt embarrassed that he didn't know how to build an addition. Still, he was afraid of drowning in the grey mother-of-pearl of Yulka's eyes and in the wide flood of her breasts on the windowsill. It occurred to him that maybe it had all been a dream — that hot coupling of theirs — because apparently nothing had changed in their relationship. She was just as distant with him as before — maybe even more so — and to reestablish their closeness, she now proposed an even higher price. Although he was attracted to her beyond words, he was afraid of getting caught in a new yoke.

"I'll talk to Kolia-the-fisherman," she said indifferently. "I'm sure he could handle the job."

This time, it seemed her words had a double meaning, and Shurka stared directly at Yulka. It was the double meaning that sobered him up, forced him to come to his senses, and maybe even offended him. "Well, fine, talk to him," he said. "Kolia knows how. Bye."

"Bye!" Yulka said indifferently and looked out at the riverscape, as if she had nothing to do with Shurka Kuksa, didn't know him and didn't want to.

So Shurka left, but she remained at the window: her face became sleepy, like a sallow moon perched there for a rest. She was so still and aloof that every man who walked down the backstreet turned, without fail, in her direction. But she noticed nothing, and had no need to move.

This happened day after day. Sometimes Shurka appeared in the neighborhood, but he never came close, and Kolia-the-fisherman's paths were such that he didn't wander into the Nameless backstreet. Indeed, Kolia's paths were very simple: to and from work, and to and from the river.

There was a devil inside Kolia-the-fisherman as well, black and fleshed out, with real horns and a tail. But this demon had a guardian who was watchful as a goose, who even resembled a goose, and this guardian was Kolia's mother-in-law. His wife, Lubka, was aware of his demon, but she was indifferent to it; there were enough other worries in her life. Whenever the devil awoke in Kolia-the-fisherman, he would either start drinking and throw his wife and mother-in-law out of the house — this was the simpler and less dangerous madness — or else he would embark on amorous adventures, and then his mother-in-law resolutely assumed the task of chasing the devil out of him. She did this by spying on him and then creating a scandal for the slut who responded to his advances. All this, invariably, ended simply. Kolia eventually returned to the bosom of his family, and the demon ended up disgraced, thrashed, and purged, with a torn tail and broken horns. In the end, the devil became so meek and scared that he withdrew into the depths of Kolia-the-fisherman's soul while Kolia once again returned to his customary paths: to and from work, and to and from the river. Although his mother-in-law might be appeased, she didn't let him out of her sight. She appeared on the island frequently to check on Kolia-the-fisherman's whereabouts and doings. If some need carried him away from the area, she knew exactly where he went, when he would return, and with whom he had business.

The mother-in-law was tiny and thin, with a sharp, goose-like face and a slight smile; it was only when she talked about lechers and whores that her voice became rusty and hoarse, her face turned furious, her eyes fumed with a copper flame, and her lips pressed together like two steel plates. This was the kind of moral guardian our Kolia had. All the women in the neighborhood knew it very well, and whenever the demon awoke in him, not one of them gave in to his advances, so he had to prowl elsewhere, such as at work, where there was a staunch security system in place, set up to keep exactly such mothers-in-law out (for it certainly didn't prevent the theft of so-called "government property," and this too everyone knew, including the security guard who had to make a living somehow).

7.

Kolia-the-fisherman turned into the Nameless backstreet one evening by coincidence and with good intentions. There, in the Swallow's Nest, lived a certain Vadym, husband of a woman who resembled a cat and owned a fantastic, lovely cat with white fluff on its tail and white fur on its chest, a cat whom she loved, in truth, more than her husband and children. And so her husband was uncomfortable at home, and became a fisherman. He had once promised to give Kolia a fishing line, or a float, or some worms, or maybe it was a sinker, or so the devil convinced Kolia, curling up his knuckles like a donut and knocking on his patron's heart. (The ancient Greeks would have described this more poetically; they would have said the little winged god Cupid, or Amor, or Eros, stretched an arrow over his bow and even though his eyes were blinded, the god shot and his arrow found its mark right in Kolia-the-fisherman's heart.) At any rate, that was how Kolia ended up in the Nameless backstreet, and the first thing he saw was an unfamiliar woman, perched in a window with her exquisite bosoms flooding the windowsill. Her face was as round as the moon, a face so calm, indifferent and self-absorbed that, for a moment, Kolia-the-fisherman forgot about Vadym, dropped to his knees, and stared at the fleeting vision.

"Well, hello, Lunar Cuckoo," Kolia-the-fisherman said softly. "Somehow I never noticed you before."

She turned her eyes toward him and drenched him in her cold mother-of-pearl gaze, or maybe she extended some icy feelers toward him and pawed with prickly but gentle fingers.

"Hello," Yulka replied indifferently.

Now Kolia-the-fisherman had no further thoughts of Vadym. Confident that he, better than anyone else, knew how to hoodwink women, he began to sweet talk Yulka. She responded curtly and indifferently, but in such a way that he gave in more and more, not so much to her charms — save her exquisite breasts, she had none — but to his demon who immediately convinced him that it would be easy to pluck a flower here. Kolia-the-fisherman didn't think about his mother-in-law; she was no longer of any concern to him. Besides, he reasoned, he was on vacation now, so while he couldn't get away with an affair at work, something might happen now. Anyway, to go without a love affair when the demon was awake was impossible, unless he drowned his sorrows in drink and again threw his wife and mother-in-law out of the house. Drinking and driving the women of his house away would have been the easier way to satisfy his demon, but he had already spoken too many sweet words for that, so he let his tongue continue to wag just as Shurka Kuksa's tongue had wagged earlier.

"So, maybe you'll invite me in for a visit?"

"You want a lot," Yulka said indifferently.

"No, I'm serious."

She became silent and once more flooded him with her cold mother-of-pearl gaze.

"Maybe I will invite you in," she said calmly. "Build me an addition out of these boards, and we'll talk. They say you know how to…"

Kolia-the-fisherman was dumbfounded. What was this? Was she making fun of him? To build an addition would take at least a week or two. Was that what she wanted?"

"And you'll pay me for it, yes?" Kolia-the-fisherman asked.

"You know that already," Yulka replied without looking at him.

Kolia-the-fisherman wavered. Should he say yes, or no? If he were to build an addition for her, this would be a superb ruse and his mother-in-law would never guess a thing. Then again, Kolia-the-fisherman's love affairs never lasted more than a week once he got what he was after. If the lady in question happened to play by the rules, it might take a little longer to win her favors, but once he had her, the affair was soon over. Such was his makeup. It wouldn't take long to win this one over, and he'd gladly start on the addition, but there was yet another consideration. If he took on an extra job, both his wife and his mother-in-law would be happy, but both of them would be sure to demand that he give them his earnings. And that meant that he himself would have to pay for the addition that he had built. Kolia had five hundred *karbovantsi** stashed away. He could tell the women that he got paid seven hundred and was keeping two hundred for himself. After fussing, he imagined, they would consent to this, but perhaps it was too high a price for the pleasure!

While he was mulling this over, Yulka somehow managed to reach an understanding with his demon, and from within, the devil began to work on Kolia-the-fisherman's heart. He grasped Kolia's eyes, one in each palm, and began to fling them at that exquisite flood of bosoms on the windowsill until Kolia-the-fisherman felt that at any minute, he would overflow like a lake. Practical considerations no longer mattered — Kolia would live only once, and the devil convinced him that his savings would soon vanish like smoke anyway. Later, it would not be so much the conquest of a woman that Kolia would remember, but the satisfaction of outsmarting his mother-in-law. That would be worth not only five hundred — but a thousand rubles! This was apparently the demon's clinching argument, for Kolia-the-fisherman suddenly said, "And do you have tin to cover the roof?"

"Don't you have any?" Yulka replied carelessly. She already knew he had agreed.

"The supplies must be yours," said Kolia.

"You'll cover it with tar paper," Yulka said. "I'll get it."

Now Kolia began to squirm a little and gaze somewhere beyond her head. "I'll have to talk over a thing or two. I don't know if I'll be free," he said.

"Go ahead and talk it over. There's no fire," Yulka responded nonchalantly.

Kolia-the-fisherman was an experienced tactician. Working for Yulka, he would be visible not only to the Nameless backstreet but to the entire neighborhood. Thus, the job had to be sanctioned not only by his wife, but even more importantly, by the guardian of his morals. Everything must be out in the open, so the women wouldn't suspect a thing. Only one event need remain secret — and the time for that would be carefully selected. The hour Yulka had meticulously chosen for Shurka Kuksa would not do for Kolia-the-fisherman, for this was the time Kolia was expected to be lying next to his lawful wife, pleasing her as other husbands of the neighborhood pleased their wives at that hour. Even this was under the anxious surveillance of his mother-in-law, because if he put his wife off, his guardian would suspect something was amiss, and would begin to investigate.

And so Kolia-the-fisherman didn't talk to Yulka much longer, but went to see Vadym. There Kolia got the fishing line, or float, or sinker, or worms he was looking for, and when he finally left and walked back across the yard of the Swallow's Nest, he felt almost like a saint, impaled by the stares of eight women. (Kolia-the-fisherman once came across an illustration of such a thing in one of his mother-in-law's religious books.) He was like a saint—Sebastian, shall we say —because all those women had witnessed but not heard his conversation with Yulka, and they were now dying of curiosity about its contents. The wind had only carried their words into a neighbor's orchard, where the only one who could have heard them was an old, scabby dog who was sullenly guarding some practically bare apple trees—and trifles such as this didn't interest the dog at all.

"So Yulka was bargaining with you to make an addition?" the former owner of Yulka's room bleated boldly.

"Oh!" said Kolia-the-fisherman stopped, feigning surprise. "You know everything, auntie. It was about the addition! But I'm not sure if I'll take on the job or not; I have to talk it over with my wife."

"She's not offering much?" the goat-woman asked.

"No, not much," replied Kolia-the-fisherman. "These days, everything's expensive."

"Yeah, sure are hard times now," added another neighbor, the owner of a bulldog, who looked like a bulldog herself.

"I don't know, don't know," said Kolia-the-fisherman. "Maybe I'll take the job on, but probably not. I'd rather go fishing. Then I can bring home a tail or two and don't need to exert myself."

"Ah, men are such laggards these days," said the owner of the bulldog.

"So who wants to break his back, auntie?" said Kolia-the-fisherman and went on his way. He was secretly pleased by the bulldog owner's words. This was exactly the kind of impression he wanted to leave—one of disinterest. Later on, he would tell them that it was his wife and mother-in-law who forced him to take the job. What could be more engaging than your own wife and even your mother-in-law, guardian of your morals, pushing you into the arms of some lunar Cuckoo? He wouldn't be a man if he didn't take advantage of such an opportunity.

And so Kolia-the fisherman calmly returned home. Neither his mother-in-law nor his son were there. His wife was alone. He teased her for a while, even though she wasn't amorously inclined; she snapped at him and pushed his advances away, but not very strongly. In a while, his mother-in-law returned. Kolia busied himself with his fishing gear. The womenfolk teased him about his activities, and then Kolia casually recalled the thing he had never forgotten.

"By the way," he said, "when I went to see Vadym, there was some new tenant at the Swallow's Nest... She wants an addition built...somehow she found out that I know how..."

"I'm the one who told her," said the mother-in-law.

("Fantastic," Kolia thought. "One-zero, in my favor.")

"She asked me to build an addition. I didn't give her an answer, thinking I would talk it over with you. I'm not very anxious to cut my vacation short, I'd rather spend it sitting in a boat..."

They both stared at him, their eyes flashing.

"A nibble," thought Kolia-the-fisherman and contentedly lit a cigarette.

"How much will she give you?" asked Lubka.

"That's just the point. A mere trifle. Five hundred."

"You bargain with her," the mother-in-law demanded.

"She says she doesn't have any more."

"She's a cocky peasant," the mother-in-law declared. "These upstarts have money."

"I didn't count her money," said Kolia-the-fisherman. "And I don't really want to ruin my vacation. I exert myself enough at work. And if you really want to know, Mama, I'm a cocky upstart too."

The mother-in-law was dumfounded for a minute.

"You're not a peasant anymore," she said. "You've been living in the city for a long time now. The cocky ones are the ones that just moved here from the village. In my opinion, you should take the job... She's such a toad, so homely," she said to her daughter. "Even that sort comes crawling into the city. What is she hoping for? You can smell the cockiness in her."

The fact that she spoke this way about Yulka was good, although it did irk Kolia-the-fisherman a bit. In his eyes, Yulka wasn't as homely as all that.

("So, it's two-zero?" he asked himself.)

"I feel the same way," Lubka put the final seal on his guaridan's sanction. "Instead of loafing on the river, you'll bring home a kopeck or two. At least it'll pay for your meals…"

This really aggravated Kolia-the-fisherman; sometimes Lubka could be so spiteful.

"And what, don't I have my own home!" he growled.

"You do, of course you do," his mother-in-law said consolingly. "As far as I know, she goes to work too. So is she going to leave you in the house?"

The question was obviously a meddlesome one, so Kolia-the-fisherman answered it casually. "I've told you that I didn't make any deal with her yet. We just talked about it. I'm not all that anxious to exert myself."

"So you'll exert yourself a little," Lubka said nonchalantly. "You'll lose some of that belly, because on that boat, all you do is get fatter."

Lubka's barb was sharp; lately, Kolia's stomach had begun to bulge while his wife remained thin and supple (and she liked to poke fun at his belly). For some reason, Kolia observed, thin people disliked fat ones. She knew very well that this comment would anger him.

But he decided to let it be. "Go ahead and laugh, laugh…"

8.

And so Kolia-the-fisherman began to build an addition for Yulka. Beforehand, he had a very practical conversation with her, because Kolia liked to have everything clear. Then, on the first day, he dug a ditch for a small foundation and began transporting rocks from the river for it. He turned down Yulka's *borsch* at lunchtime, saying he would have lunch at home, but he agreed to eat her supper, and after supper, he firmly insisted on payment for the day's work. Yulka tried to weasel out of it, as she had done with Shurka, but that didn't work with Kolia, because he threatened to abandon the job (and reminded Yulka just how much she was costing him). So Yulka submitted and obediently went to bed. He worked her over with such pleasure and skill that Yulka groaned under him softly. But she neither embraced him nor kissed him until he reproved her; then she held him but responded to his kisses only lukewarmly. Well, Kolia-the-fisherman thought, this would have to suffice the first time.

The transaction didn't take long. The women in the yard knew that Kolia was having supper with Yulka, but there was no way that they could observe how many dishes Yulka served, nor what the dessert was, though the former owner of Yulka's room did press her ear to the keyhole while they were having supper, and Yulka must have suspected the same, because she turned on the radio and thoroughly muffled all sound. The goat-woman did the eavesdropping only partially of her own initiative, for she was a friend of Kolia's mother-in-law, and although Kolia's mother-in-law was contemptuous about Yulka's feminine charms, she wasn't about to neglect her duties as guardian of Kolia's virtue. She had arrived on location early, when Kolia-the-fisherman was still at home sleeping, and asked the goat-woman to keep an eye on him.

Kolia-the-fisherman had a different problem after the vigorous dessert Yulka served him: later that evening, he had to repeat the performance with his wife and that was a bit too much for him. The first night, he was able to excuse himself by claiming exhaustion. (Lubka knew that he had been lugging rocks all day because she had gone to watch him at work). The second evening, he again used the rocks as an excuse, but that day he had mortared the foundation wall, and Lubka knew this too. She didn't go to see it herself, but the mother-in-law did. The problem occurred on the third evening, after he had built the frame for the addition. That day, Yulka was hot and eager, even though he had planned to take a break from her. He walked home in a complete daze from his "dessert," brooding over what would happen when he couldn't repeat the performance with his wife. Then not only his wife but also his mother-in-law would become suspicious. So Kolia-the-fisherman made up his mind to rely on stimulants. But earlier Yulka wouldn't give him a drink, and he hadn't been able to convince her otherwise because she claimed she would rather see him quit the job than drink. She just hated drunks.

"I'd be thoroughly repulsed by you," Yulka had told him bluntly, and so he'd given in,

When Kolia came home, he started to fuss and, as was his habit, act like a spoiled child. He said that if his wife and mother-in-law didn't give him a drink, he wouldn't go back to work the next day and would forgo payment on what he had already done.

"I'm paying myself anyway," he thought.

Besides, he told them, he was tired of exerting himself, and he had had enough. They wouldn't let him rest during his vacation, because all they knew was money, money — and they could choke on it, as far as he was concerned.

To settle the conflict, the mother-in-law had to rush over to the former owner of Yulka's room and buy a bottle of moonshine. While she was at it, she checked on the results of the goat-woman's spying.

"They play the radio," the former owner of Yulka's room reported. Since every woman in the neighborhood played the radio this didn't raise the mother-in-law's suspicions and besides, she still didn't think Kolia-the-fisherman would be tempted by such a cocky peasant. In her opinion, Yulka was just too homely, especially compared to Lubka, who, in her estimate, was a beauty. The mother-in-law told the goat-woman about the problem with her son-in-law, who had suddenly developed whims, and then hurried home with half a liter of fermented sweet homebrew. She portioned out a quarter of it in the kitchen and hid the rest, saving it for her son-in-law's future weak moments.

Nothing aroused Kolia-the-fisherman sexually as much as alcohol, so he gulped down the portion, and because his mother-in-law had gone out again, and his son wasn't back yet from play, Kolia-the-fisherman played out a passionate love scene. Whether it was the whiskey or the scene itself that aroused him, Kolia and his wife locked themselves in the bedroom at a time completely atypical for such things, and they didn't come out even when they heard the mother-in-law returning. When she began to scratch at their door, Lubka sent her away so callously that she grasped the situation instantly.

After his passionate outburst, Kolia-the-fisherman could snore with a clear conscience. Meanwhile, the flushed and enflamed Lubka went out into the kitchen where she had all sorts of work to do. She glanced at her mother with haughty indignation, and the latter huddled on a bench without a word; in truth, they were now both calm and satisfied. Most satisfied of all, however, was Kolia-the-fisherman. He awoke just as Lubka was leaving the room after throwing a robe over his naked body. He waited until she was gone, and then giggled victoriously, gloating that he really knew how to thumb his nose at the both of them.

Afterwards, for some reason Kolia-the-fisherman couldn't fall asleep: maybe he was still drunk, or maybe he had been satisfied as never before, or maybe it was because his head was filled with strange thoughts — not about his wife with whom he had just enjoyed a love tryst, and not even about his mother-in-law whose goose nose he had just tweaked gloriously, but about the Moon's Cuckoo from the Swallow's Nest. He suddenly realized that what he found most alluring about her was the very "peasantness" of her; either it rekindled memories of his childhood and youth or aromas of his parental home, for Yulka was a peasant through and through — and those were the kind of girls he had wooed as a youth. To him they were the epitome of beauty. All the more so because there was a country fragrance about them — maybe of fields, or hay, or the scented herbs in which they bathed their bodies, or maybe of that primal force that people who live close to the earth possess and plant into their fields, valleys, meadows and gardens. Once, Kolia had visited Kiev, and God knows what led him to a museum there. In front of the place stood several roughly carved stone figures of women. They had flat faces and enormous pendulous breasts, low hips and short squat legs. Remembering the figures, Kolia was stunned to realize that Yulka looked just like those stone women from antiquity.

If it wasn't for the alcohol in him, maybe he wouldn't have had such strange thoughts, but it seemed to him that Yulka was a reincarnation of one of those ancient Scythian women, or maybe it was Scythian blood, undiluted yet by life, that ran in her veins. He remembered how passionate and hot she was today, how impassioned he had been. This never happened with his own wife. He had clearly sensed the fragrance of wormwood on Yulka's body, but no, it wasn't just the scent, for a strange ache arose from Kolia-the-fisherman's chest and spinning head. It seemed, suddenly, as if he were in another life — and he was mowing grass, heaving haystacks into a thresher; he remembered the blazing sun, the scent of straw ground into dust, how it smelled of sunshine. He remembered the lovely eyed, dust-covered girls on the threshers, their hair tied with white ribbons, and overhead, the rapturous sound of a lark. Somewhere near the thresher, he grabbed one of those lovely eyed girls, and she screamed and began pushing him away, but in his hand he felt her trembling, pulsating breast, and he inhaled it all into his lungs — the earthy, rustic spirit of the girl. That was what he had sensed in Yulka today. But this trance lasted only a minute because Kolia-the-fisherman's intoxication had run away like excess water. He looked around with a satisfied, squinting eye. He was proud of the fact that he was lying not in some slovenly peasant hut, but here, in the city, and that his wife had just left the room, smelling not of herbs but perfume, because before making love she always dabbed some perfume on. He was proud, too, that she had catered to him by letting him drink today, and that he had not humiliated himself, as he might have, for it was no small accomplishment to work over and please two women in one evening. These were the comforting thoughts that lulled him to sleep again and plunged him into a dream, a dream which, more than anything, was about the village, about reincarnated Scythian women with round moon faces; about horses racing into the night, emanating intoxicating fragrances; about cows that trampled morning's golden dew and trumpeted greetings to the large rising light; about the smell of a freshly-baked loaf of bread from the oven soaked in oil and sprinkled with salt; and for that matter, about crunching a fresh cucumber right off the vine in the garden. And there — in that dream — he felt a wistful longing clutching at him. God knows where it came from or why. And then he saw a white phantom with a chalk-white face walk through the house, and the moon in the upper window pane flooded the figure from behind, and something metallic glistened around the phantom's head, and suddenly he was afraid that it might be some evil spirit coming at him, and he jumped up in fear. "What?!"

"It's only me," laughed Lubka. "I put on a cold cream mask for the night."

9.

"You'll need to find something to cover the addition," Kolia-the-fisherman told Yulka when he came to work just as she was getting ready to leave for her job. "Because I'll be finished in two days."

"So you're not going to get it for me?" Yulka asked, smiling somewhat mysteriously.

"That wasn't part of the deal," said Kolia. "You're already costing me plenty."

She didn't say anything and left. When Kolia eyed her from a distance, he thought she was indeed ugly. What did he see in her to exert himself this much, and to pay his wife a small ransom as well? He must be mad. He thought he'd give himself a rest today; that is, work without payment and convince Yulka to pay out another time, because after last night he felt as if he were made of cotton. He yawned and had a cigarette, but it didn't taste good. He eyed his work critically; it wasn't turning out badly.

"Yes, I'm melancholy!" he concluded. "And when I go mad, I really go mad."

He dreaded starting the job. He felt like a limp piece of straw. Then he realized someone was staring at him. It was the goat-woman.

"Listen, auntie," said Kolia-the-fisherman. "Maybe you could measure out a shot for me."

"Let Yulka give it to you. She's the one who hired you."

Kolia-the-fisherman sat down on a stump. "Yulka won't give me any because she objects to it. Besides, she's not here," he said. "I'll pay you. What do you charge for a glass?"

"For you — a ruble."

"O-ho!" said Kolia. "Expensive. How much goes into one of your glasses?"

"Everything's expensive now," said the goat-woman. "My glass holds a hundred grams."

"Well, then bring it out because I just can't get going."

At that very moment, Yulka was crossing the wooden planks over the washed-out dam, and who should come out from the bushes on the other side but Shurka-Kuksa.

"Hee, hee," he chuckled and grabbed Yulka. "Ah, we meet after all. So you've hired Kolia-the-fisherman?"

"Because you weren't willing," Yulka said indifferently, not reacting to his pawing.

"It was too expensive for me," said Shurka Kuksa. "Maybe you need something that's cheaper?"

"As a matter of fact, I do," Yulka spoke calmly. "Two rolls of roofing paper."

"Two whole rolls for that measly addition?" Shurka snapped. "One's enough."

"Then get one," Yulka said placidly.

"Then can I come by and see you?" Shurka grinned like a youth.

"If you're not drunk, we might reach an agreement," said Yulka, but when he tried to grab her voluptuous breasts again, she pushed him away.

"What about an advance, Yul?" Shurka asked, offended.

"You already took your advance," she replied and walked warily down the path, as if they were strangers.

"No, wait…" Shurka caught up with her and grabbed her shoulder. "So if I get the roofing paper, then you'll…with both of us?"

"That's none of your business," Yulka jerked her shoulder back. "And I'm not forcing you. If you want, then come, and if not, I won't cry for you."

She flooded him with that cold mother-of-pearl look from her strange eyes, and he suddenly realized that it was for her payment that he'd get the roofing paper. He would get it, because he was drawn to her like a magnet, and in his head he felt the familiar swoon. But he was offended that he had been replaced by Kolia-the-fisherman, that she was so indifferent to him, that she demanded payment for her love so coldly and shamelessly, and that he himself was unable to make her fall for him.

"What the devil!" Shurka Kuksa exclaimed to himself. "Am I falling in love with her?"

It made him laugh. How could he possibly fall in love with someone like her? He crossed the wooden bridge and decided to see what Kolia-the-fisherman was doing. He knew where he could get the roll of roofing paper; he had seen some in the shed where Vasia Ravlyk kept his chopped wood. The shed was near a garden, far from the house, and it would be easy to sneak in there. It'd be awkward any other way because he and Vasia Ravlyk were enemies now.

"Maybe that's exactly why I can take that roll from him — because we are enemies?" Shurka Kuksa thought and relaxed. Whistling to himself, he began to feel good. Really, what was there to worry about? There was a bright sun overhead, he knew how to get the roofing paper, and now that his problems were over, his spirit felt light. Today he'd get everything done, and then he would have Yulka's hot, burning body again, and afterwards he would be free as a bird again, without debts or obligations to anyone.

He heard the pounding of a hammer in the distance and followed the sound. He wanted to take a look at the fool that for the sake of Yulka's allurements was building an entire addition. Shurka had

turned down the prize, while this Kolia got hooked. No wonder he was a fisherman.

"Greetings, Kolia," he said when he reached the hill. "Working hard?"

"As you can see," Kolia-the-fisherman replied.

"And is she rewarding you with adequate payment?" Shurka bared his teeth.

Kolia-the-fisherman glanced at him warily. "You know everything?" he asked.

"Hell, Kolia, I put those doors in, so I know. She's one hot broad, no?" He saw Kolia-the-fisherman pale and was delighted.

"It's no concern of mine what went on between the two of you," Kolia-the-fisherman retorted sharply. "She hired me for payment, you understand?"

"Sure, I understand, Kol. A fitting payment."

"If you wag your tongue, you know what I'll do!" Kolia-the-fisherman threatened.

Shurka knew. Once, when there was some business between them, Kolia had clobbered him. "As far as I'm concerned, we're talking like buddies," Shurka said amicably. But a whiff of his breath explained Kolia's hostility.

"Just you remember," Kolia said sharply. "I was hired honestly, and I'm doing honest work. And I don't like your stupid insinuations, you understand?"

Still, Shurka decided to poke a little more fun at him.

"I understand, Kol," he said. "But do you know why I came to you? Because your mother-in-law approached me and started asking if I had noticed anything."

"And you told her about your doors?" Kolia asked spitefully, and Shurka sensed that he was right on target: Kolia felt threatened by him.

"I'm not stupid, Kol," Shurka replied. "She gave me a fitting payment. And with you, maybe it's different! I was just curious."

"Forget your curiosity." Kolia-the-fisherman peered at him with narrowing eyes. "Just don't wag your tongue!"

"There's another reason I came to see you," Shurka ventured. "Maybe you have a roll of roofing paper? This needs to be covered. I'd put a lock on my tongue then."

Kolia grabbed Shurka by the shoulders and lifted him off the ground until his feet dangled. "Don't you make an idiot out of me," Kolia hissed. "Or I'll lock your tongue myself, and I'll lock it up for good. And I'm not joking." He pushed Shurka down on all fours.

"All right, I understand," Shurka said picking himself up. "She's costing you plenty. She cost me a lot too, and it was worth it." He grinned. "What should I say if your mother-in-law begins questioning me again?"

"Tell her what you know," Kolia-the-fisherman said. "That I was hired honestly for honest work."

Too bad, Shurka thought to himself. It didn't work. He really didn't feel like crawling around Vasia Ravlyk's place for that roll, but the trick just hadn't worked on Kolia. Still, he thought, I understand everything, and Kolia understands me, too. Perfectly!

They shook hands and parted. But this chat had spoiled Kolia-the-fisherman's mood. It had seemed like everything was beautifully under control and that he had really tweaked his mother-in-law's nose, and now this oaf came along, and to top it off, the oaf had already slept with Yulka, because he'd put in her doors. So apparently Kolia was one of many who Yulka shamelessly used to improve her home, and he had thought that she was enfatuated with him. Kolia was displeased by all this, and maybe because he was in such a bad mood to begin with, he considered Yulka, for the first time, with sober eyes. Today he had absolutely no interest in her, or in woman-kind at all, for that matter. He needed to give himself a break. Maybe his weakness had passed. He had been in this state for too long! Yet just to drop everything wouldn't do either because that would create unhealthy suspicion among the women in the yard, and eventually with his wife and mother-in-law. Maybe what he should do, Kolia-the-fisherman concluded, was go fishing. That Shurka had really nauseated him. He was such a gossip. Shurka probably wouldn't reveal all these secrets directly to Kolia's mother-in-law, but he wouldn't be able to resist bragging to his street buddies, and they in turn would tell their own wives, and eventually it would all reach Lubka and his mother-in-law. No doubt about it. Then it wouldn't be Lubka or the mother-in-law who ended up with tweaked noses, but he, smart-aleck Kolia himself. He who would not only lose all of his savings, but would be disgraced as well. That was why Kolia didn't succumb to Shurka's blackmail and decided to scare him instead. It would have a much greater impact on that doddering Romeo. He had already beaten him up once before.

Considering all this, Kolia just didn't have the will to pick up a saw or ax or hammer, so he put away his tools and began to leave the yard when, of course, he ran into one of the women. It was the cat-like one, Vadym's wife. She was walking with a kitten on her breast, and both of them were purring softly.

"You've quit early today," said the cat-woman, or woman with cat.

"Can't work for some reason," Kolia grinned. "I'm heading for the river. Had a dream about a fish today."

"A live one or a dead one?" the cat-woman asked.

"A live one," Kolia-the fisherman replied.

"That's a bad dream," she said. "A dead one is even worse, but a live one isn't good either."

"That's why I can't work."

"You'd better not go to the river, Kol," said the cat-woman, and suddenly Kolia-the-fisherman looked at her with his eyes wide-open; she wasn't all that young anymore, but she was still very attractive.

"So maybe you'll invite me in?" Kolia asked devilishly.

"Oh sure, right away." The woman laughed and left.

"A nibble!" Kolia-the-fisherman thought, excited and pleased, and turned around to watch her firm calves and shapely rear end as she sauntered across the yard.

This improved his mood, and Kolia decided that once he was rested and the dust had settled, he would try dipping his line in this pond. But he couldn't return to work today, and since he didn't expect to get any payment anyway, he bolted through the gate of the Swallow's Nest, where the river glistened brightly before him, like a huge fish, beckoning him with a thousand sparkling eyes.

10.

Fortunately, Vasia Ravlyk was on the second shift today, so it wouldn't be much of a problem for Shurka Kuksa to get the roofing paper. There was only one thing he had to be alert for: that neighborhood busybody Ludka who might be spying on him. Actually, Ludka had been acting strangely lately: she didn't wind her way down the street from neighbor to neighbor any more, nor did she sit on the large stone with red-headed Nadka, or short Natalka, or Magadansha, or the taxi-driver; in fact, she didn't appear on the street at all, and Shurka Kuksa was a bit disturbed by this, because you felt safer if she was in sight; if not, you began to suspect that she had discovered some new method for spying, like red-headed Nadka's telescope. He wasn't threatened so much by a telescope at night, as he was by not knowing what to expect from Ludka. He resolved the problem simply: he decided to drop in on Ludka himself, and since they had once been classmates, he felt he had the right to do so. He'd tell her that he had run into one-or-another of their classmates, which, in fact, was actually true. So Shurka walked through the gate that led into a small enclosed garden filled with flowers and knocked on a door with peeling paint. Ludka was at home, having just returned from work, and was surprised by Shurka's visit, but then they chatted merrily about their classmates.

"Why don't we see you in the neighborhood anymore?" he asked. "You're not ill?"

"I'm sick of the neighborhood," Ludka commented indifferently. "I'm doing some sewing here."

True, there was an open manual sewing machine nearby with some fabric tucked under the needle press.

"Yes, we're getting old," Shurka said philosophically.

"Maybe you are, but not me," Ludka quipped cheerfully. "Are you still tweaking bulls' tails?"

"Nope," said Shurka. "I'm going to settle down."

"Are you still beating down Yulka's path?"

"How can you say that, Lud!" Shurka said indignantly. "She hired me to put in some doors. I worked for her for two days and that's all!"

"So what's that hammering there all day long?"

The question flabbergasted Shurka. Wonder of wonders! If Ludka didn't know that it wasn't him, but Kolia-the-fisherman working for the Cuckoo from the Swallow's Nest, then there was definitely something mysterious and unusual going on: Ludka, who knew where everybody's chicken was heading, now wasn't aware of such a simple fact.

"That's Kolia-the-fisherman building an addition for her," Shurka said, and then remembered Kolia's threats. "She hired him, too. Those peasants have money."

Ludka's eyes lit up for a moment, then faded.

"So let him build it," she said indifferently. "What's it to me!"

"Could she be sick?" Shurka thought, leaving Ludka's house. Well, let her be sick a while, at least until he obtained that roll of roofing paper and claimed his payment tonight. What happened tomorrow didn't interest him much. If it's true that every human being has a counterpart in the natural world: an animal, bird or insect, then he was, by nature, a moth. It was no coincidence that ancient people had their own animal or bird totems and had names like Wolf, Fox, Rabbit, Skunk, Eagle, Hawk, Sparrow, Bluejay, Mosquito or Butterfly. Shurka Kuksa was a night creature. He loved to hover in the dark, but whenever he spotted a flame, he dove in headfirst, spun around till he became exhilarated, lost his head and scorched his wings. Then he gradually abandoned these activities until the next time he was drawn to night flights or love fancies, and once again flung himself head first into darkness.

Darkness excited him and filled his lungs; darkness intoxicated him, moonlight aroused him, and the cricket's song inspired him. Darkness made him bold and foolhardy, and everything he did that was forbidden occurred with its blessing. Shurka became a harmless child of darkness. The damage he did was more playful than malicious.

And so he headed into a thick patch of potatoes, or what scholars call earth pears or artichokes, and crouched there listening to the shouts of drunks and the buzzing of mosquitoes who were also night creatures and didn't bite their relative much — his blood was more poisonous than nourishing to them. Shurka settled down in the potato bushes — first of all, to make sure that Ludka really had no intentions of going out to spy, and second, to await that moment when the building's residents — and there were a hundred or more living there — would finally stop going to the toilet. As soon as darkness fell, they shuffled out like sleepwalkers, one after another, monotonously and quietly. They opened doors with their own hooks (there were three outhouses near Vasia Ravlyk's garden), hid inside, stayed for a while, and then came out. Others followed suit, and the final one was another child of darkness, the pharmacy lady, who was fat, plain and angry with herself and the entire world. She was saturated through and through with medicinal smells and so slow in her movements that she resembled a turtle. It was the turtle that finished off the evening parade, because she needed to hide in the wooden outhouse a little longer than the others. Maybe that was where she read fortunes on the stars that peered in through the cracks. Sometimes, after she left, someone who had been out partying might run into the outhouse. And then, at last, came that mystical silence that occurs when everyone falls asleep: when families, after drinking tea, fall into wide or narrow beds, when worms, snails and porcupines crawl out of their hiding places, when cats gracefully leave their homes with imaginary bows around their necks and tiptoe on the dewy grass like grand dames or ballerinas.

That was when Shurka Kuksa leapt across the road and climbed through an opening into Vasia Ravlyk's garden. It was completely quiet. True, something invisible rustled as if it were whispering or sighing, and for some reason, the sound frightened Shurka Kuksa. No wonder he hadn't wanted to come here. He crept along the path cautiously, and without a sound, he entered the shed, found the roll of roofing paper, and threw it over his shoulder. When he emerged, he saw that bright moonlight flooded Vasia Ravlyk's garden and that shadows were interlaced with a delicate glimmering light that made the entire orchard glow magically. Shurka Kuksa felt his hair stand on end, because there, under the apple tree where Ravlyk's mistress, a real she-devil, had hung herself several years ago, he now saw a bright, transparent figure woven out of moonbeams. The image had a cat's head and was dressed in a white gown and white high-heeled slippers, and it stood there swaying faintly, fading and reappearing.

Just then, somewhere beyond the fence, several rockers on motorcycles roared by, and it seemed that the frail, transparent figure woven out of moonbeams was momentarily shattered by the roar. Shurka seized the opportunity to bolt across the orchard and through the opening in the fence without losing the roll of paper, which now felt like it was glued to his back. It seemed to him that the apparition's bright hands reached out for him, ready to strangle him, mashing him and that roll together into a sticky black mass. A spasm tightened his throat, and he fell on his hands and knees to crawl through the fence. Then he picked himself up, and ran as fast possible to where the mournful Moon's Cuckoo from the Swallow's Nest sat in her window.

Maybe she was sad because Kolia-the-fisherman had abandoned both her and the construction today. Maybe he wouldn't come back. Maybe he had had sufficient satisfaction. Then she would have to contend with sitting in the window again, and if someone assumed that was exactly what she wanted, they obviously didn't understand a woman's psyche at all. Not one of those brutal boars who wanted to jump into the hay with her knew a single thing about her; they understood nothing, especially not her most precious secret which was, after all, her secret. This was the source of her sadness and pain: she was trying not to wither in this world like a blade of grass, but instead to burst into bloom, into a flower that would attract bees to its nectar, because if her nectar wasn't gathered, it would be transformed into poison. This desire within her was more than mere bodily pleasure. It grew inside like winterweed that weaves in on itself as it spreads out or like a grapevine shoot that fastens itself with hair whiskers to a wall and climbs up, up to some unknown height in order to affix itself on a more promising balcony or trellis, so that later it might catch sunshine on the surface of its leaves and, in time, experience the birth of a great mystery within. That was why she built and primed her nest; she wasn't a cuckoo bird that heedlessly dropped its eggs into another's nest, even though, like the cuckoo, she took advantage of another's labor. She abhorred this but had no other choice because, just like the cuckoo, she didn't know how to build her own nest and needed help with it. She was all alone in the world, having flown in from somewhere else, with no family or dear ones; all cuckoos live without families and dear ones. She became sad and sorrowful in moonlight, and her face glowed whenever she lit up the night with pale hopes. And her only attraction were those voluptuous breasts that flooded the windowsill, like milk, because they long yearned to swell and fill with milk in order to bathe and rejuvenate this God-forsaken world. And so all she could do was to be submissive, to sit and quietly wait, because she had no other way to care for herself.

Something made a noise in the backstreet, and Yulka shuddered. The gate quietly opened, and some monstrosity with an elongated black head began to push its way into the yard. The monstrosity shook its whole head like a tuft and climbed up toward her, the Moon's Cuckoo from the Swallow's Nest.

"It's me!" Shurka Kuksa whispered coarsely, all out of breath. "I

brought you the roofing paper. You didn't expect it so soon, did you?"
"Why not?" Yulka replied calmy. "We made a deal."

11.

Whenever his mother-in-law suspected something, Kolia-the-fisherman knew it immediately, because she would open her eyes wide and bore them right into him as if she were casting a spell or enlightening him with the rays of reason. She did have something of a witch in her, undoubtedly, because those looks left Kolia's body unpleasantly agitated, restless, with the feeling that he'd be caught any minute, and all of his secrets would be revealed. Something had to be done immediately. He must throw his mother-in-law off his tracks, otherwise she was sure to sniff him out. So he decided, as they say, to stray from the straight and narrow. The next day he didn't go to work at Yulka's, but headed for the field of weeds and was warmly welcomed by the drunkards there, especially since he had sent one of them to the former owner of Yulka's room and had paid him for that mission in full. He knew very well that his mother-in-law would note this right away. She would be baffled for a while, and then would realize that her sense of impending threat was indeed accurate, but that she had been misguided about the direction from which the threat was coming.

Lubka had left for work already, so the mother-in-law couldn't send her straight into the weeds to drag her husband home. Meanwhile, Kolia-the-fisherman was drinking with the drunks, babbling along with them as they shouted incoherently, just as his mother-in-law circled the weeds, not daring to go in after him because she knew Kolia would summarily chase her out and might even strike her. Only his wife could pull him out of there lawfully, and his mother-in-law, as Kolia might say, could just butt out!

Finally, she could stand it nomore and ran to the public phone on the street to call her daughter, hoping she could get away from work somehow to put things in order. But the receiver had been ripped out for the umpteenth time and just lay there on top of the instrument. To make the call, she would have to go all the way up Prosynovska Hill, and she had no intentions of doing that as she wasn't about to let her wayward son-in-law out of her sight. She wasn't troubled so much that he might get drunk and lose at cards, as she was concerned that he might betray Lubka. She had been having suspicions about him lately but, as it turned out, Kolia-the-fisherman had veered in a totally different direction. He had strayed by succumbing to drunkenness, not uncommon for him and not a pleasant situation, but not as bad as becoming a real scoundrel and jumping into the hay with someone. This wouldn't be a mere "straying from the straight and narrow," but utter debauchery — a word Kolia's mother-in-law pronounced with such contempt, even hate, that her lips and eyelids trembled. So she was somewhat appeased by Kolia's lesser misbehavior today, though she still headed uphill to call her daughter at work. Kolia had a serious talking-to in store for him that evening.

Meanwhile, Kolia partied with his fly-by-night buddies. They began to play cards, and since Kolia vehemently declared that he had spent all his money on the booze and that he never played on credit, the drunkards were charitable and agreed to play for knuckles instead. When Kolia and his partner were losing, the others knuckled them on the head, guffawing hilariously with gaping, almost toothlesss mouths and with tongues that looked like white shovels in their throats. Whenever Kolia and his partner won, they in turn knuckled their opponents and exploded with the same Homeric laughter. Eyes bulging and mouths gaping, they slapped their thighs gleefully, and sometimes embraced, slobbering over each other. Finally, Kolia-the fisherman declared categorically: "That's it, fellows! I've had enough!"

And he suddenly took off with unexpected speed for a drunk (Perhaps Kolia wasn't very drunk, for he drank not out of want but for the sake of the comic drama he had set up.) He headed to where he figured his mother-in-law would be hiding. His calculations turned out to be amazingly accurate, because, all of a sudden, she jumped out at him like a spring, and Kolia-the fisherman bellowed: "The snake! Grab her, grab that sneaking filth! In a minute, I'm going to break every bone in her body."

She was already running from him as fast as she could, and if a bystander had clocked the speed at which she tore through weeds and gardens and down the path, surely they would report that she had set a record for old folks, though Kolia-the-fisherman had absolutely no intentions of chasing her, nor of breaking her bones, for there was no need of it. He merely smirked with self-satisfaction, knowing full well that his mother-in-law wouldn't slow down, even for a second, to look around. He knew that she would bolt into the house and lock herself in, expecting him to burst through the door any minute — and this is what she did. Kolia had no plans to return home until that evening; now he could freely visit one of his mistresses. But mistresses have a habit of not letting in someone with whom they are no longer having an affair, and there was no point in going to Yulka's because she wasn't home. Besides, he hadn't done any work for her today, so he hadn't earned any payment. So Kolia untied his boat — the oars were fastened to it on a chain — and rowed out onto the beautiful, bright, sunlit river, and since he had his fishing gear, he stopped near the shore, peeled off his shirt, and began fishing for eel among the rocks and rushes. He was lucky and snagged a sunfish, several large garfish and a bunch of eels. Then he hooked up with three other fishermen who were getting ready to cook some stew but hadn't caught much themselves. They greeted Kolia-the-fisherman with enthusiasm. One of them sneaked into a garden to dig up some potatoes and scallions; the second pulled out an apothecary flask with salt, pepper and crumbled bay leaves and claimed that this earned him a share of the stew. The third was a mushroom man, so he headed into the bushes and soon returned with one meadow mushroom, two boletes, and four puffballs, and they cooked up such a stew, you could smell it a kilometer away and it made the mouth of anyone who happened to pass within that radius salivate with hunger. But they wouldn't share the stew with the devil himself; each of them carried a spoon on him and never parted with it. They gulped the stew down right from the pot, enhancing the taste with a bottle that one of them just happened to have. All of them had "an unhappy family life" and sought diversion and consolation however they knew best.

Meanwhile, Kolia's mother-in-law sat trembling at home by the door, latched from the inside. She had a rolling pin in her right hand and a poker in the left, and waited in vain with a trepid heart for Kolia to burst through the door. It didn't occur to her that in this brief time, she had grown a goose beak and that her ears had grown like elephant weeds, thanks to her son-in-law, and, more importantly, that all she needed to do was to mount that rolling pin or poker, and with a roar of engines, she'd rise with the speed of light into the bright sky.

Kolia's mother-in-law was too naive to see herself in possession of such extraordinary talents. She failed to glance into the mirror. Indeed, she had not looked at her reflection for some time now. Kolia's mother-in-law could only think one thought at a time, and that thought was about how she would wallop her son-in-law with the rolling pin or poker when he came bursting through the door. And thus, we can say, because of self-imposed limitations, yet one more witch's talent vanished from this world.

In the evening, when Kolia-the-fisherman finally came home, there was a storm: thunder and lightning, two mighty black clouds shaped like women, with fistfuls of lightning bolts. The storm raged against a not-very-big, completely worn out, sober, practically power-less man who sat on a stool, with one eye closed and the other half-opened.

"Now wait a minute, you she-devils," he said calmly. "Let me at least get a word in..."

But they wouldn't let him say one word: one screamed and the other cackled, and when women are in such a state, is it possible to get in one wise and thoughtful word edgewise? So he sat quietly, dozing, occasionally listening to their piercing shouts. Would they mention what he thought they might? That for which he was acting out this entire comedy? Obviously, Kolia-the-fisherman had a talent for directing. But he had also discovered an important rule: when a director wants his actors to play brilliantly, they must not know that they are acting. They must be convinced that this is a real experience. Both Kolia's wife and mother-in-law played brilliantly, without realizing that they were acting out the parts of angry Furies. Kolia-the-fisherman was fair and openly acknowledged their brilliant anger. That was why he sat humbly on the stool with one eye closed and the other half-opened, so that with at least half-an-eye, he might delight in the entertainment they provided.

"Stop nagging him already, Mother. The Devil's drunkard is asleep," Lubka finally said.

He was indeed sleeping and gazing at the Moon's Cuckoo from the Swallow's Nest, with her round Scythian face, with her bosoms pouring over the windowsill. He was drawn to her once again because he was rested now, and all he needed was for these women to send him back to her.

Now a hand as hard as a poker shook his shoulder; half of his left eye opened. "Yeah, make the bed," he said. "I want to sleep."

"Don't you go bumming tomorrow. You go straight to work, got it?"

The left eye opened wider.

"Yeah, all right," said Kolia-the-fisherman. "You're right...To put in the addition...absolutely! Now can I finally get some rest? Make the bed, I want to sleep."

"I'll check, when you're gone, I'll check up on you," his mother-in-law squealed like a frightened mouse. "It's a disgrace on our family, such a worker! She may decide not to pay you. And everything that you've done so far will be worth a pile of dirt. Is that what you want?

"A pile of shit," Kolia-the-fisherman corrected her somberly.

"Phooey, what a filthy mouth," his mother-in-law replied.

Then he awoke completely, raised himself up, and looked at them. He was totally sober and alert: "So you think I should go to work tomorrow?" he asked, as if he hadn't thought it through yet.

"You're a bit fuddlebrained today," said Lubka. "And what have we been squabbling about all evening?"

Kolia-the-fisherman rejoiced. His eyes closed again, but this time it was so these two actresses, who played the Furies so brilliantly, wouldn't see how delighted he was, because he had been waiting for these very words all evening.

"As far as I could tell, you weren't saying anything, you were just screaming," Kolia declared amiably and headed for his bed because now he really was falling asleep.

"Yes," he told himself, "You really can fool women, after all; they're not all that perceptive."

12.

And so Yulka's addition was built. Without going into a lot of details, let's say that doors appeared as well. In time, the interior was plastered, a gas stove and cylinder were installed, and the doors that led to the former resident of Yulka's room were closed off with bricks.

Two weeks, or perhaps a month, went by. Autumn swept the earth, and that was when Yulka finally realized that the seeds which had been sown so generously in her by those bamboozlers Shurka

Kuksa and Kolia-the-fisherman were barren for they did not ripen inside her. Both of them had disappeared from the Nameless backstreet and didn't come around any more. The winds probably carried them into other backstreets of this world. Yulka forgot about them because there was nothing to remember. About all they left behind was a sadness which, in time, grew inside her in place of the embryo she had anticipated, and the sadness became like an enormous tree with partially yellowed leaves. As autumn swept through the earth, that invisible tree of sadness grew inside her, rustling its yellow leaves, and sometimes shedding teardrops. When Yulka couldn't stand it any longer, she sat in the window again, spread her exquisite bosoms over the sill, and looked out at God's world with empty round eyes that were no longer astonished.

Of all the protagonists in this story, only Ludka was content, because she alone had been transformed by the sacrament of the earth, and she knew this for certain even though no one in the neighborhood was aware of it yet. They merely wondered why she had become so quiet and unsocial, always a stay-at-home during her free time. Some of the busybodies sniffed out something unusual, but lacking clear evidence resigned themselves to wait, sure that a cat could not be kept in the bag forever. It would come out by itself, which it did, soon enough. Then everyone was content, and Ludka's life flowed calmly in happy anticipation, while her belly filled out and she attended joyfully to the growth inside her. There was still plenty of time ahead, so Ludka spent hours at her sewing machine, which would only occasionally fall silent as she stared out the window, lost in thought, not really seeing anything there.

Yulka sat in her own window and listened as her invisible tree of sadness rustled its yellowed leaves. Sometimes she thought that her nest wasn't completely in order yet, but she couldn't figure out what was lacking. The nights were moonlit again, but by a new moon, not yet full. And looking out at that new moon, she decided she didn't need much to finish her nest. She could build herself a coop and raise some chickens or ducks; chickens would be better. Even the neighbor women had stopped raising ducks, because dogs or drunkards or rascals kept strangling them near the river. And then she thought that maybe she could build some steps up the hill to her addition because in winter the walk would be slippery. But she considered all of this without much enthusiasm. She was tired from her endless nest-building, all the more because of her disillusionment with her helpers: muddleheads who crawled to her, carried out some task for her (can't deny the truth), but were barren like rotten trees or nuthusks. That was why Yulka was fed up and filled with contempt for those fickle cuckolds. Now, whenever someone new paused in the Nameless backstreet, she sharply turned them away. Even the women from the Swallow's Nest, as well as those beyond it, began gossiping unkindly about her, saying that she was a so-and-so. But no one knew—maybe nobody wanted to know—that she was not a so-and-so, and that inside her a tree of sadness was alive and growing, and that at night she was inundated by moonlight and sleep escaped her, and she sat by the window not to lure some old boar, but to pray to the moon and sky and earth, because they were beginning to fade around her slowly, just as she herself was gradually fading because the moon and earth and herbs had not heeded her aspirations. She sat in the window and whispered halting words to the moon, perhaps persuading him that she was not of the cuckoo family, or even if she were, that she was an outcast, and did not yearn for a cuckoo's fate, but for an ordinary human one, and that if that didn't happen, she'd wither in her window like a plant without water. She surprised herself with the stream of ancient, profound and moving words that poured from her, and she didn't understand them completely because they came not from her but from a mysterious place inside her which she obeyed unequivocally. And that mysterious source had apparently betrayed her (or so it seemed) because it brought her no real happiness after all. She cried during such moments, and her tears flowed into the night, burning and washing her face. And then something obscure awakened within her again, and in the very depths of her essence, she heard a soft whisper, so soft she couldn't make out the words, although she knew exactly what the message was. It told her that everything which existed in this world was meant to be, and everything that happened was meant to happen, and what didn't occur wasn't meant to occur; this was not her own will, nor the will of her mysterious essence, but the will of the Moon and Stars, and she should remain compliant, resign herself and wait, and listen to that mysterious voice within. Then perhaps she might be blessed in this life, because defiance and disillusionment were only a betrayal of herself. She didn't follow this reasoning to the end but felt the essence of these whispered words and that was enough, for those who can feel this don't need great understanding, and they are not yet doomed in this world.

And on one such visionary night, when the leaves on the trees had turned yellow in torrents and dropped their last seeds to the ground; when tiny beetles weaved coccoons from which they would one day emerge with wings; when crickets became silent and migrating birds obeyed the beguiling call to long and distant flight, Yulka couldn't sleep, so she got up, opened the window, and sat again without knowing why she was doing so.

Then, in the depths of the Nameless backstreet, she saw a man. He moved soundlessly, inundated with moonlight, his golden head glowing. Yulka froze in her window, afraid to breathe. Suddenly, everything in her came alive, every vein in her body quivered like a melody, but it lasted only a second. In the minutes that followed, she was calm again but didn't take her eyes off the man with the golden head. He walked up to the fence that surrounded the yard of the Swallow's Nest and paused. Yulka was startled for a moment and nervously strained to hear if the rest of the Swallow's Nest was sleeping. It was an hour when the Nest was usually sound asleep: a deep sleep in which problems and worries, friendships and animosities, falsehood and virtue, compassion and malice all were forgotten. The Nest slept as if someone had cast a spell of forgetfulness over it so that what was happening could happen. Sound asleep were the people, dogs, cats, chickens, beavers, goats, birds, porcupines and crickets — everything that was alive and real.

The man opened the gate and walked into the yard. Yulka, mesmerized, sat in the window and waited. The man, flooded with moonlight, or perhaps radiating it, paused again, and a stillness fell over everything. Then he stirred and headed up the hill, straight for Yulka's window.

"Good evening," he said softly. "You need some steps made here... And everyone here has a coop, but you don't. Do you need a worker?" He stood there smiling gently, his golden head gleaming in the moonlight.

Yulka was silent.

"Why are you silent?" he asked more tenderly.

"I'm not silent," Yulka said. "The doors are open."

"I know," he replied and looked around. "It's a strange night, isn't it?"

"It is," said Yulka and lowered her head.

"So you don't need workers?" he asked again.

"No," Yulka replied.

Then he walked up to the window and stroked her head. Yulka wept. Maybe because no one had stroked her head in such a long time, except her mother who was incredibly far away, and her distant, long-forgotten father.

"Don't cry," the man said softly and gently. "Everything will be fine. Everything will be just the way you want it. That's why I came."

Published in Ukrainian in *Suchasnist* No. 3, 1992

Notes:

Podil — The lower section of Kiev, an ancient settlement along the "right bank" of the Dnipro (Russian: Dniepr) River. The right bank is generally higher in elevation, with many of its streets leading down to the Podil district, an area that was traditionally inhabited by silversmiths, blacksmiths, and other craftsmen.

karbovantsi — Ukrainian currency; sing. *karbovanets*

Vasyl
HOLOBORODKO

Three Poems

З птахом

Пізніми осінніми вечорами
у нетопленій хаті
довго влягаєшся у ліжку — не можеш заснути
від переповнених порожнечею вражень минулого дня,
придивляєшся до темряви,
прислухаєшся до тиші,
до несподіваного сусіда — птаха, що теж не може
заснути, чути, як під стріхою у кублі
довго товчеться:
пір´я укладає різними комбінаціями,
але як не вкладе — холод дошкуляє,
заснути не дає.
Чом би зараз не встати — все одно ж не заснеш —
та не зготувати яєчні на електроплиті,
та не покликати сусіда, якому теж не спиться.
«Друже пташе, ти не знаєш,
у якій руці тримати виделку!
(Виделку — усі чотири ріжки —
устромив у дзьоба,
ніби збирався їсти не яєчню,
а виделки).
Як же ти їстимеш яєчню?
А якби ти захотів випити,
та в мене було б вино,
та ти взяв би склянку у дзьоба,
та я налив би тобі вина,
то ти вилив би собі на спину!
А тобі й так холодно:
в кублі не нагрівся,
у хаті не топлено,
та ще й облився б вином!
                    *

With A Bird

On late autumn nights
in an unheated house
you lie restless in bed — unable to sleep
flooded with the day's images of emptiness.
You stare down darkness
and listen to the silence
and to an unexpected neighbor — a bird, who can't
sleep either — hear him
making racket under the roofbeams in his roost:
arranging and rearranging feathers
to no avail — the biting cold
won't let him sleep.
Why not get up — you can't sleep anyway —
and fry an omelet on the hot plate
and then invite the neighbor, who can't sleep either.
"Friend bird, you don't know
how to hold a fork!
(He took all four prongs
in his beak,
as if he wanted to eat forks
not eggs).
How will you eat the eggs?
And if I offered wine
when you wanted a drink,
you would hold the glass in your beak
while I poured wine
and would spill it all over you!
You are already cold
you can't get warm up in your roost
my house is unheated
and in addition — you'd be all wet from wine!
*

Ти хоч скажи, чоловік ти чи жінка?
Але можеш не відповідати,
це не має значення».
Отака вийшла вечеря на самоті
з птахом.

Без одного складу

Я хотів читати —
жоден письменник не надіслав мені своєї книжки,
вибирався з'їздити до міської книгарні,
автобус зачинив двері перед моїм носом,
автори надсилали своїх агентів, і ті
вилучили їхні книжки із сільської бібліотеки
і з моєї нечисельної книгозбірні.

Я хотів писати —
наближався до чистого аркуша паперу на столі,
папір ставав чорного кольору,
чи згоряв від мого погляду,
чи чорнів від моїх думок,
ручка ковзала по паперу, як по склу,
тим, що міцніше найміцнішого клею,
прикріплювали мені в праву руку неолівець.

Так я й не прочитав те, що хотів прочитати,
так я й не написав те, що хотів написати.

Мій мовчазний читачу,
споглядальнику мого від'ємного навчання,
мої тексти, які ти спроможешся прочитати,
будуть для тебе неповними:
*

At least tell me, are you man or woman?
You don't have to answer,
it doesn't matter."
And that's the way supper turned out, alone
with a bird.

Translated by Myrosia Stefaniuk

One Syllable Missing

I wanted to read —
but not a single writer sent me his book,
I set out for the city bookstore,
the bus shut its doors on my nose,
authors sent out their agents, who
withdrew books from the village library
and from my meager collection.

I wanted to write —
approached the white sheet on the table,
but it turned black,
did it burn from my stare
or did it blacken from my thoughts,
the pen slid over paper, like on glass,
when they, with the strongest of all glues,
attached a non-pencil to my right hand.

And so I didn't read what I wanted to read,
and so I didn't write what I wanted to write.

My silent reader,
viewer of my negative learning,
my texts, those you'll manage to read,
will be incomplete:

*

у них не вистачатиме найсуттєвішого складу,
який я шукав у книжках, але не знайшов,
який я хотів навчитися писати, але не довелося.

Пам'ять

Ніби вийшов нарешті дозвіл на те,
що можна на кладовищах
садити картоплю і всяку іншу городину.
Через кілька годин після того
охочі гримкотіли по вулиці
сапками і відрами — бігли займати
грядки під картоплю і всяку іншу городину,
але то було зайве, бо в кожного
були родичі, які спочивали тут вічним сном.
Ото вони розрівняли могилки,
видрали півників і бузок,
висадили картоплю, цибулю, висіяли редиску.
(Потім вони побачили, що то не вигідно —
тільки й чути було, як туди заїздили мотоциклом
чоловіки з пляшкою, бо там закуска гарна була).
Грядочки були рівненькі та гладенькі
(прибрані, як могилки!),
і люди нарікали на долю,
що так мало їхніх родичів повмирало,
щоб можна було на їхніх могилках
садити картоплю і всяку іншу городину.

All three poems were published in *Ikar na metelykovykh krylakh (Icarus with Butterfly Wings)*. Kiev: Molod, 1990.

the most essential syllable will be missing in them,
I searched for it in books, but didn't find it,
I wanted to learn to write it, but was unable.

Translated by Myrosia Stefaniuk

Remembrance

It seems permission was granted at last
to plant potatoes and various vegetables
in cemeteries.
Some hours later in the streets
the eager hurried
with picks and buckets to reserve garden plots
for potatoes and various vegetables,
it was silly to rush, everyone has relatives
resting there in eternal peace.
So they leveled the graves,
ripped out iris and lilacs,
transplanted onions, potatoes, and seeded radishes.
(Later they realized this wasn't practical —
they could hear when men on motorcycles
went there to drink because snacks were available.)
The garden plots were squared, neatly aligned
(decked out like graves!)
and people bemoaned fate
not enough relatives had died
to use their graves
for planting potatoes and various vegetables.

Translated by Myrosia Stefaniuk

Natalka
BILOTSERKIVETS

Six Poems

Я помру в Парижі в четвер увечері.
— Сесар Вальєхо

Забуваються лінії запахи барви і звуки
слабне зір гасне слух і минається радість проста
за своєю душею простягнеш обличчя і руки
але високо і недосяжно вона проліта

залишається тільки вокзал на останнім пероні
сіра піна розлуки клубочиться пухне і от
вже вона розмиває мої беззахисні долоні
і огидним солодким теплом наповзає на рот
залишилась любов але краще б її не було

в провінційній постелі я плакала доки стомилась
і бридливо рум'яний бузок заглядав до вікна
поїзд рівно ішов і закохані мляво дивились
як під тілом твоїм задихалась полиця брудна
затихала стихала банальна вокзальна весна

ми помрем не в Парижі тепер я напевно це знаю
в провінційній постелі що потом кишить і слізьми
і твого коньяку не подасть тобі жоден я знаю
нічиїм поцілунком не будемо втішені ми
під мостом Мірабо не розійдуться кола пітьми

надто гірко ми плакали і ображали природу
надто сильно любили
           коханців соромлячи тим
надто вірші писали поетів зневаживши
          *

We'll Not Die in Paris

I will die in Paris on Thursday evening.
— Cesar Vallejo

You forget the lines smells colors and sounds
sight weakens   hearing fades   simple pleasures pass
you lift your face and hands toward your soul
but to high and unreachable summits it soars

what remains is only the depot   the last stop
the gray foam of goodbyes lathers and swells
already it washes over my naked palms
its awful sweet warmth seeps into my mouth
love alone remains though better off gone

in a provincial bed I cried till exhausted
through the window   a scraggly rose-colored lilac spied
the train moved on   spent lovers stared
at the dirty shelf heaving beneath your flesh
outside a depot's spring passed   grew quiet

we'll not die in Paris   I know now for sure
but in a sweat and tear-stained provincial bed
no one will serve us our cognac   I know
we won't be saved by kisses
under the Pont Mirabeau murky circles won't fade

too bitter we cried   abused nature
we loved too fiercely
                    our lovers shamed
too many poems we wrote
                    disregarding poets
        *

зроду
нам вони не дозволять померти в Парижі
і воду
під мостом Мірабо окільцюють конвоєм густим.

Сто років юності...

Сто років юності, а далі все — пустеля.

Околиці свого старого міста
Хіба не чуєш, затуливши очі?
Крізь мертвий дим палаючого листя
Біжать собаки нашого дитинства
І підростає кров... Сто років

юності, а далі все — пустеля.
Тут солов'ї, неначе цвяшки, вбиті
У груди доквітаючих кущів;
У вересні просушені дощі
Полощуться на сонці, як білизна,
Розвішена між вікон. А сніги!
Великі, фіолетові... Але ти

мусиш ближче підійти
До рук, плечей, до шкіри, до сорочки,
Гарячої від спеки. До стіни,
Холодної від страху і від моху.
Хіба не чуєш, затуливши очі,
Свою колишню круглу чистоту?
Хіба не хочеш увійти у камінь,
Ховаючись від перших поцілунків?

they'll not let us die in Paris
and the alluring water
            under the Pont Mirabeau
will be encircled with barricades

Translated by Dzvinia Orlowsky

A Hundred Years of Youth

A hundred years of youth and all beyond — a wasteland.

The neighborhoods of your old city
Do you not hear them, when you shut your eyes?
Through the dead smoke of blazing leaves
Hounds of our childhood run
And the blood thickens...A hundred years

of youth, and all beyond — a wasteland.
Here nightingales, like spikes, are driven
Into hearts of flowering shrubs;
September's parched-out rains
Are rinsed in sunlight, like linens,
Hung between windows. And the snows!
Mammoth and violet...But you

you must come closer
To the hands, shoulders, skin and shirt
Torrid from heat. To walls,
Grown cold from fear and moss.
Do you not hear it, when you shut your eyes,
Your own lost innocence?
Do you not want to meld in stone,
Hiding from those first kisses?

Туди, туди — у камінь і у мох,
У биту цеглу, порвані м'ячі,
У солов'їв! У лагідних собак
Дитинства нашого, що все повзуть за нами
Крізь мертвий дим палаючого листя,
Аж кров їм проступає на хребтах.
У мох! У страх!

...а далі все — пустеля.

Пора репетицій

Наша кожна закоханість кожна тісніша та ближча
смертоносною голкою вишито флер цей і дим
поверни місяць так, щоб він падав на рідне обличчя
і тремти як художник і плач як убивця над ним.

це пора репетицій дерева виходять на сцену
кров старого актора стіка листопад листопад
о наївний глядачу ти віриш ця смерть достеменна
смерть завжди достеменна тебе научає театр

і на сад що тепер помира і воскресне весною
на зів'ялі оголені плечі старої гори
і на рідне обличчя що збліднуло перед тобою
накладає мистецтво широкий підкреслений грим

це пора репетицій вже текстом великої драми
перетруджено губи ремарки горять із пітьми
хай не будуть проклятими ролі що обрано нами
ми як пізні дерева готові уже до зими.

There, over there — into the stone and moss,
Into the timeworn brick, the tattered balls.
Into the nightingales! Into the gentle hounds
Of childhood, that lope behind us always
Through the dead smoke of blazing leaves,
Until blood rises on their spines.
Into the moss! And into fear!

...and all beyond — a wasteland.

Translated by Myrosia Stefaniuk

A Time of Rehearsals

Our every love is more stifling and close
death's needle embroiders this linen and smoke
return the moon so it will fall on a familiar face
make it tremble like an artist   cry like a murderer over him

this is the season of rehearsals   trees appear on stage
the blood of an old actor flows November November
o naive spectator you believe this death is invented
it is always invented   so the theatre says

descend on the now dying orchard reborn in spring
onto the bare withered shoulders of an old mountain
and a familiar face that turned pale before you
art puts on its wide underscored make-up

this is the time of rehearsals   the text of a great drama
the overworked lips of the prompter blaze in the dark
let the roles we choose not be cursed
we are like late blooming trees ready for winter

Translated by Michael M. Naydan & Dzvinia Orlowsky

Елегія Пікассо

Тієї ж ночі сніг пішов. Іди,
Безшумний сніже, темними устами,
Мостами, наче сплетеними снами,
Дахами;

Стоять сади холодної слюди
В одежі білій з чорними руками…
Так розбуди
Цей ранок понад нами:

Художнику, іще ти молодий,
Іди ж туди, де стомлені і бідні,
Бездомні діти і сліпці безрідні,
Жінки безлюбі, матері негарні —
В нічліжки, божевільні і лікарні,
В пивнички,
            в сльози в'ялої води.
Художнику, іще ти молодий,
Ще знаєш сам знедоленість і вбогість,
Мансарди вогкий пил, і пил, і вогкість,
Стілець і ліжко.
            А в осінню тьму —
Друг у кав'ярні в голубім диму.

…Куди летять ці голубі кав'ярні,
Куди бредуть ці почуття рожеві,
Ці акробати мандрівні і ніжні?
— У зрілість, так, у спокій, у достаток,
У спогади прославлених майстрів.. —
Про що говорять дві сестри в обіймах,
Дволике людство, і святе, і грішне?
— Про зрілість, так, про хруск того портрета
Останнього, плямистого, як світ…

The Picasso Elegy

That very night the snow began to fall. Go,
silent snow, through dark lips,
Through bridges, as if through plaited dreams,
Through rooftops:

Orchards of cold mica stand
dressed in white clothes with black arms...
So rouse
This morning upon us:

Artist, you're still young,
Go to the weary and the poor
To homeless children and blind men without kin,
Women without love, mothers without good looks —
To the inns, the mad houses and hospitals,
To the taverns,
                    to tears of sluggish water.
Artist, you're still young,
You still know wretchedness and poverty,
The dank smell of garrets, dust, dampness
The chair and a bed.
                    And to the autumn darkness —
A friend in a coffee house in blue smoke.

...Where do these blue coffee houses drift,
Where do these rose-colored feelings roam,
These wandering and tender acrobats?
— To maturity, yes, to contentment, to plenty,
To the memoirs of famous masters.
What do the two sisters talk about,
Two-faced humanity, both blessed and sinful?
— About maturity, yes, about destroying that last
Portrait, fiery, as the world...

В кубічних віллах сонце пересохле —
Це старість, це здобуток, це якась
Оригінальна втрата юних літ.

...Тієї ж ночі сніг пішов. Іди,
Безшумний сніже. Як життя минає!
Як шелестить слюда, як опадає,
Оголюючи нерви-дерева!..

Ні молодість, ні старість не вгадає,
Чого шука в житті душа жива.

Спотикаючись між зірок

Знедоленим світу

Так гарно, швидко билось твоє серце.
Я пам'ятаю тільки це. Але
Вже сніг ішов зі сторони Дніпра,
Заліплюючи очі й окуляри,
Замотуючи парки та бульвари
В пом'ятий запах мокрого хутра.
Ходімо так зі мною, ти і я.

Ідуть сніги, засмічені дощами,
Ідуть дощі у Лімі і Парижі,
Так, що не видно в цей вечірній час
Вже родимок на шиї і плечах —
Всіх особливостей легкого тіла.
Але я пам'ятаю тільки страх.

Хто сльози простирадлом витирав,
Аби ніхто не бачив — опівночі,

*

In square villas, the sun has dried out—
This is old age, the reward, this is some kind of
Original loss of youth's years.

...That very night the snow began to fall. Go,
Silent snow. How life passes!
How the rainy weather murmurs, how it falls,
Exposing nerve-trees!...

Neither youth nor old age can guess
What a living soul searches for in life.

Translated by Michael M. Naydan & Dzvinia Orlowsky

Stumbling Among Stars

Of a despairing world

So nicely, quickly your heart beat—
That is all I remember. Yet already
Snow was blowing from the Dnieper
Covering my eyes and glasses,
Wrapping the parks and boulevards
In the scent of crumpled wet fur.
Let's walk, together, you and I.

Snow is falling in Kiev and Lviv,
Rain is falling in Lima and Paris,
So hard this evening you can't even see
The birth mark on my neck and shoulders —
Features of a spirited body.
Yet I remember only fear.

Someone wipes tears with a sheet
So no one could see — at midnight,

*

І той, хто вічно сам, але несміло
Випростує свої худі коліна;
Хто вже давно забув тепло житла,
І хто давно забув про запах хліба,
І хто боїться старості і смерті,
Каліцтва й радіації — усі
Поволі йдуть в Парижі і у Лімі,
І дощ їм заливає окуляри
І сірі фари стомлених таксі.

Розділимо ж цю опівнічну каву
З бездомними під сірими мостами —
Віддай їм половину сигарети
І половину ніжних слів моїх.
Розділимо свій опівнічний хліб
З голодними, не обминімо й мертвих
З голодними бездомними устами.

…Іще одна пошарпана зоря,
Коли дивлюсь крізь мокрі окуляри,
Задощений заковтуючи сніг.

Ходімо ж так, у парки, на бульвари…

And someone else, always alone, timidly
Straightens out his thin knees;
Who long ago forgot the warmth of home,
Who long ago forgot the smell of bread,
Who fears old age and death,
Disability and radiation — Everyone
Walks slowly in Paris and Lima,
And rain covers their glasses,
The wet headlights of weary taxis.
Let's share this midnight coffee
With the homeless under damp bridges —
Share half a cigarette
And half of my tender words.
Let's share our midnight bread
With the hungry: not forgetting the dead
With hungry, homeless lips.

...Yet one more tormented star,
Whenever I look through my wet glasses,
Swallowing the rain-soaked snow.

Let's walk together, to the parks, to the boulevards...

Translated by Michael M. Naydan & Dzvinia Orlowsky

Дощ… Дощ у Львові, Тернополі…
                    Дощ — на обочині
Поля, де колія рівна, блискуча — стріла…
Ти у вагоні не спиш — як тоді, серед ночі…
Ні, це не зорі навколо, це сонні тіла.

Спи, уявляй, що ця злива змиває покірні
Сльози і піт, одяг, зморшки, гримаси і грим;
Складки чужої ваги і облиплої шкіри,
Наче наклеєні кимось над серцем твоїм.

Змиється все, і залишиться кість полум'яна,
Суть і життя, і поезії — настрій і річ.
Глянеш — це склянка гойдається;
                    глянеш — це рана
Кави пролитої плямить простелену ніч!

Запах плацкартних вагонів, вологих подушок,
Запах клозету, цигарок, любові й біди,
І нетривкі імена учорашніх подружок —
Все залишиться в потоках нічної води…

"We'll Not Die in Paris," "A Time of Rehearsals," "The Picasso Elegy," and "Rain… rain in the cities of Lviv and Ternopil…" are from the Bilotserkivets collection entitled *Lystopad* (Kiev: Radianskyi pysmennyk, 1989). "A Hundred Years of Youth" and "Stumbling Among Stars" were published in her collection, *Pidzemnyi vohon (Subterranean Fire)*, Kiev: Molod, 1984.

Rain...Rain in the cities of Lviv and Ternopil...

Rain...Rain in the cities of Lviv and Ternopil...
            Rain — along the borders
Of a field where the tracks lie flat — glistening arrow...
You do not sleep in the car — as then, that one night...
No, these are not stars that surround you, these tired bodies.

Sleep, imagine this downpour washes away meek
Tears and perspiration, clothing, wrinkles, grimaces, make-up;
The folds of a stranger's weight and sticky skin,
As if glued by someone above your heart.

Everything washes away, a single fiery die remains,
The essence of life, of poetry — of moods and matter.
Take a look — the glass sways;
                    look — this wound
Of spilled coffee stains the spreading night.

The scent of third class cars, of damp pillows,
The scent of toilets, cigarettes, love, misery,
And the short-lived names of yesterday's girlfriends —
All will be left in the streams of nocturnal water...

Translated by Michael M. Naydan & Dzvinia Orlowsky

Oksana
ZABUZHKO

Six Poems

Лист із дачі

Здрастуй, любий! У нас ізнову
по кислотних дощах заіржавів город: почорнілі
  цурпалки гудиння
над землею стирчать, як на згарищі спалений дріт.
Я не певна, що сад
зціліє і цього року, хоча здалося б
його трохи попорать, підчистить, ти ж сам
  розумієш, — але,
як по правді, то я боюся ступати між ті дерева:
щокрок усе дужчає відчуття, ніби я наближаюсь
  до місця,
де у високій траві лежить піврозкладене стерво
і масною червою кишить, мов сміється на сонці.
              Я стала лякатися звуків:
позавчора в гущáвині саду щось дивне кричало —
схоже на нявкіт, чи рип монотонної гілки,
чи здушений ґелґіт гусáчий, — водно на тій самій
  розпáчливій ноті.
Чи пам'ятаєш суху берестину, оту, що минулого літа
вцілило громом, — гігантську обвуглену кістку?
Так от, мені часом здається, що це вона
верховодить над садом, і свійські дерева помалу
тратять природну тяму, мов заражені сказом пси.
Не знаю, як поводяться божевільні дерева —
може, сходять із коренів, наче трамваї із рейок.
  У кожному разі,
я тепер про всяк випадок на ніч кладу
  коло ліжка сокиру.
Втім, метелики все ще паруються, отже, шанси
  на гусінь
не підупали. В сусідки через дорогу
        *

Letter from the Summer House

Hello, dear! The land is all rusty again
with acid rain: blackened cucumber vines
jut from the earth like burnt wires.
I'm not sure about the orchard this year.
I've been meaning to get in there and clean it up,
but to tell you the truth, I'm scared of those trees.
I get this feeling when I walk between them
that I'm very close to a place in the grass
where a corpse lies, something teeming with worms,
something hot and laughing.
And I get nervous over sounds.
The day before last, a cry rose up from deep in the garden,
like a meowing or a single grating branch
or a goose being strangled.
It had that despair —
do you remember the elm? Summers ago?
The one that was struck by lightning, and stood there,
a gigantic charred bone?
Sometimes I think it still lords over everything,
infecting the plants with rabid madness.
I don't know how crazy trees act —
maybe they shake off their roots and run amok.
In any case, I keep an axe by the bed.
At least the butterflies are mating. We should see
caterpillars soon. The neighbor's daughter across the way
*

обродилась дочка — кажуть, трохи переносила:
хлопчик відразу з зубами й волоссям, можливо,
   й мутант, бо вчора,
тобто маючи дев'ять днів, закричав:
                «Погасіть же ви врешті це небо!» —
і замовк, і більше нічого не каже; а так — цілком
   здоровéнький.
От і всі наші новини. Якщо тобі вдасться
вирватись і приїхать на ту неділю,
привези мені щось до читання, найкраще —
незнайомою мовою. Ті, що знаю, вже геть зужилися.
Цілую. Твоя О.

Клітемнестра

Кассандра (до Клітемнестри) ...*Ти правда, і не жінка.*
                        — Леся Українка

Агамемнон іде —
піднімається сходами, й сонце
світить у спину йому, і увесь він відлунює міддю,
мов налитий війною бовван, і риплять
шкіряні поворозки бляшаних його обладунків...
Приберіть, не хочу!
Не бажаю звіриного запаху з рота,
ані рук його в нігтях, лямованих чорним, — ці руки
   зривають одежу
із мене, як з мертвого тіла на полі бою,
                *

gave birth — a boy, long overdue. He had hair
   and teeth already;
maybe he's a mutant too, because yesterday,
nine days old, he shouted, "Shut off the sky!"
Then he grew quiet, hasn't said a word since. Otherwise,
he's the picture of health.
So there it is. If you get a chance
to come this weekend, maybe Sunday? bring me
something to read, in a language I don't know.
The ones I call mine are exhausted.

Kisses, Your O.

Translated by Larissa Szporluk

Clytemnestra

"You're not really a woman." †

Agamemnon's coming home.
He's climbing the stairs, the sun
Is behind him, he's clanging with brass
Like a war-bloated idol, the leather thongs
Of his armor are squeaking.
Take it off, I don't want it!
I don't want the animal smell of his mouth,
Or his hands with their black-rimmed nails — those hands
Rip off my clothes as from a corpse on the battlefield,
                              *

---

† In the version by the great Ukrainian poet and playwright Lesya Ukrainka
(1871–1913), these are the words spoken by Cassandra to Clytemnestra when the
two meet on the threshold of the Mycenae palace upon Agamemnon's return.

і можливо, під нігтями ще догнивають ворсинки
і лупа — із одежі й волосся забитих.
Може, я і не жінка —
я не хочу вищати й звиватись од смертної втіхи,
навиліт прохромлена лезом сліпучим, у скалках
   смердючого поту,
що опливає на мене липкими соками смерті —
   ненавиджу
тонке скавуління суки, котре заляскоче
мимо моєї волі в ту мить у мене в гортані,
ненавиджу хвилю змори, котра огорне,
й розбухлу од вільгості пористу таранкуватість
його глевкого підгорля понад собою,
коли буду розплющувать очі... О сину Атрея,
так під тобою пручалась розпластана Троя —
стріла поціляє в пругке, і живе, і охоплене тремом:
це лань? Брісеїда? Чи горяч жіноцької крови,
по стегнах спливаючи, робить тебе переможцем,
що кров добуває із тіл, наче праведник — воду із скелі?
Не перелюбство, не скотолюдство, але скотоложство —
змагать Клітемнестру, і лань, і Кассандру, і Трою,
   й Мікени!
Може, я і не жінка.
Агамемнон надходить, і довшають тіні із запахом
   пітьми і поту.
А мені таки зимно.
Я стою і дрижу з осяяння: вбивати — то також робота!
Прясти, ткати
(розпускати — як та, що з Ітаки), трояндове тіло Егісфа
(ах, причім тут Егісф!) натирати пестливим олійком —
*

And under the nails the flakes
And fuzz from the clothes and hair of the slain are probably
    still rotting.
Maybe I'm not really a woman.
I don't want to scream and squirm with mortal pleasure,
Stuck on his gleaming weapon amid gobs of stinking sweat
Beneath a burden more overwhelming than the regal power
    under his body
Trickling its sticky death-juices on me — I hate
The high-pitched bitch's whimper
That will escape my throat,
I hate the wave of languor that will embrace me
And the doughy, pitted neck above me
When I open my eyes. O son of Atreus!
That's how Troy, outstretched, writhed under you.
Your arrows target anything alive, elastic, quick —
Is it the doe? Briseis? or hot female blood
Flowing down thighs that makes you the victor,
Able to draw blood from a body like a sinless man water
    from a stone?
It wasn't lust, or beastliness, but bestiality
To have conquered Clytemnestra and the doe and Cassandra,
    Mycenae and Troy.
Maybe I'm not really a woman.
Agamemnon's coming home, and the shadows smelling of
    darkness and sweat are growing longer.
I'm cold.
I'm shaking from the realization: killing is also a job!
Spinning, weaving,
Unweaving (like that woman from Ithaca), rubbing
    Aegisthus' rosy body
        (what does *he* have to do with this?)
With soothing oil —
            *

насолода для пальців, заняття для пальців,
    та *не* для цариці:
це нічим не шляхетніш, ніж, приміром,
    мацання віспин,
і стократ уже ліпше було б із якимось молільником
утекти — хоч до Дельф і, можливо, пошитися в жриці,
де щосвята належати всім перехожим калікам,
віддаючись незряче тій силі, позбавленій лику,
що не прагне спиняти (удар — на бігу: вгородитись!) —
що снується повсюди, мінлива, текуча й незрима…
Ах, як зимно.
Сходиш, освітлений сонцем зі спини, —
о богорівний!
(Що богорівніший, то ненавидніший, то притягальніш
ступа́ твоя сходами — кожен-бо крок в ній заважить
з рік Іліонський — ах ну ж бо, ну ближче,
    ну ближче…)
Завмираючи з захвату,
сліпнучи з чорно-білого розчерку тіней, осоння
    плит мармуро́вих, —
на всю силу уяви держу собі перед зором
одним-єдиний покоїк,
де заслона — вся вибухлий пурпур: коли ти зайдеш
    за неї,
я, єдиним божистим жестом
руки, твердої од холоду вірного їй металу,
все переваршу, на що ти досі спромігся:
я засную нове царство —
світ без Агамемнона.

These are pleasures for hands, occupations for hands —
   but not those of a queen.
They're no more noble, for instance, than fingering
   pockmarks.
It would be a hundred times better to run off with
   some pilgrims,
Say, to Delphi, and become a priestess,
To belong at every feast to every passing cripple,
To give myself up blindly to that faceless force
Without malevolence
And omnipresent — shifting, coursing, unseen...
Oh, how cold I feel!
You're climbing the stairs, backlit by the sun —
Oh godlike
More godlike, more hateful, more compelling
Is your stride up the stairs (each step weighs
One year of the Trojan war) — oh, come closer, closer...
Stiff with excitement,
Half-blinded from the black and white — this graph of
   shadows, patches of sun on the marble tiles —
I'm keeping in my sight, with the whole strength of
   my imagination,
Just this one small room
Where the curtain's like burst crimson — when you step
   behind it,
With a single lordly gesture
Of my hand, steady with the cold of obedient steel,
I'll out-do everything you have accomplished,
I'll set up another kingdom —
A world without Agamemnon.

Translated by Lisa Sapinkopf in collaboration with the author

Визначення поезії

Знаю, що вмиратиму тяжко —
Як усі, хто любить точену музику власного тіла,
Хто вміє легко просилювати його ув отвори страху,
Як у вушко голки,
Хто ввесь вік ним протанцював — так, що кожен порух
Плечей і лопаток, і стегон — світився
Далекою тайною смислу, як слово санскритської мови,
І м'язи під шкірою грали,
Мов риби в нічному ставку, —
Дякую Тобі, Боже, що дав нам тіло!
Отож коли помиратиму, гукніть майстрів,
Аби зняли наді мною покрівлю
(Так помирав мій прадід, кажуть, відьмак), —
І ось тоді, коли крізь розм'якле вже тіло,
переливаючись, мов крізь некруто зварений білок,
Проблимне натужно набрякла душа,
Випинаючись потемнінням
(А тіло тимчасом тектиме корчами,
Мов ковдра, що хоче скинути хворий,
Бо вона його душить), —
А душа все пнутиметься прорвати
Стиск плоті, проклін ґравітації, — ось тоді
У вилом стелі шумким крижаним зорепадом
Рине Космос
І тягом в свою галактичну трубу
Видує душу, закрутить, як аркуш паперу,
Мою молодісіньку душу
Барви мокрої зелені —
Ах, на свободу! — і:
— Стійте! — скрикне вона в мить прориву крізь тіло,

*

A Definition of Poetry

I know I will die a difficult death —
Like anyone who loves the precise music of her own body,
Who knows how to force it through the gaps in fear
As through the needle's eye,
Who dances a lifetime with the body — every move
Of shoulders, back, and thighs
Shimmering with mystery, like a Sanskrit word.
Muscles playing under the skin
Like fish in a nocturnal pool.
Thank you, Lord, for giving us bodies.
When I die, tell the roofers
To take down the rafters and ceiling
(They say my great-grandfather, a sorcerer, finally got out
    this way).
When my body softens with moisture,
The bloated soul, dark and bulging,
Will strain
Like a blue vein in a boiled egg white,
And the body will ripple with spasms,
Like the hot blanket wrestled off by a sick man...
And the soul will rise to break through
The press of flesh, curse of gravity.
The Cosmos
Above the black well of the room
Will suck on its galactic tube,
Heaven breaking in a blistering starfall,
And draw the soul up, trembling like a sheet of paper —
My young soul —
The color of wet grass —
To freedom — then
"Stop!" it will scream, escaping,

*

В мить на щонайсліпучішім лезі
поміж двома світами, —
стійте, **отут** зупиніться,
Ось де вона, Поезія,
Боже, нарешті!

...Пальці востаннє шарпнуться в пошуках авторучки —
Вже застигаючи, роблячись вже не моїми...

Од такої тоски
Сопілками стають кістки,
Од такої жаги
На мокві горять шелюги,
Од такого зняття
Землетрусом іде життя,
І з-під стіп
вогняний вибухає сніп...

День по дню, день по дню
Я в собі корчувала усе, що тобі не потрібно.
Я уже дудоню
Од найслабшого дотику, легка, блакитна і срібна.
Я уже впорожні,
Наче дута китайська фігурка — долонями вгору:
Простягни і візьми —
Я тепер акурат тобі впору.
Що було — **не** було:
Ми невинністю рівні: всередині — навіть намулу...
Ледь похрускує скло,
                    *

On the dazzling borderline
Between two worlds —
Stop, wait.
My God. At last.
Look, here's where poetry comes from.

And fingers will twitch for the ballpoint,
Growing cold, no longer mine.

Translated by Michael M. Naydan

From this kind of longing...

From this kind of longing
Bones turn into flutes,
From this kind of craving
The bog will catch fire,
From this kind of knowledge
Life cracks open
And bundles of flame
Explode underfoot.

Day after day
I've uprooted from myself everything you didn't need.
Already I clang
At the slightest touch — light, silvery-blue.
I'm hollow,
Like a Chinese statuette with upturned palms.
Reach for me —
I'm a perfect match for you now.
What was, never was.
We're equals in our innocence — not a trace of ooze inside.
The shards crackle slightly
*

Коли я, мов Русалочка, йду
босака крізь минуле:
Всюди вирви од бомб,
Брухт по пущених в діл
поїздах…
якщо це не любов,
То — в міжбрів'я-упала-звізда,
Що прошила поздовж,
Не зоставивши більше нічого.
Якщо **це** не любов —
Весь наш світ не од Бога.

Од такої тоски
Починають родити піски,
Од такої жаги
Переходять ріку береги,
І гора з горов
Ізійдуться, як пальці рук…
Якщо це — любов,
Все колишнє — порожній звук.

Дорогою до пекла

Ти — тіло, втиснуте боком в розбухлу валізку автобуса:
обличчя якраз уміщається в чийсь черевик,
    од якого нога
десь в протилежнім кутку заповнює звільнену рурку
    простору
вкупі з дамською парасолькою; ззаду до сиднів
міцно, насмерть приваривсь чоловічий низ і, попри
    тисняву,
якось там навіть мусується, — краще б цього не робив,
        *

When I walk barefoot, like the Little Mermaid, across
   my past.
Bomb craters everywhere,
Scrap from blown-up trains...
If this is not love,
Then it's a star that struck me between the eyebrows,
Pierced me to the ground and left nothing standing,
If *this* is not love —
Our world isn't of God.

From this kind of longing
The sands become fertile,
From this kind of craving
The banks ford the river,
And mountains join
In a finger-clasp.
If this *is* love,
What was doesn't count.

Translated by Lisa Sapinkopf in collaboration with the author

On the Way to Hell

I'm a body shoved edgeways in the bulging suitcase of a bus.
My face is a perfect fit for someone else's shoe, its foot
Somewhere in a far corner thrust into a free tube of space
Alongside a woman's umbrella; behind me a man's hips
Are soldered to my buttocks, and despite the crush
Make rubbing motions; he'd better not come

*

бо наколи, боронь Боже, спуститься,
то геть поплямить мені спідницю,
і коли розчахнуться поздовжні «блискавки» клапанів і
  нас повитрушують,
то мене доведеться насамперед запирати.

Найгірше, однак, що в цій тичбі я вже не знаю,
чи думки, котрі думаю, є насправді моїми —
чи, може, вони прийшли з-під цієї злямченої перуки,
яку я вже дві зупинки (чи два роки, чи два життя…)
  силкуюсь відплюнути, —
а це серце, котрим гадала, ніби страждаю,
калатає з вивороту краватки, що заломилась
у мене на самому переніссі, і всі відчуття —
позрізнені, здеформовані, — котрі сочаться крізь мене,
комусь належать, і я — лиш громадська вбиральня
  злоби та безсилля.

О! — здогадуюсь. — Знаю, вже знаю, де вихід:
хочу Голготи, хочу хреста — от де можна
випростать руці-нозі, не боячись зачепити
ані розбійника зліва, ні розбійника справа,
і звести очі д'горі, і згадати власне ім'я!

Ідіотко, — відказує десь в мікрофон металевий голос
  центуріона, —
найзручніші хрести розібрали ще в минулім столітті,
  а решту,
рознявши на перекладини, порозпилювали на дошки:
з одного хреста таким робом виходять нари,
на які можна вкласти покотом шість чоловік,
а якщо в два поверхи, то й дванадцять.

Господи, що ж це діється, — хочу розгублено бевкнути,
та тимчасом мого язика передано на компостер.

Because if he does, God forbid,
I'll be all stained,
And when the exits' zippers open and spew us out
I'll need a good hosing down on the spot.

What's worse, though, is that in this throng I can
    no longer tell
Whether the thoughts I think are really mine,
Or whether they originate, say, from beneath the matted wig
I've been trying to spit out for the last two stops
    (or years, or lives?),
Or if the heart for which I believed I was suffering
Is beating under the necktie draped over the bridge of
    my nose.
And if all the chaotic, crippled senses that I'm drenched with
Are really someone else's, and I'm just a public toilet for
    viciousness and despair.

But wait! There's a solution!
Give me Golgotha, give me the cross—there you can stretch
Your arms and legs, certain not to touch
The thief on your left or the one on your right,
And you can raise up your eyes and recall your real name.
"You idiot!" clangs the centurion's amplified voice,
"The best crosses were taken last century, and the rest
Were broken apart and sawed into planks—
That way, from a single cross you get a pallet
Where six people can fit side by side—or in a bunk,
    even twelve."

God, what's going on here!—I try to blurt out, perplexed.
But meanwhile my tongue has been punched.

Translated by Lisa Sapinkopf in collaboration with the author

Прощання між зірок

А просто — жоден інший: я — це я.
Я теж умру. І кари не уникну.
І смисл, моїм означений ім'ям,
Як жовтий порох, витрусять за вікна
З моїх речей, паперів і кімнат
(Розкиданих і так — на півпланети!) —
Лиш, може, десь мій неназваний брат
У котрусь ніч спросоння схлипне: «Де ти?..»
І цього — досить. Так: пилковий слід
На пальцях, що торкнуть старе свічадо,
І світлий свист — мов нарти крешуть лід —
Ще довго буде в просторі звучати.
І, захлинувшись тайною, дитя
Закине ввись лице, од зрячих сліз студене...
І цього — досить: справдилось життя.
А далі — розбирайтеся без мене.

"Letter from the Summer House," "Clytemnestra," "From this kind of longing...," "On the Way to Hell," and "Farewell Among the Stars" are from Zabuzhko's collection, *Avtostop (Hitchhiking)*, Kiev: Ukrainskyi pysmennyk, 1994. "A Definition of Poetry" is from *Dyryhent ostanjoji svichky (The Conductor of the Last Candle)*, Kiev: Radianskyi pysmennyk, 1990.

Farewell Among the Stars

It's just that I'm myself, and no one else.
I will die too. And I won't escape punishment either.
Everything my name designates
Will be beaten like yellow dust
Out of my belongings, my papers, my addresses
(Which are scattered over half the planet).
Still, some future brother of mine, name unknown,
Might sob one night in his sleep: "Where are you now?"
And that will be enough. Look: the pollen-like smudges
On fingers touching an antique mirror
And the luminous whistle like skates slashing ice
Will long resound in open space.
And a child, gasping with wonder,
Will turn skyward his face chilled by sentient tears —
And that will be enough: my life will have been realized.
Then — keep on without me.

Translated by Lisa Sapinkopf in collaboration with the author

Viktor
NEBORAK

Two Poems

Риби

холоднокровні істоти
доживають у нашій ванні
останні дні
їх продовгуваті гнучкі
тіла закінчуються прозорими хвостами
їх очі дивляться як будуть дивитися і
з відрізаних голів

вони існують завдяки повітрю отриманому з води
відокремлені стіною від моєї кімнати
і ще стіною від листопаду і туману
вулиць будинків автомобілів
усіх тих предметів серед яких звик жити я

для них важлива вода і їжа
можливо зміна освітлення
для них не важливо що вона досягається
завдяки сонцю чи там вимикачу

для них важлива вода і їжа
можливо передчуття смерті
для них не важливо у яких родинних зв'язках
перебувають рухливі продовгуваті плями

ось так

їхні тіла тріпотітимуть на підлозі
чорні удари сплющать їх мізковиння
їхні нутрощі будуть старанно вибрані
і разом з лускою відправляться на смітник
*

Fish

cold-blooded things
living out their days
in our bathtub
their long slippery bodies end
in see-through tails
their eyes bulge
just as someday they'll bulge out
from their chopped-off heads

they live on oxygen in the water
separated from my room by one thin wall
by another from the mist, dry leaves,
street, buildings, cars
I live with

water and food? crucial
but light may not be so crucial
from either sun or socket

water and food? crucial
but knowing someday they're all
going to die may not be crucial
unaware as they are of their family connection
to other long slippery bodies

on it goes

bodies quivering on the floor
sharp blows flattening their brains
their insides scooped out
and dumped with their scales into the garbage
                *

жива риба перетвориться на заливну і смажену
а голови підуть на юшку

цей випадок не винятковий
цим займається все людство
кровоточать рибні заводи
дехто пише про це вірші
малює це знімає про це фільми
і примовляє смачного

і позирають на землю німотні риб'ячі душі

X

Вона піднімається, як голова.
Відрубана голова волоцюги.
Вона промовляє уперше, і вдруге,
і втретє свої потойбічні слова:
Я ЛІТАЮЧА ГОЛОВА!
Над юрмищем площі нависло навкіс
її всевидюще летюче барокко.
Кров гусне в повітрі, розчахнутий зріз
тінь відкидає, важку і глибоку:
Я ЛІТАЮЧА ГОЛОВА!
Сокира невидима в місто ввійшла,
стягнули з помостів тіла безголові,
роззяви напились дешевої крові,
Та зішкребе слід іржавий з чола
ПРИВИД ЛІТАЮЧА ГОЛОВА!
Жереш мелодрами телевізійні?
*

then they're poached, or fried, their heads
dropped into the soup

no fish is an island
this involves all of us, all of us
processing plants drip with their cold blood
some of us object in poems,
paintings, documentary films
still they make good eating

even while the fish spirits are watching

> *Adaptation by Lloyd Schwartz*
> *of translation by Virlana Tkacz and Wanda Phipps*

Flying Head

It lifts up, like a head,
a head chopped off a derelict.
It speaks, and then again
and again, its other-worldly words:
I AM THE FLYING HEAD!
Its all-seeing flying baroque-eye
streaks across the sky above the crowded square.
Blood thickens in the sky, the cut is ragged,
its shadow's heavy and deep:
I AM THE FLYING HEAD!
An invisible ax is in the city,
they dragged the headless bodies off the scaffold,
so gaping fools can drink blood cheap.
Scrape that rusty smear off the forehead
A PHANTOM — A FLYING HEAD!
You devour television melodramas?

*

Ти розглядаєш драконів за склом!
Стіну тобі проламає чолом
ожила куля з "Оркестру" Фелліні —
Я ЛІТАЮЧА ГОЛОВА!
Запам'ятай, не сховатись ніде!
Площа приходить у схови, площа!
Бруківку темну свято полоще
і в небеса Ренесансу гряде
МАСКА — ЛІТАЮЧА ГОЛОВА
Я ЛІТАЮЧА ГОЛОВА
ЯГОЛО ВАЛІ ТАЮЧА
ЯГО ЛОВАЛІТА
ЮЧА ГОЛО ВАЯ
ЧАГОЛО Ю АЯ
АО А О

"Fish" was published in Ukrianian in Neborak's collection, *Alter Ego* (Kiev: Ukrainskyi pysmennyk, 1993). "Flying Head," of which this is part ten (X), appeared in *Litayucha holova (Flying Head)*, Kiev: Molod, 1990.

You're watching monsters under glass!
The wrecking ball from Fellini's *Orchestra*
will break through your wall head first —
I AM THE FLYING HEAD!
Remember, there's nowhere to hide!
The crowd scrambles to hide in the square!
The dark pavement is ritually washed,
and in the Renaissance heavens the beast slouches
A MASK — A FLYING HEAD
I AM THE FLYING HEAD
I AM THE HE AD FLY
ING HEAD AM I
ING HEAD FLY I
FLY I LY I

Translated by Virlana Tkacz and Wanda Phipps

Oleh
LYSHEHA

Two Poems

Пісня 352

Коли вам так забаглось погрітись,
Коли вам так хочеться перекинутись хоч словом,
Коли вам так хочеться хоч крихту тепла —
То не йдіть до дерев — там вас не зрозуміють,
Хоч архітектура в них просто космічна
І з комина в'ється прозорий димок..
Не йдіть у ці гори хмарочосів —
З тисячного поверху
На вас можуть висипати жар..
Коли вже вам так не терпиться за теплом,
То йдіть на завіяний снігом город,
Там скраю стоїть самотня хата хрону..
..А ось і вбога хата хрону..
Світиться? — світиться.. він завжди дома —
Стукайте до хати хрону, стукайте до цієї хати..
Стукайте — і вам відчинять..

Він

В горі, аж мокрій від перестиглої ожини,
Темніє його житло.
Як міцно треба було стискати
Затесаного дрючка аж доти,
Поки в глухому закуті кам'яної нори
Зі здибленої тіні великого самітника
Не хлине з горла тобі на груди кров..

Song 352

When you need to warm yourself,
When you are hungry to share a word,
When you crave a bread crumb,
Don't go to the tall trees —
You'll not be understood there, though
Their architecture achieves cosmic perfection,
Transparent smoke winds from their chimneys . .
Don't go near those skyscrapers —
From the one-thousandth floor
They might toss snowy embers on your head . .
If you need warmth
It's better to go to the snow-bound garden.
In the farthest corner you'll find
The lonely hut of the horseradish . .
Yes, it's here, the poor hut of a horseradish . .
Is there a light on inside? — Yes, he's always at home . .
Knock at the door of a horseradish . .
Knock on the door of his hut . .
Knock, he will let you in . .

Translated by James Brasfield in collaboration with the author

He

for Ivan Franko

On the mountain, wet with overripe blackberry,
His dwelling darkens . .
With what force a man clenches the sharpened stake
Till at the end of some stony burrow
A hunter draws the rush, the blood from the throat,
From the reared-up shadow of a great ancestor . .

*

Але, крім здертої шкіри, відрубаної лапи,
Де затиснулась його сила,
Крім густого духу дикого часнику,
Над самим лігвом на стіні лишились
Глибокі знаки, проорані кривими пазурами:
Тут він їх загострював.
І рука їх запам'ятала на потім..
Ясно — коли збирала гриби
Чи намацувала пстругів під каменем —
Те знаття їй не згодилось.
Але пізніше, втомившись за плетінням сітей
На більшу, набагато більшу рибу,
Монотонна робота таки змусила шукати
Трохи легше заняття: знаки.
Вони могли якось виправдати
Примітивні вбивства..
Це було просто — досить вмокнути палець
У свіжу кров.. або чирганути гостряком
По кістці, на корі чи вже пізніше,
Й на папері: риски в певній послідовності..
Але що таке папір?
Чи знала рука, що то підрубаний ліс,
Обвалені шахти, занедбана земля?..
Певне, ще не хотіла знати,
Бо весь час пробувала
Вибілитись від гною, диму,
Стати делікатною, власністю самої себе,
Досконалим інструментом, чого нема в нікого..
І прикро було їй здогадуватись,
Що друга, ніби така сама рука день і ніч
Кує залізний ланц на молодого ведмедя,

*

Yet besides his being skinned,
Besides his cut-off paw —
Where his strength might be grasped
Alongside the smell of wild garlic —
The signs remain, drawn by claws
Around the stony pit:
He used to sharpen them there . .
And a hand just memorizes them for later . .
Of course, when a hand gathered mushrooms,
Or fumbled for trout between stones —
That knowledge was of no use . .
But later, tired from forming nets
For a bigger, much bigger catch —
The tedious job led to simpler work:
Signs — they were able in some way
To justify the rough slaughter . .
Rather, it was an easy occupation —
Just to plunge one's finger in blood
Or slash with some sharpened thing
On a bone or bark, or later, on paper:
Signs in some order . .
But what is it — paper?
Does a hand know it? That it
Is barren land, hewed wood, mines crumbling?
Perhaps the hand doesn't want to know
Because all the while
It strikes to bleach itself of dung and smoke,
To become more delicate,
A possession of itself,
The perfect instrument no one else possesses . .
And how pitiful to find out
That the other, almost same hand
Was shaping, days and nights, the iron chain for a young bear,

*

Аби навчити його танцювати
На розпеченій блясі..
Та сама рука підкидає поліна у вогонь,
Затесує перо — справді досконалий інструмент,
Але той, що висушує руку,
Притискає скалічілу до грудей, на серце..
Як воно має боліти,
Що мусить йти від себе,
Знов повертатись назад, в їдку ропу,
В рідний підгірський ґрунт,
Де кожен камінь чи кущ ялівцю
Пирскає нафтою,
Аби відмокнути в ній,
Аби та рука знов знайшла легше життя,
Аніж блукання аравійськими пісками..
Близька гора аж темна від солодкої ожини —
Але навіть верткий птах,
Не сідаючи на обтикану колючками галузку,
Ніяк не може склювати цілої ягоди,
А лише роз'ятрює її, скроплює соком землю
І летить голодний далі..

These poems were published in Lysheha's first collection, *Velykyi mist (Great Bridge)*, Kiev: Molod, 1989.

To teach him to dance
On a hot tin plate . .
Nearly the same hand puts wood gingerly into the fire,
Sharpens the pencil —
Indeed, a perfect instrument —
Just to emaciate the hand,
To press it closely to the heart . .
What pain the heart must suffer —
To return again to the oil and salt,
To the native and stony ground,
Where each stone or juniper leaf
With each touch bleeds an acrid drop,
To be immersed in it,
To find a little easier life
Than wandering Arabian deserts —
The mountain is so close,
Dark with sweet blackberry.
Yet even a quick bird perched on a thorny twig
Can't peck the whole berry,
But tortures it, sprinkles the ground with juice,
And hungry still, flies on.

Translated by James Brasfield in collaboration with the author

TANIA MYCHAJLYSHYN-D'AVIGNON was born in Lviv, Ukraine and emigrated with her parents to the United States in 1949. She received a degree in Photography from the Maryland Institute of Art in 1964. Soon after, curiosity and a need for ethnic reconfirmation inspired her to return to the land of her birth. She made numerous subsequent trips as a traveler and tour guide for various American visitors. In 1986, she was invited to be part of a *National Geographic* team that traveled to Ukraine; she has worked with *National Geographic* on several other projects since. Her photographs have been published in numerous books, newspapers and magazines in America as well as in Europe and Ukraine. In the late 1980s she was invited to show her photos about Ukraine in many cities in the U.S. and Canada. Since 1978 she has been associated with the Harvard Ukrainian Research Institute as a photographer. In 1989 she was invited to hold a photo exhibit in Kiev, which later traveled to other Ukrainian cities. In 1995 her second exhibit was held in Kiev and is currently in Krakow, Poland. Since 1991, she has divided her life and work between her adopted city of Boston and Kiev. She is preparing an album of photographs for publication.

76: Pechersky lavra (Cave Monastery), Kiev
78: Cafe Ararat, Lviv
79: Uspenska tserkva (Dormition Church), Lviv
84: "Forbidden Zone," the 30-kilometer zone of
exclusion surrounding Chernobyl
85: A returnee to an abandoned village within the Zone
87: "This holy cross has been erected in memory of those who
perished in the famine of 1932–33."

199: Bandura player
200: The group Malvy performing at the Chervona Ruta
music festival, Lviv, 1989. The poster is of charismatic singer/
songwriter Volodymyr Ivasiuk. He was found dead in woods
near Lviv in 1979. KGB involvement is suspected.
202: Protest of Donetsk miners, Kiev, 1993
203–204: Student occupation of Revolution Square (later
Independence Square), Kiev, October 1990. This student action
was one of the galvanizing events that led to Ukraine's
declaration of independence in August 1991.

225: Russian graffiti on Andriyivsky Descent, Kiev

Yuri
ANDRUKHOVYCH

Observation Duty

Translated by Christine M. Sochocky
with George Packer

Y ou grew weary wore yourself to death so it's time to cast anchor
in any port and you go on shore under a flaming sun and the
yellow-skinned Singaporians in colorful parrot shirts are standing
on both sides forming a solid wall, you walk among them as through
a corridor; perhaps they are your bodyguards. You recall: a country
of minarets — thus said that lieutenant when the plane landed in
Kabul — and I love the exotic! You walk past the colorful Chinese and,
finally, before you is a bungalow or rather a pavillion. You know that
inside there is a Tahitian woman dancing and a hump-nosed Arab
barman prepares the mixer for cocktails with ice. Patrons languish
around tables stained with stale beer foam. This is the port dive and
an electronic disco is blaring from somewhere and everywhere as ever,
and you step inside. You find everything in its place: the Tahitian
woman's legs are so long that they end somewhere just under the ceil-
ing, the hump-nosed Arab has just set up the mixer and confidently
pours the gin into the glasses arranged in a row and visitors who seem
to be mummified beat out the rhythm of the music over the canned
Dutch beer. You're tired, you sit at the bar and the Arab hands you
something cool in the glass, with ice cubes floating. Suddenly he turns
to a smeared-faced dark boy with a bare belly button and wearing
linen pants exactly like that Afghani urchin who haggled you for some
sugar. You meet him again and the electronic metronome measures an
infallible disco-rhythm within you; two beats to the second, and only
two beats to the second inside you and over you, an energetic Afro
syncope. You want to hide from everything your head is falling lower
and lower, you hide it under the table and the eyelids glue together,
you grow too weary...with incredible effort you open your eyes....

   I am already in a half-sleep. I love this state when you seem to be
still sleeping, yet awareness has already set in, like a motor which
cooled down overnight — at first it shudders and coughs for a long
time, but you are already capable of directing your dreaming, arrang-
ing the random and meaningful subjects for your personal pleasure.

   Nowadays I awake much earlier than before — as soon as the skies
turn grey outside the windows. And, though there is no need to hurry,
I cannot sleep longer. The sweet thought of another completely free
mid-May day, with its rain and sunshine, bounces within me like a
happy little devil. Just then the front door bangs loudly: the old man
has left for work, as soon as he comes out of the doorway he will begin

to cough sharply and deeply. This happens every day. I anticipate his cough, and I am not wrong. Our entrance doors slam downstairs and immediately after I hear the familiar coughing in the morning silence of our courtyard. Now, for ten minutes he will wait for the bus on the corner. I can almost see him as he paces the sidewalk and sucks on his first "Verkhovyna"* of the morning, having finally halted that cursed cough. We will see each other only late in the evening, when I return from my escapades. He will be sitting in the kitchen over the inevitable game of solitaire. We will greet each other.

Before evening comes, there is still a whole day, however — the light and carefree day of a butterfly, or so I want to believe. There is no place to hurry to — I draw closer to my bed the old family ashtray which is shaped like a Hutsul* moccasin and a package of "Lviv." The cigarettes have dried out overnight. Fingering the next one destined for destruction, I listen with pleasure to its dry rustling. I have an infallible French lighter. I bought it on a train from a talkative fatso — we shared a bottle of champagne and he kept asking me how things were "over there," where I had come from, if there were many victims and whether there were any instances of mass heroism. Finally, as he was getting off at Kaharlyk, he offered to sell me his infallible French lighter.

I find pleasure in watching the aimless tongue of fire that seems to have escaped from the prison of this miniature lighter. Taking my time, I put a cigarette to my mouth and draw the first gulps of smoke.

I feel good. I really exhausted myself and now I desperately need such carefree, unclouded days. Cigarette smoke fills up the small, still half-dark room and hangs there in curious, amorphous designs. I pull myself toward the radio, find the necessary buttons — the speaker on the Polish station promises a clear day for today and furtively announces the world news — I don't listen to him — he finally grows silent and drowns in a tide of music: Dixieland at first, then piano variations on themes of Chopin and then stable, synthesized disco, perhaps the kind I had dreamed of.

The doors to the room open slowly. On the doorstep is mother with her daily, "You've smoked the place up already?" I don't answer, but yawn and turn toward the wall, pretending that I intend to sleep some more.

Mother is also leaving for work, she only came to tell me that there are fried potatoes on the stove. She puts some money on the table, underneath the vase — perhaps finally today I'll buy some summer shoes for myself. After waiting long enough for me to grunt something (in her thoughts she consoles herself that there was acquiescence in my grunting) she quietly closes the door. In a moment, the entrance doors close behind her — that is all, I am left in the house alone and ahead of me is the day, light and joyful.

I shut off the Polish chatterbox as he is announcing car theft statistics. I light another cigarette and notice that it's getting brighter outside; the sun has already emerged from behind the five-story buildings which ring the courtyard in an imposing circle. Elton John is grinning at me encouragingly from a poster on the opposite wall, as if to say it's time to move on, old man, along the yellow brick road, hah, hah.

The first steps turn out to be difficult for me: my right leg has to be exercised first and only then can I limp along more or less decently. Mother fears that this is a permanent condition and that I will never marry due to this "old man's" defect. Alas, if I never marry, it will be for another reason. I brought it, too, back from that place, the land of minarets, although the captain of the medical service said that I had been awfully lucky. As far as the limping goes, in this slow-paced life, without an automatic rifle and pack on one's back, without marches in full gear, without dug-outs and trenches to jump over, in this new and different life, lameness is not such a hindrance, and I shall never forget to be grateful to destiny that I *was* awfully lucky.

Television had quite an erotic entertainment in store for me: a session of rhythmic gymnastics performed by overripe fillies of the Ostankino* studio. Oh, aerobics! The disco, which resounds within me from last night, disturbs me even now, as the commanding voice of the trainer urges everyone to s-t-r-e-t-c-h more often and further. I don't like this at all. I shut off the TV and shuffle along to greet the unchanging procedures of the morning.

The bathroom tiles shine. It's pleasant to notice how bourgeois we are becoming. The shelves are heavy with colorful creams, shampoos, deodorants, pastes — and all that is "state of the art," according to the latest labels, serves hygiene and fosters moral healing. Some aromatic foam and hot water, and I feel as if I were amid the humid lianas of India. Peach nectar is splashing in the cavity of my mouth, my cheeks are soaped with a golden lemony cream and excellent Dutch razor blades are here to serve me. The arrangement of vials, bottles and tubes reminds one of the dance of joyous colibri* around a young python, capable of aquatic excesses. I feel very good.

I turn on my cassette player to support this light festive feeling. The devil take the boy — in my absence he recorded all kinds of junk in disco style interspersed with Italian *canzoni*, and because he did not have new cassettes he erased my favorite rock stars and it was his luck, yes, yes, he was awfully lucky that a few weeks ago he had left home for two years in order to pay his sacred debt as his older brother had done. Otherwise I would have arranged for him a "course for the young warrior" while he was still at home.

While I am breakfasting on the promised fried potatoes, the group "Exile" replaces the Gibson brothers and Gloria Gaynor is interrupted by the very delicate, very lyrical Puppo — finally it is the turn of the Osibis and Eruption groups. "Blackskinned monkeys," I think of them good-naturedly, but this disco-service had become mightily boring and I stop Stevie Wonder in the highest flight of his unique voice.

The time comes to leave for the city. I pause in front of the mirror — well, buddy, it's not the best of looks but it's there, the moustache is growing, the hair seems to have gotten longer, the wrinkles on the forehead and around the eyes are an unqualified plus, the somewhat swollen eyes, a minus. I put on my good old velvet jacket. I don't know if such are worn in Paris or New York, but in our Kryzhopil (Zhmerinka, Shepetivka, Okhtirka) this is just fine. The jeans are not at their most blue, even three years ago friends still called them *bliuvaisy** but the very thought of the highs I lived through in the years of my snotty pre-army youth in the company of L., my first (or was it second?) love, the very thought compels me to treat respectfully their benign greyness and virile patchiness.

The street reflects the freshness and grace of morning. I don't rush so long as it smells of trees and gardens and not of exhaust, so long as sparrows are splashing in yesterday's puddles.

This is where the landowners live. This is the street of two-storied houses and tulip plantations. Here live the cherry and strawberry magnates whom we, the inhabitants of ordinary government housing, understandably call *kurkuli**. They are always making additions to their yards or sinking into the soil up to their elbows, picking the latest harvest. And although their daughters are already wearing original American or Canadian jeans, their too-fully-developed figures give away their remote village origins. No, I prefer the bare-assed aristocrats.

A seedy old man, hanging onto the gate of one of the houses, has probably read my thoughts. He looks at me as if I had come to expropriate his parcel of land together with the building and that he would like to send a few bullets from a sawed off shotgun into my back…

I am an observer. For three weeks now, I've done nothing but examine my surroundings "in all variations of their forms and appearances" (as my learned classmate Liufa, who is today a doctor of philosophy, would say).

For I understand now that to live is to be present at a feast and, when I remember how near I had been to having that presence cut short, when I think about that cursed "land of the minarets" where I had been so awfully lucky, I throw myself into observing life with even more avarice.

A picturesque group of pensioners huddled around a chessboard, the queue around the carbonated water dispenser, secretive young mothers with baby carriages, pigeons picking up bread crumbs in the square around the cathedral, even some fanciful balcony, some ornamental gate or an unexpected turn of the cobbled street between the neat buildings and orchards — all of this makes me utterly happy.

Of all the approaches to life, I have chosen active observation. I relish chance conversations with unknown people — this exchange of everyday phrases which might seem boring and a waste of time to a more troubled or serious person. I like to appear suddenly amidst a throng of soccer fanatics who, gathered in the market place, are arranging mythical teams and prognosticating the outcome of matches. I have nothing against watching auto races on TV, or trying my luck at a shooting gallery. And the marketplace! What a luscious setting for the true observer. I delight in watching how things are displayed, sold, weighed and counted: how pompous butchers, filled with corpulent dignity, apply their axes, how unshaven southerners* in nylon shirts wink at their fair-haired customers, pushing rotting pomegranates at them, and with what skill the modest collective farm women in kerchiefs, setting prices worthy of the most desperate of times, ransom off the surplus of their kitchen gardens.

I walk by stores, kiosks, barbershops, museums. The sun has jumped from the tip of the city hall building to the tops of the metal baskets near the dairy store — these were just being loaded into their cart by two caps — a lean fellow with blond fuzz instead of eye brows and a very young snotnose whose work coat hangs as if on a corpse. Through the window of the dairy the reflection of a lame young chap approaches them; our paths shall cross here right now and never again.

They're selling Czech crystal in the street. A throng of amateurs of opulence besieges the crystal displays, and huddles by doors which bear the sign "Merchandise Entrance." Upstairs, on the second floor, is the fashion atelier, young seamstresses in thin blue coats run out to the balcony to rejoice in the spectacle of *Sturm und Drang* in front of the building. They giggle, loudly exchange impressions and probably don't even suspect that they have also turned into a kind of spectacle: two porcine wanderers from the trade school, having taken a convenient post at the entrance to the building, are observing from below with undisguised pleasure the blowing in the wind of those coats and all that is promised by such blowing.

It seems that I am not the only observer at this time. It is perhaps given by nature but we are not aware of it that, in spite of themselves, most people are taken in by the wave of some contrived activity. But I am too tired for such waves. I can only take in their resonance, like ripples on the surface of a pond formed by a thrown stone. I just collect and swallow. It's a strange occupation, but it is mine and this is the heart of the matter.

And while I search for ways to justify my inactivity, an odd old woman comes along pushing the most tattered baby carriage in all of Europe. The carriage is generously decorated with lilac branches and from its aromatic deep peer out three comical heads with wet nostrils and pointed ears — three pups. They look around seriously as the old woman speaks to them quietly, then angrily shoos away a group of kids who had assembled around the carriage. In the land of the minarets, we shot dogs. We were given such orders because, in the summer, with heatwaves of 40–50°C all kinds of epidemics are possible. One sergeant killed almost twenty of them.

I light the next cigarette. There is very little beer left in the mug.

Here by the barrel, in the sun, lively debates are going on, exchanges about dry and hard carp, of the odors of the river and of salt. Across from me two veterans in semi-military trench coats are talking. Perhaps they are recalling some details of the operations of 1944 in the Iassy-Kyshiniv region. They drink beer in greedy swallows which make their sharply protruding Adam's apples move like crazy. There is a stern decisiveness in their eyes.

And now, across the square to the book vendor's stalls. Perhaps I can turn up a not too shabby Polish detective novel. The main thing is that such reading does not obligate one to anything and perfectly accommodates over-tired, lame people such as I.

I am being watched as I dig through the stacks of books. These girls are the owners of the stall, or at least its charming faeries. They are both of average height, pleasantly rounded and soft. Two kittens with treacherous movements. It's curious what they might think of me if I bought this yellowed tome of Novalis in German for twenty rynski*.

"Perhaps you will make me a gift of this book?"

The first one smiles slightly, the other studies me attentively. I like the first one better. She even jokes — shaking her head as if to say, "Nuts to you!"

Finally she permits herself to continue the conversation — perhaps this could lead to something?

"Do you read German?"

"I not only read it, I even understand it a little..."

It was a poor joke, but both of them are laughing now. The ice has been broken! I have a great urge to ask one of them (the first one) when she finishes work and to arrange a date. I feel sure she would agree. Maybe she is waiting for me to ask.

Don't get excited, little soldier. You'd better go across the street and be on your way. I put the book back and walk away slowly. (As she follows me with her eyes, I probably limp ten times worse than usual.)

I could have tried, if I had not been so...tired. I wave to her from the opposite sidewalk — she is still looking. Good bye, my love, good bye! *Ciao, bambina*, sorry!

I should speed up a little. The sky has become overcast, the air is heavy, there is even a threat of thunder. Therefore, before the typhoon hits and a tsunami drowns our miniature atoll, I must climb up the tallest palm tree. The first raindrops have arrived already but I have no urge to run. I operate as best I can among the disturbed crowd of natives.

Oh, here is the blessed sign: "The Globe Café-Bar," a marvelous place for tired seafarers and retired leaders of armies. Although the rain is already striking forcefully and purposefully and muddy streams are swirling on the pavement, carrying papers, cigarette stubs and cherry petals toward the gutters, this does not disturb me. Feeling in my pocket for the "yellow devil,"* I descend confidently (it seems to me) the stairs to the basement room of the cafe. Here I enter intimate surroundings, the unchanging disco; there is no Tahitian woman on stage (it must be her day off), but Borya Fishkin, the barman, truly resembles an Arab.

I spot my familiar uncrowned kings! My former brothers in spirit, the founders and leaders of the rock group "Dombey and Son" — Dombey himself (Slavko Dombrovsky) and Nestor "America" (the best bass guitarist in the European part of the Soviet Union), and with them a young woman in a cream-colored outfit, dark-haired, semitic looking, I recall that three years ago she was a singer in the "Dunay" restaurant. In those days I wrote the lyrics for "Dombey," I even suggested their name (Dickens notwithstanding*), inasmuch as they already had a Son, a drummer, who was small and thin and resembled a sparrow. Later the Son was jailed for contraband (he used this noble word to refer to plain old black marketeering), but the name stuck.

"America" has already recognized me and his face has lit up as he waves his hands about and even tries to hug me as I sit down beside him. Just don't tell me how much I have matured!

Then "America" introduces me slowly and ceremoniously. I was not wrong about Raiechka; it was she who sang at the "Dunay."

I dive into my cocktail, and a strained silence sets in. Her hands trembling, Raiechka cannot pull out a cigarette from the package. In silence I observe my old buddies: "America" has changed a lot, he's grown heavier; he has a short haircut and is wearing a good wool suit, and with his giant dark glasses he more resembles a chief of the Paraguayan secret police than a good old rocker. They said that he had married well — to the daughter of the rector of some institute and that he even enrolled at that institute (strange things can happen!). Of course they had a separate cooperative apartment and a car — one's chin does not double from poverty. Dombey, however, looks as if we had just parted ways yesterday (at my send-off party he had gotten drunk and at three in the morning kept proclaiming from the balcony the freedom of creative expression). He is just as hairy, in a faded leather jacket and still resembles Ian Anderson of Jethro Tull. He nods to me slightly and turns again to his plate laden with a colossal fatty cutlet. He gives the impression that he is here separately, on his own, and that he has nothing to do with verbose "America" and some de-mobilized invalid.

Now Nestor takes the initiative: something must be done about this silence! He sings some lines from old songs with my words (for Raiechka's benefit), recalls "Linotype Rock," "Green Tennis Rackets," "A War on Mars," "Asphalt Man"...

O, this was ingenious, Raiechka — an asphalt man in a yellow vest with a shovel in his calloused hands — a social "blues," psychedelic rock! The clamor on the dance floor would subside when we began to play "Asphalt Man."

Raiechka smokes silently and gives Nestor a bored look. Dombey finally finishes chewing the cutlet and after swallowing some white wine, announces:

"We've had enough of shuffling through old underwear. I'll tell you an abstract anecdote. It's about a crocodile who asks a frog how far it is to the Mississippi..."

The anecdote is not only abstract but also as long as *The Iliad* and it ends with a vulgarity, but it gets a pretty good reception. (Raiechka laughs loudest, as if to say, see what I'm like?) As soon as he finishs the joke, Dombey seems to separate himself again — he sips his wine and intently examines the artificial daisy in the vase.

Silence returns and "America" cannot think of anything better than turning to me:

"You seem so secretive, old man... Tell us about the Dushmani, don't be so silent..."

Raiechka raises her eyebrows:

"So it's from over there that our hero returns?"

I don't like such questions and such curiosity and I try to stave them off with a joke. I go to the barman for another cocktail and for a bottle of "Viorika." When I return to the table "America" displays an ugly insistence:

"What's wrong with the leg, old man?"

Raiechka cannot let it go, either. In her eyes I am an intrepid paratrooper, a professional killer with iron muscles, palms and nerves. Only Dombey (holy soul!) meditates on the plastic daisy and doesn't give a damn about anything.

I answer sparingly, not out of modesty but because truly there is not much to say, but they — especially that wench — are holding me in a lethal grip (why do they need to know?) and I slowly unwind. The cocktail flowing through me, I begin to talk in fragments, clumsily, about things better left unsaid:

"The heat... In the daytime, the heat. The food was horrible... you could barely swallow it. The boys grew thin, suffered from jaundice... They smoked pot, they drank cologne... In the evenings the barracks smelled of 'Carnation' and 'Red Moscow' ad nauseam... The sergeants would hit you for this... In the morning even piss in the latrine would smell of cologne."

"What about the minarets? What about the exotica of the East?" intrudes Nestor.

"Minarets? Why are you clinging to those minarets? And what else, harems with nude dancers? None of that exists! It's a savage and hungry land — the desert and the mountains... Dirty people, spreaders of disease. The grownups sold us pot and their kids placed the mines."

I shut up and light another cigarette. It's too bad that I got so upset — they might think that I've become a psychopath.

"America" shakes his head pathetically and Raiechka looks at me somewhat differently now — without provocation or faked curiosity. Her outfit is unzipped quite deeply and a small medallion on a chain moves delicately in the tanned cleavage between her breasts. She catches my gaze and, as if automatically, pulls the zipper up higher.

Dombey offers a joke about a little pink elephant and a grey rat, but "America" interrupts him and turns again to me:

"You know, old man, you are quite stupid, sorry to say...you could have avoided the whole ugly thing. Everyone told you, get yourself into an institute, the army can do without you... You would have been accepted — none of us doubt it, not even Dombey (Dombey nods his head seriously), but you were so stubborn. You went to work in some underground print shop and kept ruining your eyesight through the nights — you liked transforming metal into words, you see! — and when the time came to go to war, you didn't even bother to get yourself a medical excuse..."

"Poor chap!" sighs Raiechka.

"And imagine," continues "America," "imagine, Raiechka, while this idiot [pointing at me] exposed himself to the bullets over there..."

"Why don't you drop dead with your oratory!" — I interrupt.

"Yes, yes, while he was there twirling the flag about, life did not stand still, people turned into people, seized the free places under the sun, in other words, they settled in..." — "America" pauses for a minute, drawing in the smoke of the cigarette — "they settled in as comfortably as possible and even Liufa, quiet, nerdy Liufa, married his girl, didn't he? — he had found a free slot."

"I wish them happiness!" burst out of my mouth, probably not as dryly and indifferently as I would have wanted.

"Poor fellow!" Raiechka said again.

"Tell me the truth," "America" pushes on. "Weren't you ready to kill yourself when you read in a letter about their wedding? I heard that there are many cases of this in the army and you could have been stupid enough to do this..."

"In the army this is called 'receiving a bad letter,'" I said. "Those soldiers are watched closely and are not put on guard duty."

"And how did you get over this letter?" "America" looks at me with an indifferent kind of curiosity, as if to say, and what did you pull then?

I answer as I put my hand on Raiechka's small hand:

"How did I live through it? Quite calmly: there were many like her and and there will be many more. Isn't it true, little girl?"

She pulls away and, in return, poses the idiotic question:

"And were there any Afghani women?"

As if awakened from his lethargy, Dombey adds:

"Forgive me, girl, but those Afghani women don't even wash..."

Again Raiechka laughs harder than the others, but I feel that she is already tired of sitting here. And, in truth, she says that she's sat with us too long already, that she must go and, not taking her hand out of mine, she gets up and then suddenly says to me:

"Will you see me home?"

Dombey gives "America" a significant look; he, in turn, looks at the daisy; over us flows the sound of the next Italian hit, the Adriatic voices pronouncing the words clearly (*mare* usually rhymes with *cantare* and *piazza* with *ragazza*); and I, still holding her damp hand, follow her through the labyrinth of the lower hall...

The rain has stopped. According to the rules of May, the sun is shining again, there are terrific puddles with sparrows and passers-by who furtively turn toward the buildings when cars go by, splashing the sidewalks with with muddy sprays. It is four in the afternoon.

"Let's go to my place," Raiechka says huskily. She is standing too close and some of the passers-by look at us a bit too curiously. "Let's go, we'll drink to our acquaintance..."

She seems to be made out of alcohol and cigarettes.

We succeed in hailing a taxi and throw ourselves into the back seat. The driver, who looks like Jean Gabin, evaluates us as a couple, in terms of the fare, having barely looked into the mirror. The trip is long enough for her to smoke a cigarette. We stop in some micro-district totally unknown to me — a nine-storied, uninteresting jungle.

"Have a good time!" shouts Jean Gabin, winking at me surreptitiously. The old lech!

The apartment is on the third floor. Raiechka is nervous for some reason, she has a hard time with the key and the door as I talk to her about islands full of palm trees and Tahitian women with breasts as heavy as coconuts...

"Here we are at home," says a tall, thin type with a beard and an icon-like face, after we finally burst inside.

"Oh, oh, Petrov!" Raiechka feigns surprise — get acquainted, this is my husband Petrov! And right on the spot, with a charming directness she whispers into my ear: "He is leaving shortly."

Petrov shakes my hand amicably. I recognize him: he is also an old rocker, who used to play at club dances; he had an admirable synthesizer with a fanciful and delicate sound. Petrov is hurrying somewhere, yet we have time to drink a glass of wheat whiskey which he takes out of the portable cooler. We top it off with yesterday's dry bread while Raiechka busies herself, turns on the disc player — this time it's Amanda Lear. She prepares sandwiches on the run so the kind master of the house and I drink another glass and the slightly drunk Petrov whispers to me confidently:

"Don't get bored here... Raiechka, she's all right... We have complete freedom, you understand? I'm going — as you well know, work is work. The Chaika Restaurant, do you know it? That's where I play now."

Their apartment is small, one room, the walls are covered with superstars (there's Elton John) and with all manner of strip teasers — all this is colorful, shiny and effective. In the place of honor by the window is a drum with the name "The Catafalque Supergroup," a phonograph, a tape player, stacks of journals, sheet music, pliable LP's — everything evoking an atmosphere of active musicianship. A child's bed and a few toys scattered carelessly on the floor testify that Petrov has not completely neglected his family duties.

While I'm examining all of this, Petrov announces yet another time that he is leaving us, again he presses my hand sincerely and at length and, now from the doorstep, he shouts:

"The Chaika Restaurant, don't forget. Come somehow — you'll hear how we play. We'll sit, have a drink. Well, *Ciao* for now!"

We are alone. I don't quite understand how I ended up here and what will happen. My head is spinning somewhat from all that I've drunk and all the mixtures and Raiechka disappears into the kitchen to wash some dishes. The Beedoo orchestra is blasting in the room, Elton John grins encouragingly from the poster (Ha, Ha!), I go out on the balcony to smoke and to let the noise in my head subside a little. Evening is approaching, some unusual birds are sitting on the rooftops and tree branches. Toddlers are playing in the sandbox, one can smell the lilacs — this would be an idyll but an infantry major passing underneath the balcony spoils the general impression as I suddenly remember everything: the heat, the dusty, overheated BTR's*, and the smell of cheap cologne in the barracks.

I throw the butt at a pigeon on the next balcony and return to the room. Raiechka is standing over the ottoman, her back towards me and she is taking off her clothes...

How did it happen that I fell asleep? I open my eyes — we are lying side by side, naked as our pre-human ancestors and she is staring at me. I know that I should be offering explanations; instead I light a cigarette and ask in an unnatural voice:

"How did it happen that I fell asleep?"

We are lying in silence, somewhat distanced one from the other, yet there is an inexplicable closeness between us.

"Poor chap..."

Then she jumps up and begins to dress quickly.

"You can lie here a while longer," she says to me. "I have to run and get the kid at the nursery..."

Now she is gone and I am alone in a strange house.

I have to get away, of course, although I know that she will be hurt not to see me when she returns. Perhaps she wants to show off her son? ("What do you say?" "Say hello to the uncle! That's a good boy!")

I get dressed quickly and leave the apartment. The lock clicks dryly. It's half past six.

I'm lucky in meetings today. Not far from Raya's house I bump into Wasyl whom I know from God knows where. He is a well-regarded plasterer and painter, tortured by the need to drink, and, since right now I want the same thing and in large doses, our selection falls on "Mitsne."

Now we are sitting on children's swings in the midst of some courtyard, drinking the cheap red wine out of the bottle. The wine gurgles pleasantly in the throat and flows through the veins like warm fire. We are swinging, and the poplars are swinging with us. Then, cursing and gesticulating, I tell Wasyl about the bestial Dushmani, about exchanges of fire in the mountains, about punitive actions, and also about an ace of American intelligence whom I personally detained on the Pakistani border for which I was awarded the prize of the infallible French lighter which I demonstrate to Wasyl right there and then for emphasis. He listens to me so intently, with such enthusiasm and understanding, that I make him a gift of that lighter.

Then I decide to go to the Chaika. Really, why shouldn't I go, since Petrov had invited me? The idea of having a drink with him and of parting as honorable people, is so attractive to me that I leave Wasyl in the entrance he had ducked into to urinate.

The Chaika Restaurant is situated in a park along the shore of the city lake. I can see its lighted terrace from far away and can hear the hoarse, lusty roar of the saxophone which sounds out traditional, vulgar melodies.

I climb the stairs to the terrace and can hear Petrov's voice from the hall, for he is too close to the microphone:

"For our dear friend Givi Nakhurtsidze — a song about an iceberg!"

I want to enter the room, but am blocked by a powerful doorman: "Hey, there! Where are you hurrying?"

I would not succeed in ignoring him. So I shout something long and complicated into his ear — the music is thundering and the waitresses in green, low-necked dresses pass by, laden with orders. He growls and pushes me aside — a doorman with a glass eye, probably some amnestied thug, a veteran of the underworld. I have the strongest urge to spit into that glass eye.

Finally he surmises who it is that I want to speak to ("Petrov, the musician?"). He's still examining me with his glass eye and hesitating. But a good impulse takes hold of him, and he stops a green waiter in flight with two bottles of champagne and orders him:

"Call for Petrov!"

I wait on the terrace feeling very jolly; I observe. The dancing is in full swing: hysterical embraces, drunken, greasy lips, heart to heart talks, danced-out ladies congregating by the washroom, exuding sweat and perfume.

For some reason that Afghani runt with the bare belly button appears before me. I stand at my post and he runs up to me, laughs stupidly and begins to beg, "Sugah…sugah!" I make horrible faces, I want to chase him away, but he is not afraid and keeps on repeating: "Sugah! Give me some sugah!" I reach into my bag, get four cubes and put them into his dirty palm. He stuffs his mouth full of that sugar — all four cubes — chews on it, slurps, sucks and a greyish saliva rolls out of his mouth. Then he runs a circle around me again demanding "sugah."

Petrov's appearance on the terrace brings me back to reality. He is wearing an orange vest and a dark-blue bow tie. His beard juts out aggressively, but he himself is the soul of friendliness:

"Oh, how nice that you came, old man! I was not even expecting it…" He slaps my back and for some reason asks me to wait for him by the bushes below, behind the terrace.

Down below is just fine with me, why not? The bushes smell of the evening freshness of leaves, rather thick and heavy after the rain.

Somewhere nearby a nightingale exudes a lovelorn frenzy, but here it's calm and the restaurant noises do not quite reach me. It's dark and quiet. I wonder what time it is.

I hear quick, nervous steps on the grass. I turn around toward them — there are five of them (the whole jazz band, "completto"!). Petrov is first, the leader of the orange vests. There is an unnatural raspiness in his voice, as if to say, there will be no mercy!

"You scum, now tell me, how was it with my..."

They'll be afraid to kill or maim me (they're intelligentsia, after all), but they'll give me a good workout. Well, I'll strike first.

"You, bastard," I shout as the heroes of Westerns sometimes do. "Just for your information: I served in the paratroopers! I would kill twenty Dushmani with one swing of my palm!"

No one has the nerve to strike first, they seem affected by my paratrooper speech. They push their leader forward:

"Go ahead, Petrov! Go for it!"

I am the first to strike. I succeed in punching someone in the teeth and then everyone turns on me. Feet, arms, elbows and fists are pummeling me as if they were let out of a sack.

"Don't hit me, I'm only the pianist" — for some reason this Elton John refrain is spinning in my head.

I am lying on the wet grass, curled tightly and tensed up as they kick me — elegantly and painfully. Then I hear someone's light steps and a frightened female voice.

"What are you doing? Stop it. You might kill him, God forbid. Everyone is looking for you. Where are the musicians, where are the musicians. The manager is running about and you're here, it turns out. Hurry up!"

So they leave me to resume playing their music — out of breath and content; only the one who had his teeth punched is cursing.

I am lying on the damp grass and have no urge to get up, to move my arms or legs. I am very tired. This is the heart of the matter.

The nightingale has grown silent for some reason and I can hear Petrov announcing, having caught his breath:

"So, for our dear guest Givi Nakhurtsidze — a song about an iceberg!"

Is there no one alive in this city? What darkness and what emptiness — the streets are dead. Where did everyone go? Why is there no light in their windows? There is only the editor who is finishing the final page of tomorrow's newspaper. In five minutes he will sign off on it and "tomorrow" will begin.

I walk home. Blood is oozing from my lip and nose and I cover my face with a sticky palm. If only a policeman would turn up! Most of all, I would like to see that girl from the book stall — right here, right now, in this depeopled, nocturnal city. I would fall to my knees in front of her in the middle of the street and, kissing her hands, I would declare my love...

But she is not here, and I am walking home. The old man is probably still sitting in the kitchen, pretending to play solitaire, but he is really waiting for me. I'll enter and I'll say:

"Good evening, father..."

Published in Ukrainian in *Prapor* No. 7, 1989

Notes:

Verkhovyna — a brand of very strong cigarettes

Hutsul mocassin — The *Hutsuly* are highlanders who live in the Carpathian Mountains of western Ukraine

Ostankino — Moscow television studio

colibri — large, violet-eared hummingbird

bliuvaisy — a play on the words "blue" and the word for "to throw up"

kurkuli — Ukrainian equivalent of *kulaks*, the term applied to all but the poorest peasants. Kulaks were exiled, sent to labor camps, or killed in the 1930's, during Stalin's campaign to collectivize Soviet agriculture.

"southerners" — a common reference to people of the Caucasus region

rynski — a colloquial name for an Austro-Hungarian coin

"yellow devil" — money, in Soviet jargon

Dombey and Son (1848) — novel by Charles Dickens

BTRs — military vehicles

ВРАГ
НЕ ДРЕМЛЕТ!
© J.R.R.T.
ТРАКТИР
ЗЮ
СВОБОДУ
ЛЕОНАРДУ
ПОЛТЕРГЕЙСТУ!
СПИД НЕ ПРОЙДЁТ!
ДЖОРДЖ

Bohdan
ZHOLDAK

The Seven Temptations

Translated by Michael M. Naydan
with Charlotte Holmes

There lived, if you can call it life, a certain ascetic. He lived and perfected himself by doing battle with the temptations that so fill our lives — in contrast to the rest of us, who seek them out with all their might, intending to submit to them.

The first temptation: living space.

When Mykola Semenovych was offered a separate apartment instead of his communal one, only one thing was demanded of him: that he organize a feast in a restaurant for his provider, a certain Fedir Serhiyovych. Mykola had spent eighteen years on the waiting list for apartments, but instead of getting shorter, every year the list left the ascetic farther from his desired goal. Someone else would have fed that Fedir Serhiyovych in restaurants for his entire life, but not Mykola Semenovych. So in this way he condemned himself eternally to communal life, thus overcoming the temptation of living space. One should add that living with people has many more potential temptations than living in a separate apartment, especially when all the windows look out into a single inner courtyard.

The second temptation: television.

His neighbor to the left acquired video technology. Completely by accident and without premeditation, he placed the screen in a corner that could be seen marvelously from Mykola Semenovych's windows. Mykola Semenovych took to fasting as every day in the neighbor's room, movies glowed on the screen — lavish, saturated and abundant with the culinary treasures of life abroad. That neighbor treated information as existence, so the set was practically never off.

Mykola Semenovych had been planning to hang curtains at the window, but upon reflection ascertained that in this way he would not undergo a true trial. With all his effort, he placed himself under these living color video visions.

The third trial: drugs.

The neighbor to the right turned out to be a drug addict.

The new neighbor hated Mykola Semenovych, precisely because Mykola Semenovych had a goal in his life. Thus he secretly added various drugs to the kitchen pot to accustom his antagonist to the greed of evil. After eating, Mykola Semenovych could not comprehend what was happening to him, but he struggled with these phenomena with the aid of new fasts. How much hash the neighbor fed him in vain! And he gained nothing — as usual when tempters provoke a true ascetic.

When other druggies cut up the addict for a suitcase of hash, the expiring neighbor hauled himself up to Mykola Semenovych's window by mistake, expecting that he'd get out of this alive with a small bag of Yakutian diamonds. This unexpected wealth, however, did not fluster the ascetic. He immediately took the bag to the police station and turned it in, not even asking for a receipt. Soon after, his old mother came to him crying that her roof had blown off and the cellar had flooded, and there was nothing to shore up the domestic economy.

The fourth temptation: avowal.

It assumed the guise of working for the general good. Recognizing in Mykola Semenovych certain aptitudes, his neighbors proposed that he become involved with a grand social group, one more influential than all the others. Their main argument went like this: you will then be much more able, Mykola Semenovych, to apply your love of people to progress and the common good than if you cling to your ascetic proclivities.

Perhaps he would have succumbed had they not rashly disclosed that being in this group was incompatible with ascetics. So he turned them down, however alluring it might have been to help his neighbors.

The fifth temptation: motherhood.

Finding her son in an awful state (he was fasting), his mother forgot about her troubles. She settled in at his place and every minute instructed him, drawing on her folk wisdom, about a righteous life. After a year he was forced to kick his own mother out of the apartment, while giving her all his savings for repairs.

The sixth temptation: seduction.

At that time a young woman, a medical student, moved into the communal apartment to live in a corner of her grandmother's room. She immediately grasped that it would be a lot cheaper to move in with a bachelor, which Mykola Semenovych had been for twenty years. On several occasions she entered the wrong room at night wearing only her underwear. And once in the bathtub, covered only with suds, she was inspired to suggest that he wash off her back. Mykola Semenovych nearly declined, but decided that the victory would not be a very big one. So he rubbed her back, relying on asceticism to the very end.

The new occupant of the drug addict's room was a former graduate student of the Asia Insitute. He knew Sanskrit and used to translate the sutras, until that got him kicked out of the university. And when he began to preach them to others, he earned himself a decent prison term.

Mykola Semenovych did not believe his eyes when he saw that winter a naked man on the opposite balcony, lying on a board of nails. After seeing this, the ascetic decided to forswear beans.

On the second day, he observed the man clenching his teeth and whipping himself in the snow with a triple-lashed riding crop. Mykola Semenovych reflected on this and decided he'd better abstain from honey. Then he decided to add to this abstention three hours of his sweetest early morning sleep.

But the man seemed to exist only on the meager offerings of his students. In return he read them Sanskrit without bothering to translate it. To Mykola Semenovych's misfortune, two friends of the ex-graduate student ended up in his apartment—disciples not only of Zen, but of Christ. They conveyed to him in rapturous tones that this man was wholly capable of nourishing himself on the smoke from an incenser, for he was linked by a telepathic bridge with the Universe, from which he was drawing energy.

Mykola Semenovych, who a week before had begun to sleep on iron planks, now also renounced drinking water and went on an autotrophic diet, living exclusively on his own saliva. Had it not been for conjuctivitis, acquired by washing in icy water, he might have noticed two mighty radiators just inside the neighbor's balcony doors that wafted hot air over the sutra disciple during practice. His whip was a stage prop, borrowed from a stunt man friend. And how was our poor fellow to know that this guy, in fact, was hiding in the mezzanine a two-door refrigerator, stuffed with extravagant sausages? How was he to know that the disciple's two peaceful novices were really models from the art institute, for whom the disciple purposefully contrived the teaching of Zen-shaktism, so that they would screw him, one after the other, in the most shameful positions of the Kama Sutra, ones that not even female students in the medical schools could hazard a guess about?

How was he to know that the conscience of his neighbor was stained by several papers signed in the Gulag, and that he silenced those pangs of conscience only by swigging homemade moonshine? How was he to know that the incense burned in the apartment every day was just to kill the stench of the mash?

Mykola Semenovych found out that this Sanskrit wasn't Sanskrit at all, but rather a Buryat language, which the disciple learned while on a compulsory work detail cutting trees in Siberia, and that it was for his insufficient knowledge of Sanskrit that he was thrown out of graduate school. How was he to know, lastly, that the book of prayers was a translation into the Buryat language of Mayakovsky's poetry with the title page torn off?

Nevertheless, thanks to this hippie — who, while eating peppered Hungarian ham and observing the sufferings of Mykola Semenovych, cynically called the spectacle "a game of ascetball" — our hero attained the ideal of all earthly ascetics — he died from utter exhaustion. He, who believed he had attained the illumined pinnacle of self-sacrifice and had passed through all temptations, perished, not having endured the seventh:

The temptation of asceticism.

Published in Ukrainian in *Spokusy (Temptations)*, Kiev: Radianskyi pysmennyk, 1991

Yuri
VYNNYCHUK

Max & Me

*Translated by Michael M. Naydan
with Elizabeth Searle & Ed Hogan*

I was, maybe, fifteen and my brother Max — six, when our old man acquired permanent ownership of a wooden villa, whose sole inconvenience was that you could only lie down in it horizontally, and that it was two meters beneath the ground. He arranged his journey into a better world this way: he fell down drunk from a footbridge into a stream, the water only knee high. He managed the fall so well that it's possible he had help, though we certainly wouldn't know anything about that.

It's true that on that very evening Mom ordered my brother and me to lay a rope across the footbridge and to loosen the hand rails. She didn't say why, and I'm still wondering about that. When the corpse was found in the morning, the ropes were gone.

Mom started wailing:

"O woe is me! How terrible! Who have you left us to?"

It would have been a sin to complain, since our mother was in the not-so-bad hands of her suitors, who, even when our old man was alive, trampled a path to our house and paid decent money, confirming Mom's sexy wiles.

At those times Mom chased us out of the house, but we're not dopes. Sneaking up to the window, we watched everything with pleasure. I lifted my little brother on my arms so he could see how our momma was playing hoppity-hop on the bed with the guy.

We knew all her guests by sight and always fondly greeted them. We liked them and showed them respect, because they brought us candy and other sweets.

There was just one windbag we couldn't stand. He was such a fat pig that he could barely crawl into the house. So as not to hurt our momma, he didn't mount her, but put her on top. It was like this: poor momma was hoppity-hopping till sweat poured out, and he just lay there like a log, wheezing.

Ha, you're such a dog! We're going to make you bolt out of here. Just before his arrival one day we took pepper and liberally sprinkled it on the bed under the sheet. Then we planted ourselves behind the window and waited.

We watched him arrive and get ready to go at it with our mom. Mom started to do her thing, and he — whether he wanted to or not — scraped his backside. The pepper even went up there. Whichever way he was thrown, up or down, our mom, like a sparrow, flew up, then quickly fell down with a bang. We began to object so our mom wouldn't fall on the floor. But God showed mercy. Our piggo, though, after all that jumping around began to sneeze his brains out. He was already getting dressed with fiendish exertion and that sneezing!

Then Gramps finked on us under the window, bawling:

"What are you scamps doing here?"

And we answered him:

"Hush, Gramps! You'll frighten away the client!"

"What kind of client, dammit?"

"Come here and just take a look!"

From that time our gramps began to hang out under the windows. He was about to punish us:

"Look, don't forget to call me when those... Cause I'll take a crowbar and break their legs! Take that, blockheads!"

It wasn't even a year since Dad's death, and our mom had exhausted herself to nothing from riding. Then the suitors disappeared somewhere — as if the wind had blown them away.

As though for spite, an adventure arose with Gramps. Gramps, ya see, was busy checking the neighbor's chicken coop. He liked order everywhere.

"I," he says, "don't take anybody else's stuff, just what's left over. And when I begins to count the chickens, I sees an uneven count, and I sez to myself: if there ain't no pair — then leave it for the bear. And I takes away one chicken. And when I count an even number, then if I takes one — you break up the pair. So I takes two."

At a certain unfortunate hour, Gramps was caught in the chicken coop just as he was screwing the head off of the second in a pair of chickens. Gramps, of course, tried to explain that his activity was directed exclusively for the benefit of the economy. But the eight-balls didn't take him seriously and skillfully counted up the paired nature of Gramps' ribs. Since then, no one has had any doubts about Gramps not having an extra rib.

After such a counting out, the poor guy didn't get up out of bed. But we already knew quite well that our breed has more lives than a cat and Gramps has, God knows, many more years of tumbling in bed till he even thinks about giving up his spirit to God. This wasn't the point for us, and we didn't complain much when at night Grandpa puffed and panted underneath the feather comforter that covered his head. So that feather comforter wouldn't slide off and our Gramps, God forbid, wouldn't catch a cold, we sat on top with Mom.

The poor guy couldn't even quack because our Mom was a stout little woman. Though she had a rump the size of two, all the same, Gramps' pretty little head hurt her for sure, especially his long hooked nose.

Thus as Gramps, God rest his soul, was croaking, we were left standing on sheep dung. His diploma for soundless penetration into the chicken coops lost its validity from the time his authorship of the deeds became known to everyone it served. So it wasn't a surprise when our mom said:

"Well, you've already grown up, time to get on with business. Cause I'm not planning on supporting any spongers."

That this was the holy truth, we were assured through Gramps, and to insure ourselves against various surprises, at which our mother was very adroit, we started up an entirely respectable business: we grabbed everything lying around that wasn't bolted down.

Little Max was a uniquely clever boy, but already much too screechy. Somehow that screeching burnt me up so much that I couldn't take it:

"Shut up," I says, "or I'll cut off your ear."

As much as I warned him, he wouldn't stop. I really loved my little brother, but you have to keep a promise. So I take a knife, slash-slash — and the ear's gone.

Max fell silent, and suddenly his tears vanished. First they dripped like from a down spout, then it was as though they were licked up by a cow. He looked at me with such bulging eyes. His mouth gaped, and from his ear ever so quietly, the brrr-brrr trickling.

"Idiot!" I couldn't hold back. "If you'd just cover it with your hand!"

Not even a peep from him. He stands there as though he's kicked in the head. It would have gone on for a while if Mom had not come out and asked:

"What happened that he's not crying? First he wailed like a stuck pig, then he quieted down and hasn't stirred since. What did you do to him?"

"Nothin'. I just lopped off his ear cause he was freaking out too much."

"Did you at least clean his ear before you lopped it off?"

"No, but so what?"

"The 'what' is that you can spread infection. Lord, what am I to do with you? You never ask the grown-ups, you decide everything yourselves. Max, go into the house. I'll cover your wound with dough. Just look at how it's bleeding all over! Instead of bugging out your eyes like a frog staring at it, just cover it with your hand!"

I hid the ear in a matchbox, covering it with cotton, and Max never parted with it. His ear soon became the envy of all the boys on the street; even kids from the edge of town came to catch a look at it. With pride Max showed his ear, explaining:

"Vlodzyo cut it off when I was screaming like a stuck pig."

Then everybody turned their gaze to me, filled with respect and envy: that's some brother!

Fortunately I realized that you could make some decent dough from displaying a cut-off organ. I began to collect a nickel from every onlooker. In rare cases, when an onlooker was too young to control his own finances, the payment was exchanged for some valuable objects. These might be colored glass lenses, buttons, a dead mouse, a strange little beetle, or even a piece of candy.

Momma couldn't have been more thrilled with us:

"I always said: my blood's flowing inside you."

She never mentioned our dad's blood, since she could never be sure which of her countless suitors really was our dad.

But all things come to an end. When our audience dwindled, our profits declined. Poor Max couldn't take this. With tears in his eyes, he begged me to cut off his other ear. But well I knew that this would hardly interest anyone again.

Then we began to reflect upon what else we might cut off Max. We thought for a long time until Max finally suggested with a secret glance that he had one other strange thing that was completely unnecessary, and happily he would part with it. But when he showed me the thing, I didn't want to take upon myself such a heavy sin.

"Max," I said, "you're still much too little and can't appreciate the value of that thing. When you grow up a bit, you'll really need it once in a while."

In short, whether we wanted to or not, we were forced to look for other earnings.

2.

About the same time a lush wandered into our yard and fell asleep, and our sow ambled over and bit him on the neck. She, as rarely happens with a sow, wasn't miserly and called over the boar to share the sweets.

Upon hearing the loud snorting and smacking, we ran out with our mom and chased off the gluttons. But it was too late; the lush had already departed for a better world. And at that moment a bold idea visited Mom's gray little head: so as not to waste good stuff. Before the meat began to stink, she decided to make schnitzels from the lush.

Without thinking much, we dragged him into the barn and quickly chopped him apart into bits and pieces.

Since the skin was already damaged, we buried it, and separating the meat from the bones, we put it through a grinder.

The next day, a new sign adorned our house:

> UNDER THE GREEN DOG
> *Here you can tastefully dine*
> *and lodge overnight*
> *in the company of an incomparable Lolita.*

The incomparable Lolita was, of course, our momma. She got a shaggy black wig and didn't look bad at all, even though she had no rubber or corsets tucking her shape in.

Our work lay in making sure our overnight guests were fed with the most varied of meat delicacies, liberally flavored with hemlock. When the guests dispersed to their designated bedrooms, they got interested in the incomparable Lolita. What confusion when it turned out to be our momma. But there was no other way out — the incomparable Lolita visited each room in turn and forced them to copulate, combining the profitable with the pleasurable.

By dawn not a single one of the clients was breathing, and then our real work began. Although "Under the Green Dog" also had visitors for lunch, so much sausage was left over that we had to take it to the market. And so many damn bones collected that the entire barn was cluttered. The work piled up and we, no joke, were huffing and puffing.

One evening, after a long discussion, we decided that Max would care for the garden. We'd planted hemlock and henbane everywhere, so that we'd have seasoning for the meat. The butcher's work fell to me, and to Momma — the cook and the incomparable Lolita.

Despite this, later on, we still couldn't manage everything, and so Momma suggested that we look up her brother.

3.

My uncle lived outside of town on a farm, and he had three underswine: Bodyo who was my age and two twins — Milko and Filko. I'll tell you about the daughter later.

Uncle occupied himself with a nice little business: he'd catch cats and dogs and make soap out of them. Auntie then would sew mink and fox furs from the cat and dog skins, which gave off a suspicious odor. Their owners complained that they were always followed by cats and dogs on the streets, perhaps relatives of the fox fur.

Thus I was designated negotiator. Just in case, I picked up an ax and hid it beneath my belt under my jacket.

Quiet reigned on the farm. An autumn wind consoled the last leaves. Auntie was sitting at the doorstop kneading butter. It was hardly cow's butter.

I politely said "hello" and asked whether Uncle was there.

"Yep, yep, go back of the house — he's there, landlording."

In back of the house my old blockhead uncle and his three little blockheads were tanning cats.

"Lord, help me!" I greeted them.

"Oh, look who's come to us!" Uncle exclaimed, pretending to be pleased. His three ferrets stretched their mouths from ear to ear, baring sparse yellow teeth. "What wind brought you here?"

"The wind that sweeps in money."

Uncle looked at me with interest. Then he wiped off his bloody hands in the grass and stepped closer.

"Well, okay, let's talk. But first let my boys check if you don't happen to have any kind of silly thing under your shirt that might cut a finger."

With these words the three jerks rushed toward me, baring their teeth, eager to fulfill their dad's command. But I stopped this impetus, welcoming the eldest with a shot to the head with the blunt end of the ax.

"Eh-eh," Uncle got fidgety, "I was just kidding."

"Keep these kind of jokes for a job that I'm about to toss your way."

They poured a bucket of rainwater on Bodya and he came to. We sat on the grass under a tree, and I explained:

"Well, the deal's like this. With our mom we opened up an inn, 'Under the Green Dog,' which a lot of guests frequent, but no one notices whether they ever come back out."

Uncle looked back and forth at his den mates meaningfully, and I continued:

"We treat them to meat, and the leftovers of the meat we sell at market. In addition we make soap from the high quality bones and fat. Maybe you've heard about the brand 'Chinese Orange?'"

"Why wouldn't I have heard about it? It's the best soap there is. I use it a lot myself."

"Yeah, we make it. Though, true, we don't use it ourselves."

"And you get the meat after the overnight guests disappear?"

"Right."

"And you feed the overnight guests with meat that appeared after a place is freed up by their predecessors?"

"How quick you are, Uncle!" I shouted rapturously.

Uncle sat lost in thought. The three ruffians wrinkled their stunted brows, pretending that thoughts oppressed them, too.

"Hmm..." Uncle finally mumbled. "And you want to propose that we work together?"

"You just read my mind."

"And you aren't afraid I'll sell you out?"

"Naw."

Uncle raised his eyebrows in surprise:

"Why?"

"Because Max and I are juveniles, and the court would decide that Momma threw us off the righteous path. But Momma won't end up in jail because she's too smart. They'll lock her up in a palace of culture for crazies, and they'll release us to all the four corners of the earth. But then, dear Uncle, your judgment day would come along. There's lots of fat on you, the soap'd be luxurious."

Uncle grimaced.

"I see. Well, I agree. How about you, my lovely kiddies?"

The lovely kiddies immediately nodded their heads. I liked their reticence. We squeezed each other's hands, and Uncle said:

"Well, it wouldn't hurt to wash down a few. Let's go to the house."

Auntie set the table. Uncle got some kind of bottle overgrown with moss out of the credenza and poured out a shot glass for everyone. In my life I've never had to drink a more abominable poison. A corpse would have cursed had someone sprinkled that contagion on his lips. I bit a pickle, but the dumplings that appeared on the table failed to inspire.

4.

From then on our business was so successful that we made oodles of money and began to think about how to expand. It's true, things didn't go without altercations, because Uncle and Momma never missed a chance to cheat each other.

Once Momma said to Uncle:

"Listen, Lodzyo, why don't we become relatives?"

And so now the time comes for me to say a few words about Uncle's daughter, who was 17 and considered herself marriageable. Her name was Ruzya — a creature born quite stupid, who was good only for being kept in a dark garret, so she wouldn't frighten decent people.

Imagine an emaciated, greenish, and, if that's not enough, mustachioed babe. And they were planning to hitch me with her.

I resisted with both hands and feet:

"She's as ugly as world communism! When I see her, everything gets limp and hiccups take over."

"My son," said Momma, "our business needs this. And if you don't agree, then I'll have to take extreme measures."

She looked at me in such a way that I envisioned one leg in the place my beloved dad was.

5.

The wedding was grand. The number of wandering cats and dogs in town decreased noticeably, and they shot down so many crows you couldn't count them. Auntie baked such chicken in cream from them that the guests nearly swallowed their fingers. I won't even speak of stewed rabbits from cat and dog liver. Auntie applied all her culinary talents, so that even the most discerning gourmet wouldn't doubt the provenance of the sausage, the pate and hams.

I sat with a sour look on my face, and next to me my Ruzya stuck out like a skeleton. Her mustachioed smile gleamed from ear to ear.

For a long time I tried not to look her way, so as not to ruin my appetite, and scrupulously consumed those several natural sandwiches that my momma had stuffed into my pockets. But those greenhorns, her off-their-rocker brothers, screeched awfully — so to speak, the liquor was bitter (but can it be sweet if it's made of animal dung?), and they weren't going to drink, you see, until the young couple sweetens it up*.

I turned pale and felt goose bumps prickling along my back. Forget about sweets, mother damnedest! Let a fence post kiss my boots; then, maybe, they'll glisten from her lips like tar. But her brothers lamented till their mugs turned red as beets from the exertion.

Meanwhile Ruzya cuddled over to me like a little dog, and I heard something gurgling in my stomach, as if someone was pushing a wheelbarrow of bricks uphill.

As I rose to my feet with a heavy heart, Ruzya stuck her mug at me and, spattering me all over with saliva, nearly bit off my nose. ·Sucking like a leech, that nag attached herself to me, and I thought she'd suck out my soul. I barely tore her off me, and fell on the bench. Her muzzle glistened with saliva. It wouldn't have been apropos for me to wipe my face, so I grabbed a piece of wedding cake, though it was baked from sawdust, and stuffed it into my mouth to kill the taste of Ruzya's lips.

Meanwhile the parents figured I was burning to be alone with the bride and, grabbing us under the arms, shoved us into the bedroom and locked us in.

My little wife, red from indefatigable thirst and brimming with desire to finally destroy the concrete and iron Maginot Line of her innocence, instantly slipped her rags off her bony form, and became naked as a jay bird.

My numb gaze travelled the smooth flat surface of her chest and sank to her sunken stomach, covered with blue veins and tough enough to straighten out nails on, and then with horror got snared by a black distaff that protruded from between her legs. This broom stunned me with its disproportionate size, and I immediately suspected the talented hand of my auntie.

Laughing malevolently, I tugged at that nest. Ruzya let out a scream. An ordinary wig ended up in my hands, one adapted for a different function — and not without skill. On the spot where there had been impenetrable debris, there now reddened a timid little Ho Chi Minh-like beard that Ruzya chastely covered with her bony hand.

To dispel the tense atmosphere, Ruzya giggled and, jumping sprightly on the bed, threw her skinny legs apart, so that I shouldn't doubt the reality of the spot they had married this dope to. I found that everything there was in order and that a disguised grinding machine wasn't lying in ambush for me. From my relatives you could expect just about anything.

But I wasn't having any of it. Ye-es, I thought to myself, if I don't teach her common sense right away, when will I be able to teach her? And taking off my strap, I went up to her as the fool grinned like a cat. I grabbed a pillow, covered over her snout and marked her with a criss-cross. Like a snake, she writhed and rocked, so much so that her bones rattled, but I didn't stop — striking crosswise — until the strap stuck to her skin.

I pulled away the pillow, sat down next to her and said:

"Just tell anybody this and I'll kill you on the spot. I'm that kind of guy. Comprendez?"

"Uh-huh," she said through tears.

"I don't want to have to see you naked any more. Your goddess-like looks tempt me as turpentine tempts a cat."

6.

After all her intimate relations, you'd think we'd be living like dumplings in butter, but our mom had shriveled up. Now the "incomparable Lolita" could satisfy the kind of guy who'd been sitting in prison for 15 years, and only then if you got him good and drunk.

Our whole family gathered together around the table and debated how to overcome our difficulties. I suggested that we rope our auntie or my beloved wife into this business.

You should've seen how Uncle reacted! All of a sudden he sprang up on his crooked legs and started pounding his fists on the table:

"I won't allow it! I won't give her to you!" he said, along with similar exclamations flavored with peppery words.

His three dork sons grabbed for their knives and forks, as though mistaking me for a cooked turkey.

"Aha," I said to uncle, "when your sister abuses her power for the sake of the communal pocket, you don't say boo, but when your turn comes, you hit the brakes?"

"I'm too weak for that kind of work," Auntie said.

"She's very weak," Uncle repeated. "I don't tussle with her more than twice a week, and even then it's scratch-scratch to get it over with quicker."

"And that's only when he smacks me across the mouth," Auntie moaned. "Cause for me even twice a week is too hard. It's good that I take out my lower plate at night, or my whole mug would be mutilated."

Momma shook her head. "Those guys are all barbarians. One guy just wanted to cut out a piece of my rear-end. He said that when he sees it, he begins to slobber and wants to wolf it down. After I heard that, he never saw me again without my undies on."

"But how did he…?" Auntie got interested, but Momma, casting a look at her children, whispered into her ear. Auntie said: "Aha!" And she got lost in thought.

"Well, that's fine," I thrust in. "You've got a point about Auntie. Keep her exclusively for your own petty bourgeois kulak needs. Pound the sand and sniff if she's breathing. But I'm a guy of the present, my morality isn't messed up by bourgeois superstition. I'll give up my beloved wife for the communal business."

On hearing this, Ruzya flared up like a fire, and lowered her eyes. It was immediately clear that she looked on my sacrifice as the greatest gift fate had offered her. Finally she would shake off her heavy shackles of innocence and sate her thirsty flesh.

All the rest pondered the proposition, feverishly calculating their percentages of the take. To help them out, I continued:

"Since I'm her complete owner, I require 40% of the profit for myself."

I knew what I was saying. Uncle, catching scent of money, suddenly forgot that we were talking about his daughter, and threw himself into the negotiations, knocking down the price. Auntie inserted her own:

"And how much for me? I gave birth to her! Carried her for nine months, I was almost broken in two! I request payment for each month."

"Not nine, but seven," my momma said. "I remember well. That's why she was born so emaciated."

"How's that 'seven'?" Uncle became alert. "I counted well. I know what I was doing. Everything went according to plan. It can't be seven, because they would have taken me into the army right after the wedding."

"But Ruzya was born in the seventh month, I remember that as if it were today. You were already serving your ninth month."

Auntie, her eyes to the ceiling, had gone completely white.

Uncle turned slowly to her, gave her a long look and, without thinking long, drove his fist so hard into her teeth that Auntie collided with the armchair, throwing up her arms and legs. In her left hand she clutched her lower plate, which she had managed to pull out.

"Yep, that's the way it is with dames," said uncle, shaking his head and gulping down ten double-shots of moonshine without taking a bite. "Twenty-five and not a point more."

"Good," I agreed.

Ruzya didn't grumble about her fate, because she got all that she could ever dream about — five or six boys each night, sometimes more. This wasn't just life, but paradise. I almost envied her.

But that was the beginning of our problems. The ex-Lolita now concerned herself only with containing the voluptuous shapes that tumbled from her clothes, while the new one had ribs that jutted out like a ladder.

In order to fully survey the parts of her body that required the hand of a maestro, Momma ordered Ruzya to strip. By that time Auntie had convalesced, having received from Uncle two cuffs on the mouth and a cup of water on her head. She put in her lower plate and got down to business. Momma and the two boys circled around like bumblebees. They all conferred about what to do with this treasure.

"I'll make titties from oakum," Momma said. "I'll sew them around with cheesecloth so they hold together when the client feels them up. And you, Ruzya, should moan heartily, because even though it's oakum, a girl has to moan and roll her eyes when somebody grabs her by the tit. But what can we do with the ribs? You can drum out a march on them. I'm surprised, son, why you haven't knocked on them from time to time."

"Maybe we can cover them with dough so they don't stick out so much?" put in Uncle, chewing pork rind.

Auntie took a spoon from the table and knocked herself on the forehead, looking Uncle straight in the eye. But Uncle, for sure, didn't understand her transparent hint, because he stretched for a pickle instead of a strap to tie her down.

"There's no other way out," said Momma. "We'll just have to feed her with dog lard for several days. That'll make her fill out real fast."

"I don't want dog la-a-rd!" Ruzya began to shriek.

"To melted dog lard you need to add a little honey, whiskey and whipped eggs," Momma added. "This is a solid-as-a-brick-wall recipe when someone wants to quickly put on weight. And it's not as vile as you might guess. I used to drink it, and it wasn't bad."

"What kind of eggs?" Auntie asks. "Chicken?"

"No. Cat testicles," answered Momma*.

"Oo-oo-ooh," Ruzya grimaced.

"Hush," Auntie interrupted. "If you needa, you needa. We have testicles, why complain?"

"It'd be nice to broaden her rear end a bit," Momma said, "because this is a lump and not an ass. How does the poor girl sit on it? Well, bend over."

Ruzya obeyed, showing us a butt that was hard as a knee cap, at the sight of which Uncle reached for his bottle and quickly downed ten more double-shots.

That very day they tied poor Ruzya to the bed and every hour fed her a cocktail made of dog lard and whipped cat balls. And so the lard would satiate her body with as little loss as possible, Ruzya was kept in bed around the clock. Toward evening the whole family gathered by her bed to follow the results of Momma's diet.

Ruzya's muzzle virtually shone from the lard but she looked sad and oppressed. Little by little her body took on the fat, and now it veritably beamed in the darkened room, which was thick with the odor of dog and whipped cat balls.

But despite Momma's and Auntie's sorcery, after a week Ruzya still hadn't put on enough weight to let her loose among clients, and we had to continue the fattening regime. After another week, Ruzya looked so elegant that even my saliva drooled, and I contemplated having a taste of this morsel, but after recalling the special ingredients contained therein, I quickly lost my appetite.

Ruzya had become puffy and round everywhere. On her chest two pastry fluffs dangled and with each step bobbed cheerfully. Momma taught her to walk in such a way that her rear end stuck out as eloquently as possible. My Ruzya turned into a mare on which hardly anyone could resist taking exercise.

That's how it happened. Ruzya enjoyed constant success, and our business bloomed in all its many colors.

7.

We were ill prepared when the police surrounded our farm-yard.

Uncle and Auntie were busy with their cats, Max was tending his garden, Ruzya was upstairs entertaining a client, and Momma was making hunter's sausage from cat intestines. I was sawing wood for smoking ham, and my cousins were distilling their beloved animal dung.

At this peaceful moment, when the sky above our heads shone in translucent azure, sirens and brakes suddenly began to scream, triggers were cocked on carbines, and tens of voices commanded us to raise our hands and give up one by one.

"Better death than slavery!" my momma shouted out, and in seconds we hid in the house.

Everyone armed himself as well as he could. Uncle stuck through the window his double-barreled Austrian rifle which he'd been using to hunt cats, and Auntie pierced the thatched roof with an ancient machine gun.

Ruzya ran downstairs with her client, completely naked. The client screamed that he was here accidentally and right now was going to give himself up.

"Good," Uncle said. "The road is clear."

Ruzya gave him a good-bye kiss, and he dashed out into the yard, shouting:

"I'm one of yours! One of yours!"

Perhaps if he'd chosen a different password, everything would have gone well, but in that shout the police sensed an insult to their honesty. An automatic rifle barked and stitched through him — first up and down, then sideways.

After this the police moved to the attack. On the thatched roof the machine gun began to snarl. The bullets hopped first along the trees, then the plank fences while Auntie swore royally at the police. I think those curses annoyed them more than the bullets. The three brothers dragged out from the basement a cannon painted orange, which looked more ridiculous than threatening.

Meanwhile, Uncle, sniffing heavily with his potato-like nose, threatened the police with his double-barreled gun.

Max and Momma grabbed pitchforks and took up defensive positions by the doors.

At the same time, I gathered into the basement everything that could give evidence against us, and liberally doused it with gasoline. Soon there would be enough to throw a match on, and in a single blow the police would lose their case.

Finally the brothers loaded the cannon and, opening the doors, pointed the barrel at the assault force. On seeing such a monstrosity, the police instantly fell to the ground.

Bodyo lit a stick, raised it to the end of the barrel and shouted: "Fire!"

How can I describe what happened? A deafening explosion shook the whole building, and a poisonous black smoke smothered all of us. One shot smashed all the windows and frames, and the doors with their jambs. Behind our backs, right across from the doors, the shell sent another door off the wall. The cannon had shot in the wrong direction.

When the smoke cleared I saw two ragged heads. The twins had virtuously done their duty. Bodyo was luckier — they simply tore off his hand.

Uncle coughed heavily.

Momma and Max shook their heads and beat themselves on the ears.

Auntie had crawled out onto the roof and shouted to us: "Lodzyo!"

"Whoa!" The old man's throat rattled.

"You alive?"

"Who got killed?"

"The twins."

"They never gave me any pleasure. Even on a day like today they got on my nerves."

And in a minute:

"Lodzyo!"

"Whoa!"

"Tell Ruzya to put on her underwear because the police are almost here."

After this Auntie's machine gun began to rattle, and Ruzya searched for her pantaloons.

I understood that not much was left for us.

Bodyo was one-handedly reloading the cannon.

But it made little difference when it managed to shoot, because the police were closing in from all sides.

Momma and Max stuck their pitchforks through the windows and then through the door so our adversaries could behold the weapons that awaited them.

Uncle asked:

"Bodyo, you going to shoot?"

"Yep."

"Well, then, bye."

The cannon thudded so that on the opposite wall another door appeared, and one of the police cars flared up. Too bad that Bodyo didn't see that.

There was a commotion on the roof, and Auntie's voice came down to us once more:

"Lodzyo!"

"Whoa!"

"I'm flying off!"

"May the heavenly kingdom be yours," Uncle replied, crossing himself as Auntie crashed heavily into the yard.

From the cannon fire we all had blackened mouths and looked like Angolan rebels.

Ruzya crawled out on the roof in her underwear.

Max wailed:

"What've we done to them that's so bad?"

"We'll die like heroes," Momma answered.

Upstairs the rattling of the machine gun reverberated again. I felt a sudden pride in my wife. Strange, although I'd never slept with her even once, at that moment I felt such an overwhelming attraction for her that I was ready to rush to the roof and make love to her amid the bullets.

And perhaps I would have, but a rattling reverberated on the roof and Ruzya called:

"Daddy!"

"Whoa!"

"I'm flying!"

"The Heavenly Kingdom to you!"

Ruzya fell along with the machine gun.

Uncle turned away slowly from the window, and I saw his mouth fill with blood. He sank onto the floor.

I picked up the double-barreled gun and knocked off a policeman's cap. The weapon, it seems, couldn't manage anything more.

Momma and Max courageously defended the door, but the sides were uneven. The police wanted to take at least some of us alive and shot above our heads, but when Momma stuck one of them with the pitchfork like a dumpling, the infuriated policeman tore her stomach apart with bullets.

"You bandits!" Max became enraged and threw himself into the attack, a forked weapon in each hand.

The end was in sight. I tossed a match into the basement, then I raised a small log from the floor and with all my strength whacked myself on the head.

I found out what happened later at the trial.

They put me on trial because I was the only survivor. The evidence and the house had burned to the ground. I assumed the role of an idiot, feigning that I didn't understand a thing.

I got what I wanted. They diagnosed me as ill and sent me off to the asylum at the Park of Culture.

Now I'm sitting by the window, admiring the wintry park. A fine snow is falling, crows are cawing, I'm wearing clean pajamas, and on my knees there's a plate of sweet kasha. Life is beautiful.

When Spring comes, I'll ask Olya, the nurse's aide, to take me for a walk in the garden. I'll behave so well that all will wonder how I could have done such evil deeds. Some even say that I'm suffering only because I was left alive; everything was thrust on me alone. Olya brings me candies, pats me on the head and says: "So young, so nice, but terribly ill!" I try to lick her hand, but she hides it behind her back and laughs.

Olya will say: "He's earned it," and take me for a stroll in the springtime. My pants and shirt will be hidden beneath my pajamas.

"Be careful that the director doesn't notice," her older sister smiles to Olya as she opens the door.

We're going to walk slowly, very slowly, since over the past year I've grown unaccustomed to walking. Olya will hold me beneath my arms and will caution me:

"Careful, a hole... Careful, a bump..."

There in the garden's depth behind the thick bushes I'll smile at Olya and take her by the throat with both hands. Her cartilage will crumble easily. Her body, small and tender, will hang on my hands.

Maybe I'll kiss her good-bye, and maybe not.

Quickly getting changed, and leaning back on a linden tree, I'll take respite on a wall. A farewell look at the house of crazies, and — welcome, freedom!

But for now it's winter. I placidly chew my kasha, and when Olya asks about a second helping, I quickly lick her palm and say:

"He-he-he!"

Published in Ukrainian in *Chetverh* No. 5, 1993

Notes:

"...and they weren't going to drink ...until the young couple sweetens it up" — In the Ukrainian wedding tradition, the guests clang their silverware and plates until the bride and groom kiss to sweeten the wine.

"'No. Cat testicles,' answered Momma" — *Iaitsia*, the word for eggs, also means "testicles."

Oleksandr
IRVANETS

The Tale of Holian

Translated by Serhiy Zaitsev
with Jhumpa Lahiri

R ight here, please, I'll get out here. That's good, thank you. Here's some money. Go on, take it. Buy yourself a beer. These days even chickens don't lay eggs for free. Take care!"

The door slams shut and the engine starts again. Just wait for this truck to pass, then quickly cross the highway. Right into the ditch. Ditch, hitch…which is it — hitch? To hell with English words. I can never remember them all. I'll cut through the woods if I can get behind this fence and around the transformer.

"Hello! Hello! Natashka? I can't hear you very well. When did you get back? Really? I'm finally calling you. Where from? From the dorm lobby. Hello! I can't hear you again! Hello! Can you hear me now? I worked at a young pioneer camp the whole term! We had an incident there. One guy… OK, I'll tell you later. The bus stop in half an hour? See you there."

"Nice sneakers, Natashka… great brand. Your parents got them for you? A gift from him? Wow! As for my life… There's a bench, let's sit down before the bus comes. So, there was one guy in the camp who was just gorgeous! Black hair, tall, blue eyes… Dressed in all the best labels, right down to his shorts. Yes, I saw them. Is there anything wrong with that? Seryozha was his name. Please, don't interrupt, let me explain in some kind of order, though it won't come out like that anyway. He had been there since the beginning of the term, working as a sports instructor. He usually woke up early to do morning exercises with the kids, then went back to sleep until lunch time."

I can cut through the woods and save myself two kilometers. There, below that sandy mound of pines. Nobody's around. I'd love to sit down in this gray-green thicket, stretch my legs and pull out a cigarette. Here it is, a Bilomor. I bought a pack in the dining car of the Leningrad express that stops at our shabby little station for a whole four minutes. A forgotten flavor. Tastes great!

And now, behind my back, Izelina appears, still invisible. She's wearing a flimsy outfit that matches the dusty gray-green of the thicket. The sleeves droop down to her elbows, exposing tanned skinny arms that stick out like epaulettes. A worn skirt barely covers her knees. And her legs, filled with little white scratches from the weeds. The main thing, of course, is that there is a naked body beneath her clothes. Blood rushes to my head. The humming of a gadfly in the sweaty torpor of the afternoon — Izelina.

"Here's how we met. I worked in the kitchen during the first week, until they hired another shift. He arrived for lunch one day and smiled his dazzling smile — the girls just melted. Then he said, 'Let's eat, girls, 'cause I'm hungry, 'cause I missed breakfast and overslept.' Everyone rushed to serve him: one girl poured borsch in a bowl, another heaped a plate with goulash. Meanwhile he came to the kitchen window, peered through and said to me, 'Hey, darling, did you lick all the spoons yet? Give me a clean one.' I just stood there paralyzed, though generally I'm not shy. All I could manage to say was, 'Can't you eat with your fingers?' I don't know what came over me. He smiled, reached through the window, grabbed a spoon, eyed me again and walked away. On his way to the table he turned a bit and said over his shoulder, 'I only use my fingers to squeeze cuties like you.'

Gazelles and fallow deer in the green lap of the summer — Izelina. I created you so long ago I can't even remember. You've been with me ever since. You're always at hand; it's not hard to summon you. You know, Izelina, tomorrow is Saturday, a day-off in the city, or at least, a partial day-off: everybody is dressed up and groomed and holding bunches of flowers, white Volgas decorated with ribbons, wedding rings, teddy bears and dolls — all line up in front of the Registry Office; mothers-in-law fuss around, fathers-in-law look wooden in their dark suits, grooms smoke nervously and brides perspire in their bulky outfits... Tomorrow he will carry her in his arms through the Registry Office doors, after the sacred ritual, where by law, right, name and so forth... On the last step at the exit she will jump up a little; otherwise he will fail in his final burst to the finish line — she's quite hefty, with those strong legs and a body widening at the bottom — "Chess queen," he used to call her.

"That night we had a dance for the monitors in the camp, after the kids were already in bed. The music and lights were terrific. To be honest, I was exhausted — I wasn't used to working so hard. But I went to the dance anyway, wearing my Lambada blouse, you know the one I mean... Then he walked in, looking rested and cheerful — he didn't care if we were tired because he'd slept during the day. Here comes our # 3. Wait a second, I'll get the tickets. Sir, could you pass them over for validating? Thanks. When he came in I was sitting on the window-sill — I was dead tired! The next moment he started walking towards me across the dance floor. He asked bluntly, 'Can I dance with you?' What was I supposed to do? I couldn't say no. At that moment they started playing music from this American movie... They had it on tape... I can't believe I don't remember the name of the movie. The music goes like this: ta-ra-ra-ra-ra, ra-ra-ra-ra, ra-ra-ra! . . You should know! It doesn't matter, I'll remember later. So there we were, waltzing together, oblivious to the others — he was so tall and calm. Then he said, 'Doesn't your tongue ache after licking spoons all day?' I smiled and replied, 'Not just spoons, but bowls and plates, too, four hundred of them, after the first and second courses.' — 'And, of course, the glasses after the juice.' — 'That's right.' Then he put his mouth to my ear and murmured, 'Let's go for a swim in the river.' We're getting off here, Natashka, this is the Officers' Club.''

"Chess queen"... in a stalemate situation... But why? See, Izelina, see how she is surrounded by bishops and rooks — by the officers on the small plaza in front of the Registry Office? Too bad a Bilomor doesn't last very long. I can't even tell when it's out because of the long cigarette paper. Got out of the habit, since I've been smoking filter cigarettes lately. Let's move on. Behind that mound with the pine trees I can take a sandy trail traveled by no more than one or two horse carts a day. There are pines there, too, and a grassless forest that bears good mushrooms only in the fall. Somewhere among the trees is the decomposing corpse of a boar which was probably hit by a truck — the stench spread around for half a kilometer, the corpse swarming with worms. It's over now. I can't smell it anymore. The wind blows it away.

There is really nothing wrong with it — girls have to marry. It's the law of nature, so to speak. The world is big enough, there are other fish in the sea, but... But why are you lying to yourself, why are you trying to put your mind to rest? You know that what will happen tomorrow will take her away forever. And ever. Strangely enough, I don't feel the slightest urge to rush to the city and save the situation by looking for chances to steal her from the wedding procession in front of the Registry Office. Really, what could I do? Wear a black mask, burst in on a horse, snatch her from the crowd and throw her across the saddle?... Kidnapping of a Sabine woman. I don't even want to go back to the city. If it were up to me, I would stay in this forest forever. By the way, here's a good place to sit, to lie down, even — nice long grass below the track where the pines recede and make a small clearing. Where is our favorite Bilomor?

"I didn't really expect he would suggest something like that, but then I thought, 'Why not? There's nothing wrong with it!' So I said, 'OK. But let's wait a few minutes.' Yes, this is their main check-point, and the cafeteria is right behind it. You can see it from here. Hello, this is our new employee, she will be working in the cafeteria. Go on, Natashka, the Personnel Office is that way. Hurry. I'll wait for you in the locker room."

"Did you apply? But they should be thrilled. Nobody wants to commute to this suburb. A military regiment!... The name itself makes me sick... What happened where? Oh yes, in the camp... Well, after a little while I looked around to make sure nobody was watching, and we slipped outside. The camp was very quiet — probably those degenerate young pioneers weren't sleeping yet, but at least they were in their rooms. Everything was still. Not even a gust of wind, and you could smell the fragrance of pines in the air. We walked together downhill, to the hole in the fence and then to the river. It wasn't dark, because the moon was throwing shadows from the trees. Still, I was a little scared, so I held his hand. It was so tranquil. All of a sudden he said, 'Would you like to hear some poetry?' No, it wasn't 'poetry' that he said, it was 'verses.' His voice was very beautiful and ornate. I said, 'Sure, go ahead.' He recited something in Ukrainian which I didn't quite get: a guy and a girl walking through an old house looking at tapestries. There were some strange words I didn't understand and then the girl and the guy saw each other in mirrors. When he had finished reciting I said, 'As for me, I prefer Asadov. Do you know his poems?' He coughed and said hoarsely, 'I saw it coming.' No, wait, how exactly did he say it? Oh, he said, 'It was to be expected.' He was quiet for a while, then added, 'At any rate, this poet's name also starts with an A.'"

*

Our Bilomor. Urytsky factory, the so-called "Three bananas." Look, they've changed their trademark. When I got home from the army I still had a few packs with me. I was finishing the last one when I met her. What possessed me to go to that disco in the Polytechnic College? It was so stuffy, with the lights flashing and Tina Turner moaning through the speakers. I went outside for a cigarette, and there she was, standing on the steps getting some fresh air. She was wearing a red dress, and she was flushed from the heat in the room. I moved down a step, leaned against the railing, blew some air into the cigarette shell and bent it so the tobacco wouldn't get into my mouth. We didn't go back in. For about an hour we strolled in the park around the college building, and then I walked her home through an old cemetery, a historical landmark, that cuts into a new neighborhood. That's why they can't wipe it out with a bulldozer, and it's a good thing. By the fence was a long row of concrete German crosses that have survived since World War I. Behind the crosses were angels, genies and maidens wailing and mourning on the Polish tombs. The cemetery is narrow and lit by lamps on the side streets. Otherwise it would have been a little eerie. There, near one of the angels, you took her hand in yours, turned her around to face you and quickly kissed her parted lips, your teeth tapping hers.

And all this time, all this time you knew about him, but it didn't matter. In her bookcase at home, near the table, between the panes of the middle shelf, was a studio photograph of a gallant cadet with blonde hair and a pin recognizing his achievements as a first class athlete. Smiling, you asked, "A boxer?" "No, swimmer," she replied, not catching the humor and nervously looking at you with her gray eyes. At the time, the cadet was away for a month at a remote training camp, anxiously waiting for his three-week vacation before his last year in college. You spent those three weeks at your aunt's in Moldova, drinking home-made wine and taking commuter trains to Odessa to go for a swim in the sea. You happened to get back the day before he left, and out of curiosity you asked Dima Hordiychouk to give you a ride to the train station. They came by bus half an hour before his train for Riga was leaving. Dima parked right by the bus stop, and hiding your face behind a newspaper, you took a good look at him. Broad-shouldered and long-armed, he jumped off the bus, grasping a suitcase with stickers on it. Instantly he turned around and offered his free hand to help her. She leaned on him and stepped down, wearing that same red dress she wore the first time you met her. She stood by his side and put her arm through his. In no hurry, they climbed the stairs to the platform. You put the article aside and said, "Let's go, Dima." That evening you were kissing her near the mailboxes in an entrance to a high-rise apartment building.

It was she who didn't want to change things. But you're just looking for excuses. You didn't even insist that things change. Once, on a moonlit night, she explained it all: she had been dating him for a long time now, since the sixth grade; after the eighth grade he went to a cadet school, and she had given him her word. But to make the waiting shorter and easier she found you. There was no reason to be offended, she just told you the truth. You could have left then, left forever, but it was all just as she had explained. You didn't leave, though you got the hint. You only pressed her to yourself, because you'd grown used to her, and you needed those rounded shoulders, big lips, and the cool eyes of her immobile face. Then you told her about Izelina.

The Bilomor is almost out again, but I don't feel like leaving — it's so nice here in the shade, I can throw the cigarette butt into the grass and lie on my back. And there, head to head with me, lies Izelina. This time she's wearing a dark green dress — green with a tint of blue.

Then I told her about you, Izelina, because I didn't have anything to say about other women. That's why I told her about you. I had to say something...

"Well, we finally reached the river. It was absolutely quiet, and the water was still. There were algae here and there and some bushes on the bank, and the moon was shining above the pine-trees. He stood by my side and lightly touched my shoulder with his. 'This night makes me think of... what's his name?... oh, Gogol,' he said. I didn't quite understand why he said that, but I guess Gogol wrote his great works on nights like this. He lowered his face to mine and said, 'All we need is a mermaid... But that's okay, we'll have one right now...'" The next instant he called out a name to the bank across the river — it was something like Izabella or Elizaveta, some bizarre name. I didn't know what was going on, but all of a sudden I saw a girl on the opposite side. I felt strange and confused and wondered why she wasn't scared to sit in the bushes by herself at night. I'm telling you, Natashka, it was a ghost. You won't believe it, but he shouted to her, 'Come over here! Come to us!' She went down to the water, grabbing hold of some branches to keep herself from falling down. Then I saw her approaching us! She was walking on the water! No, you don't understand. Yes, really! You don't believe me, and I wouldn't have believed it myself if I hadn't seen it with my own eyes. She crossed the river, coming closer and closer, then stood smiling about a meter and a half away . She was so beautiful! Shining in white... Wearing a dark dress that glittered like water in the moonlight... Okay, Natashka, go change. We'll be together on the serving line now, I'll tell you the rest of it then..."

Two weeks ago he caught you at the entrance to your apartment building. He wasn't really spying, he was just sitting on a bench, smoking and waiting. Tired and relaxed, you were returning from a session at the gym. You were about thirty meters from the entrance when he saw you, stood up and stepped on his cigarette butt. "Let's go talk?" — "Okay, let's go..." Together you walked to the construction site of an unfinished apartment building, where he found a nook surrounded by trailers for workers. Then he quickly turned around and hit you in the face. He only got you once, because he caught you off-guard. After that you pulled yourself together and parried most of his blows. You were satisfied with your performance, but he increased the pressure, and step by step you began retreating to a wall. There he tried to kick you, but you slipped aside and he smashed his foot so hard that he saw stars. You realized that he was completely disarmed, and turning away from him and picking up your exercise bag, you rushed past the trailers and headed home without once looking back. That evening she — I guess it was she — called you and kept silent for a long time. With your shoulder you pressed the receiver to your ear and went on reading the soccer page in a newspaper. Finally you heard the short buzzes — she'd hung up. You turned off the light and, using no sheets, quickly fell asleep on top of the covers.

"Then the girl just melted into the air, that was it. Of course I was scared and asked him, whispering, 'What was it?' He said, 'Izelina.'

That's it, I remember the name finally! Then he said, 'It's all right, there's nothing to be afraid of,' and taking my hand, he led me to the water, where the bank was cleaner. 'We can swim here,' he said, and I suddenly remembered that I wasn't wearing a bathing suit. I figured it would be okay to go in my underwear, and he said it was okay, too, since he didn't have his bathing suit, either. 'I won't look', he said, so I asked him to turn away and then took off my blouse and skirt and quickly ran into the water. It was still warm after the hot day. He took off his pants and his tee-shirt and dove in. We swam to the algae and back. Everything was so still, the moon was shining and the mosquitoes were all over us. I was quite chilly when we got out of the water, so I pressed my body against his. He didn't react to me at all. I went into the bushes to wring out my underwear and got dressed. He did the same. After that I asked him, 'Should we go?' But he stood there, deep in thought, then said, 'No, wait. Can you see this spot?' He pointed to the small beach where we had just been swimming. 'Yes,' I said, and he replied, 'Remember it.' I asked, 'What for?' But he only smiled and said, 'Now let's go.'

"When we got back to the camp the dance was over. He said, 'Let's find a bench and sit for a while.' Yes, these are the meatballs we serve. What is it you don't like about them? Go see the manager, she has the list of ingredients: how much meat, how much bread. Look at him, he sniffs it, too! They're fresh, don't worry! What are you trying to smell? What a customer! What is he doing here, in the officers' cafeteria? Must be some clerk. Why doesn't he just sit in his office?"

Don't be alarmed, Izelina. I'm not thinking clearly. I'm so exhausted for some reason. This is the way it goes. Come here, give me your hand. This is what I've decided, Izelina: I'll stay here for about six weeks, until the end of the summer. What always maddens me is the thought that under your clothes...

"We don't have any more goulash. Never mind what's on the menu. We ran out because we didn't make enough. There are meatballs left, do you want any? Wait a minute, Natashka.

"These people are really getting to me. I hope it's slow until dinner. Let's get something to drink and sit down. Here's what happened next. We sat down on a bench, and I felt a bit calmer; I was even getting sleepy. But I sat and waited for him to start something… Instead he began telling me about stars and constellations, about their names and about legends in which stars merged and turned into other stars. I dozed off and yawned, then cautiously pressed myself to him, but he didn't even think to put his arm around me. Eventually he noticed that I was falling asleep and said, 'Are you sleeping, my darling? Well, I'll let you go to bed now.' He walked me to my room, and when I was about to go in he said, 'Listen, I got my pay yesterday, but I'm afraid I'll lose the money. Could you keep it for me?' He pulled an envelope out of his pocket. I didn't understand the reason for his request, but asking nothing, I took the envelope and stuck it in my skirt pocket. That was it. He left and I went to bed. We didn't even kiss. You don't believe me? Just listen to the end of the story… I actually looked inside that envelope before going to bed. There were 150 rubles in it. I put the money in my purse because I thought it would be safer there…

"The next morning they couldn't find the sports instructor in the camp. He didn't show up to conduct the morning exercises with the children; he didn't appear at lunch time and wasn't in his room. At first everybody thought he'd gone to the city for the weekend, but he couldn't have left without letting someone know… They called his apartment in the city, but he wasn't there, either. All of a sudden I remembered what he had said to me by the river the night before. I quickly washed the cups after the afternoon snack, hurried out of the cafeteria and rushed down to the river. It was a weekday, so there were no fishermen or picnickers. I crossed the meadow below the poplars to get to the beach and found a pair of pants and men's underwear near a bush by the water. Scared to death, I ran back to the camp to report to the director what I had seen, but I was so out of breath that I couldn't say anything when I saw him. Finally I managed to explain it… They all ran to the river — the director, the monitors, everybody else. You can't imagine what a turmoil it caused. The sports instructor had drowned! A rescue crew arrived, which was located on the river not far from the camp. They dove again and again, searching everywhere without finding a thing. The next day they returned, this time with the police, asked me questions, searched the river again, and again found nothing. For some reason I was afraid to tell them about the money he'd given me, so I kept it. I still have it with me. I can show you.

"But that's still not the end. A week or so later, after everybody had quieted down a little, I went home for the weekend. I stayed one day, rested a bit and came back to the camp by the last bus in the evening. It was getting dark, and I saw a taxi parked near the administration building. The yellow light in the front window was on — that meant it was in service. I passed through the gate and was walking by when I heard someone in the taxi quietly call my name. 'Are you so and so? Work in the kitchen?' 'Yes,' I answered, and stopped. A young woman wearing a red dress got out of the car. I noticed a wedding ring on her finger. 'I would appreciate if I could have a talk with you,' she said. I was surprised by her politeness and said, 'Sure. Go ahead.' She said she wanted to find out more about Serhiy. At first I didn't understand who she meant, but then I remembered. The first thing I said was that I had told the story to the director and the police a hundred times already, and that I didn't have anything new to say. I asked her who she was, if it wasn't a big secret, of course. 'It's not a secret,' she replied, 'I was his close friend and I want to understand what really happened.' I heard tears in her voice as she added, 'If you don't want to tell me, could you at least show me the place where it happened?' 'Right now?' I asked. 'Yes, now,' she said quietly. I dropped off my bag in my room and by the time we were ready to go it was pitch dark. It wasn't like the night he and I had gone to the river. Clouds covered the moon and stars. Still, she wanted to go, so we went. We had just reached the hole in the fence when all of a sudden it got very windy and started pouring. I asked her if she wanted to give up and head back, but she insisted. Ducking our heads, we ran across the meadow to the little beach. It was pouring in buckets by the time we got there, thunder, lightning, very scary! It took us about five minutes to get to the place, and after we had stood in the bushes for a while, I asked her again if she wanted to return to the camp. She said no and asked me to wait. I was wondering why we had to wait — I would have gone back alone, but I was afraid of the thunder and the dark. Just at that moment I heard someone call us from the opposite bank, but I couldn't hear clearly because of the rain and wind. We both got scared, and she said, 'Did you hear?' The next instant we saw that same girl, Izelina, walking towards us on the water. We were petrified, standing motionless in the pouring rain. The girl came closer and closer, but she was moving so slowly that it seemed to take her

263

half an hour to cross the river. Finally she stepped onto the ground, walked up to us and said right in the girl's face, 'Serhiy Holian is dead!'

"Is it dinner time already? Okay, we're coming. Can't they wait a bit?"

Published in Ukrainian in *Suchasnist* No. 5, 1994

Halyna
PAHUTIAK

To Find Yourself in a Garden

Translated by Michael M. Naydan
with Charlotte Holmes

A s a rule, gardens don't grow at train stations. But one grew here. From behind a high brick wall, branches with red apples peeked out. Only sparrows flew through the fence. If the builders had understood that poets had wings, they'd have thought up a more complicated system of defense than this wall and impenetrable steel doors. But the poets who had wings died a long time ago.

Hrytsko imagined that one warm night he'd crawl from the last train, and when he reached the station, he'd see the doors open. He'd enter the garden, lie down in the tangled fragrant grass, bend his cheek to Mother Earth, then weep and ask: "Who have I become — an unhappy tramp?"

The police from the southwestern rail line knew Hrytsko and didn't bother him. What can be taken from someone who doesn't have a house or a wife, only a haromonica and the black illness from the war? The hospital was his only refuge. The hospital and Nuska, his sister. He lived at her place for a while, but in mid-winter he bolted from her warm house and searched for the wind in the fields.

As he walked, he talked to himself. "Quiet, Nuska, quiet... The black illness will do everything in the world to a man. What have I done? I need people to see me, and I need to see them. And there are so, so many like me — even those who've never had the black sickness. And there are enough even without the black sickness. Skovoroda also wandered through the world, and is my harmonica worse than his philosophy? I'm happy that there were people like Hryhory Savych in the world. Not for everyone are walls oppressive, not for everyone..."

Hrytsko hustled through to the first car of the train. He smoked lazily in the aisle as others arrived, sat down and gazed out the windows. Then he buzzed the harmonica. The people saw a scrawny man in a green cap and wide pants. Though Hrytsko wandered aimlessly, he made sure that his clothes were clean. He stood by the first bench and, bobbing his head, began to play "In the Hills of Manchuria," then "Farewell Slavic Woman," and finally, "Neighbor Lady, Neighbor Lady, Lend Me a Sieve." These were the only songs he knew, but people threw kopecks into his cap anyway. Hrytsko said, "I kiss your hand," to everyone, even to a child, and went on to two more cars. Then he sat down on a bench, and though people asked him to play, he refused, because he was weary. When Hrytsko didn't feel like playing, he just didn't feel like playing.

Hrytsko's father had taught him to play after returning from the war minus a leg. Hrytsko already had the black sickness from the time that a German, in jest, had fired a shot over his ear to spook him. He'd had seizures ever since. After the war he began to frequent bazaars with his invalid father. His father played the harmonica, and Hrytsko collected money in an army cap. His mother couldn't bear the shame of this and died, and the old man froze to death one night as he returned, drunk, from town.

Hrytsko tried to write this sad story down on paper, but God hadn't given him Skovoroda's* talent. Only when he played his mournful harmonica did his invalid father stand before him again — in a patched cotton quilt jacket, inebriated, unshaven, with bright blue eyes. Some invalids get everything without being put on a waiting list, but nothing good ever came to his father, from the beginning of his life to the end.

Hrytsko got off the train and went to the buffet counter in the station for his favorite meal — a beer and smoked fish. When he'd eaten, he took the heads and skins with him to offer to a dog or cat; those old ladies who ran the buffet counter always stuffed their pigs with leftovers. Hrytsko didn't like the old ladies because long ago one of them had called him a beggar. People could see he wasn't a beggar. It was easier to be a crook than to play the harmonica on the train. Hrytsko had told the police of his ill fortunes and shown them his invalid's ID card, and now they mostly left him alone.

So he paced to and fro on the platform, waiting for the train. When his friend Styopa called out to him, Hrytsko pulled a handful of change from his pocket and gave it to him.

Styopa licked his moist lips. "Listen, Hryts, it's good I've run into you. Our friend Mykoltso is really weak. He'd like you to drop by." Styopa was trembling.

"What's with you? You froze?"

"Oy, I've froze, brother. Winter's coming soon."

"You should go to your mother. Maybe she needs you to chop wood."

"A-a," Styopa waved his hand, but he thought a bit and agreed. "That's the truth. She doesn't have any firewood."

"Let's go, it's on our way."

"We should have a sober up drink."

"I already had one."

"Then I'll go to her later."

Hrytsko scratched his nape. What can you do with the guy? He's a jack of all trades...

He watched as Styopa, hunched against the wind, ran to the tea counter. His back was covered with chalk dust.

"Misery," said Hrytsko. "Misery."

He left the station, picking his way over the tracks, and eventually entered a little street with leaning picket fences. Dogs looked out of their houses but didn't bark.

"I'll give these scraps to Mykoltso's dog Bosko," Hrytsko decided.

The street was to be demolished, and in its place tall brick blocks of flats would be built. The homeowners said "screw it" and had stopped painting their window frames and patching their picket fences.

"Misery," Hryts yawned, and his heart tightened as he felt the black illness approaching. The last time, it had knocked him to the pavement so hard he needed stitches on his head.

Mykoltso lived in a tiny house with one window and made a living from fixing shoes. Suddenly, he had taken ill. He was an old man, nothing strange here. But just recently he had painted the window frames and his front door white, and he spared no expense to do it.

Bosko wasn't in his dog house. Hrytsko wiped his feet on the wooden grating of Mykoltso's porch and pushed the door open. The warmth wafted onto him, and he felt weak, but managed to compose himself.

"Is the master of the house at home?" He removed his hat.

"Yes," Mykoltso answered quietly. Bosko wagged his tail, smelling Hryts's pocket. Hryts unwrapped the package and gave the dog the fish scraps.

"You didn't expect me? And I ran into Styopa... He says our Mykoltso has gotten weak."

"If he hadn't grown weak, he'd have come," Mykoltso said reproachfully, and his eyes were almost gleaming. "You warm yourself up. Even though I'm weak, I've managed to light a fire."

"Your heart?"

"Yep."

Mykoltso's limbs were bloated, almost blue. "Well, Hrytsko, let me see you. Hey, brother, take care of your shoes... If you don't fix'em, watch out, you'll need to throw 'em away."

"Don't worry!"

"I know that you're not looking at the ground, and it's carrying you..."

"You have to go to the hospital."

"If you stay, maybe I'll manage without a hospital. Play for me. Music — that'll be my medicine."

"I can play."

After the song Mykoltso sobbed like a child, then slowly wiped his nose with his hand." Things are good with you, Hryts. Live at my place. I'll die, then I'll give you the house and Bosko."

"But then they'll take me to an old folks' home!" Hrytsko said cheerfully. "That's what they told me at the hospital. They'd take me right away, and it'd be years before I get out. Or maybe I'll get married, huh?"

"Whether you're stupid or blessed, ain't nothin' like your own home. It's your sister, and wife, and mother. And I'm gonna die soon. Look..."

Mykoltso pulled back the blanket that partly covered him, and Hrytsko saw his shining, swollen legs.

"When water fills a man up, watch out. It's the end."

Hrytsko stroked Bosko's ruddy back, and the dog nuzzled his armpit with his gray snout.

"I feel bad for Bosko. The dog catchers'll take him away."

"I won't leave Bosko, you can be sure of that, Mykoltso."

"All right. But if you ever have to leave him, it would be better to take an ax and kill him."

Hrytsko shuddered. "God be with you."

"Then you won't leave him?"

"No."

"I have money in the bank. Use it for my funeral."

Hrytsko gustily played "Oy Neighbor Lady, Neighbor Lady" until his ears stung, then put down the harmonica without looking at Mykoltso, who said, "You can leave Bosko with me for a day or two if you have to go somewhere. He won't be confused. He's a smart dog."

"You know," Hrytsko said, "maybe I'll die sooner than you will. But if I go out for a while tomorrow, don't be surprised. I'll come back. I have business to do."

Mykoltso could barely swallow his saliva, but he replied, "I know what kind of business you have...you and that harmonica! It would be better if you stayed in the house. I'll help you. Maybe I won't have to go to the hospital after all. If they grab you on the street or at the train station, they'll take you to the hospital instead of me."

Hrytsko looked around the room, empty except for a table covered with an oilskin cloth, a box of shoemaking tools, and a bookcase.

"Take down *The Kobza Player** and read to me a little," Mykoltso said. "I like the way you read."

Hrytsko obediently took down the book bound in coarse leather.

"Please read the 'Perebendya'!" Mykoltso said.

At night the wind rose with rain, and Hrytso couldn't sleep. He listened to Mykola's breathing, and Bosko's, too. The walls shuddered.

"It'll knock us over yet," thought Hrytsko. He didn't know that old houses stand strong.

"The wind tears off all the apples. May it not break the branches," he thought, and remembered the garden at the station." On the other side of the wall, it doesn't blow so hard."

From the collection *Potrapyty v sad (To Find Yourself in a Garden)*, Kiev: Molod, 1989

Notes:

Hryhory Savych Skovoroda (1722–1794) — the itinerant philosopher who was called the Ukrainian Socrates

The Kobza Player — Ukrainian bard Taras Shevchenko's first book of poetry which, when it appeared in 1840, helped to define Ukraine as a nation

Author Notes

YURI ANDRUKHOVYCH was born in 1960 in Ivano-Frankivsk, Ukraine. He began publishing in literary journals in 1982. In 1985, together with Viktor Neborak and Oleksandr Irvanets, he founded the popular literary performance group "Bu-Ba-Bu" (Burlesque-Bluster-Buffoonery). This alignment was a seminal part of the literary culture of the Eighties and its members continue to be active. Andrukhovych's first book, *Sky and Squares* (poems), appeared in 1985. Military service in 1983 and 1984 inspired him to write a series of seven "army stories," which were published in 1989. The life of a soldier in the "red army" was the subject of his screenplay, "A Military March for an Angel," which was the basis for A. Donchyk's film *Oxygen*. He has published five other books: *Downtown* (1989), *Exotic Birds and Plants* (1991), *Recreations* (1992), *Moskoviada* (1993), and *Perversion* (1996). He edits, with M. Izdrik, *Thursday*, "an irregular journal of texts and visions."

NATALKA BILOTSERKIVETS discovered her muse at an early age; her poem, "A Word on Your Native Tongue," written when she was 13, became immensely popular when it was published in the late Sixties in the newspaper, *News from Ukraine*. In 1976, while still a college student, she published her first book of poetry, *Ballads of the Unconquerable*, and became the youngest member of the Ukrainian Union of Writers later that year. A song was composed to the words of her poem "We'll Not Die in Paris" by the Lviv-based band Dead Rooster and received the 1992 Chervona Ruta national music festival award. Born in the village of Kuyanivka in 1954 to a family of teachers, she received her undergraduate degree from the Philology Department at Taras Shevchenko State University. The American literary journal, *Agni*, awarded the Tkacz/Phipps translation of her poem "May," dedicated to the Chernobyl disaster, its award for the best poem published in the journal in 1992. She works as an editor at the journal *Ukrainian Culture* in Kiev, where she lives with her husband and two children.

Born in 1951 in Donetsk, VOLODYMYR DIBROVA has been, is, or will be again: a writer, translator, literary critic, and teacher. He has published two books of short stories, two plays, and a novel. His novellas *Peltse* and *Pentameron*, translated by Halyna Hryn, will be published by Northwestern University Press at the end of 1996.

VASYL HOLOBORODKO studied at universities in Kiev and Donetsk until he was expelled for "acts irreconcilable with the title of Soviet student." He subsequently served two years in the Soviet army, then worked as a coal miner and a collective farmer. He began publishing in 1963; between 1968 and 1986 he was prevented from publishing in Ukraine. His award-winning book of poems, *Green Day*, was published in 1988, followed by *Icarus with Butterfly Wings* in 1990. He was awarded the Shevchenko Prize in 1992 for *Guelder-Rose on Christmas*. His poetry has been translated into English and Portuguese, and published in Canada, Brazil, and England. Born in 1945 in eastern Ukraine, he continues to live and work in the village of his birth.

Born in a Lviv University classroom in 1961, OLEKSANDR IRVANETS gravitated naturally toward higher learning from an early age. He studied education, received a teacher's certificate, and taught school for eight years in the village of Kanonychi, before publishing two collections of poetry: *Fire in the Rain* in 1987 and *The Shadows of the Great Classicist* in 1991. He spent two months as a fellow at the Akademie Schlöss Solitude in Stuttgart, Germany and has written five plays, some of which have been performed in Kiev and Stuttgart. He left teaching in 1988 and has since worked in the theater and as a literary advisor at a newspaper.

EVHENIA KONONENKO studied mathematics and engineering at Kiev University and received her degree in 1981. In 1990, her life took a literary turn when she published, in the journal *Vsesvit (The Universe)*, a group of translations from contemporary French poets. In 1993, the French Embassy awarded her translations its Zerov Prize, and the following year she graduated from the Kiev Institute of Foreign Languages with a concentration in French. In recent years, she has published short fiction in *Vsesvit* and has completed a poetry collection, *Kievan tercets*, a book of prose, *A Hot Subject*, and a translation of a children's book. She works as an academic researcher at the Institute of Cultural Politics.

"I'm a very old man," writes OLEH LYSHEHA. "My age? A few years ago I would write one poem a year. It seemed to me, the main matter in the poem should be my soul's matter gained by a year of experience…, not a momentary burst of tears or anger, nor a day or week. I'm writing these lines on a street bench. It's October. I feel cold. In my bag are two books — *The Songs from this Earth on Turtle's Back* and another by Henry David Thoreau. God, never been to America…"

KOSTIANTYN MOSKALETS was born into a family of writers. After army service, he worked in radio broadcasting while studying at the Moscow Literary Institute, from which he graduated in 1990. He is the author of two poetry collections: *Dumy* * (1989) and *Songe du vieil pelerin* (1994). His novels *Where Am I to Go?* and *A Crowning Experience* have been published in journals, together with numerous stories, essays, and translations. He has also performed his own songs in numerous productions of the theatrical group, "*Ne zhurys!*" (Don't Worry!). He has lived since 1991 in his native village of Matviyivka.

"I write about 'the country between light and dark'," writes HALYNA PAHUTIAK, who loves re-reading Richard Bach, Hesse, and medieval Latin writers for literary inspiration. "When I communicate with children, write or read, I come to terms with reality, with which it is a tough business to find a common language. Skovoroda taught me not to contribute to the evil in the world. There are also ways of preventing it. Enough." She has published four books of prose: *Children, Master, Getting into the Orchard*, and *Wild Mustard Seed*. She has also published a novella, *The Sun*, set in the small provincial town of Urozh. Born in 1958 in the Lviv region, she graduated with a degree in Ukrainian Philology from Kiev University.

YEVHEN PASHKOVSKY felt compelled to leave Ukraine for health reasons following the accident at the Chernobyl nuclear power plant. During this period he traveled widely across the Soviet Union and returned to Ukraine only after independence had been declared. His literary debut was in 1988 in the anthology, *Sails* (Kiev). He is the author of several novels, including *Holiday* (Dnipro, 1989), *Wolf's Star* (Molod, 1991), *Abyss* (in *Suchasnist*, 1992) and *Autumn for the Angel* (published serially in various journals, 1994). He was born in 1962 in the Zhytomyr Region and has worked at various jobs in Ukraine and Russia.

Since 1985, SOLOMEA PAVLYCHKO has been working as a research associate of the Institute of Literature, Ukrainian Academy of Sciences. Since 1992, she has headed the editorial board of Osnovy Publishers, Kiev. She has written three monographs in the field of American and English literature, and numerous articles on Ukrainian and Western

---

Dumy — Ukrainian epic tales, mostly about Turkish or Tartar captivity, dating back to the 17th century and performed to the accompaniment of the *bandura*, the Ukrainian national instrument.

literatures, the women's movement, and feminism. The drastic political and social changes she witnessed during Ukraine's struggle for independence were the subject of her book, *Letters from Kiev* (St. Martin's Press, 1992). "There was a burst of political ideas and identities; political life became so intense and life changed so drastically that I felt compelled to put everything down and not forget it because it was what was happening to Ukraine," she said. She has translated into Ukrainian D.H. Lawrence's *Lady Chatterly's Lover*, and William Golding's *Lord of the Flies*. She has also edited Ukrainian editions of poetry collections by T.S. Eliot and Emily Dickinson. She admits to having a longstanding attraction to American literature and chose it as her major at university. "It was quite inexplicable at the time because it was during the Cold War."

Born in 1939, VALERY SHEVCHUK is one of the most respected contemporary novelists in Ukraine. During the 1970's he translated medieval and Baroque Ukrainian literature into modern Ukrainian. He has published many novels, including *Naberezhna 12 (12 The Esplanade*, 1968), *Vechir sviatoi oseni (A Blessed Autumn Evening*, 1969), *Na poli smyrennomu (On a Submissive Field)*, *Dim na hori (The House on the Hill*, 1983), *Try lystky za viknom (Three Leaves Outside the Window)*, and a short story collection, *Kryk pivnia na svitanku (Cockcrow at Dawn*, 1979).

YURI VYNNYCHUK takes his name from an uncle who was killed by the secret police in 1941. In 1973, he completed the Stanislav Pedagogical Institute where he developed a reputation as a prankster. He became involved in student publications and the *samizdat* underground. By 1973 he had become a target of the KGB. His writing was blacklisted from official publications and his house was searched in an attempt to find incriminating evidence. The search proved a failure, but for fear of his safety, he went underground in Lviv, a city in western Ukraine. He chronicled his adventures during these years in his book, *Divy nochi (Ladies of the Night*, 1992), which caused a sensation among young Ukrainian readers. In 1987, Vynnychuk created a stage singing group called *"Ne zhurys!"* (Don't Worry!) which became an overnight success in Ukraine and toured the U.S. and Canada two years later. While residing on the periphery of the Ukrainian literary establishment he continues to publish his own work, and edits and writes for the Lviv newspaper *Post-Postup*.

"Language — any language — that's what I would call the capital love of my life: nothing else has the power to synthesize music and myth, two things without which the world would be a totally unliveable place," writes OKSANA ZABUZHKO. A Fulbright scholar in the U.S. in 1994, she resides in Kiev and works as a scholar for the Ukrainian Academy of Sciences. Prolific both as a scholar and as a poet, she cites *Winnie the Pooh* (read at age 4) and *Hamlet* (read at age 14) as the great literary influences of her life. "Since then, no more crucial literary influences, other than numerous 'literary sisterhoods' with a very strong feeling of kinship, across epochs and languages — with Marina Tsvetaeva, Sylvia Plath, and Ingeborg Bachman." Since 1985, she has published three books of poetry: *May Hoarfrost* (1985), *The Conductor of the Last Candle* (1990), and *Hitchhiking* (1994). Translations of her poetry have appeared in *Agni, Poetry Miscellany, Harvard Review,* and *International Poetry Review.* In 1996, she published a novel, *Field Research in Ukrainian Sex,* which has become a controversial bestseller in Ukraine and has "inflicted upon me a boisterous fame of either 'enfant terrible' or 'femme fatale' of Ukrainian literature." Her scholarly work includes a translation of Sylvia Plath's poetry into Ukrainian and *The Chronicles of Fortinbras* (forthcoming). *A Kingdom of Fallen Statues: Poems and Essays,* her first book in English translation, has been published by Wellspring (Toronto, 1996).

"I am the biggest living writer in Ukraine," claims 300-pound BOHDAN ZHOLDAK, who also boasts of having lived several lives — all in Ukraine. Born into a family of writers in 1948, he studied at Shevchenko State University in Kiev, taught Ukrainian language and literature, then directed a children's film studio until 1978, when he began more actively to write prose and drama. His plays *Who'll Betray Brutus?, How the Cossack Mamai Achieved Immortality, The Fairy Tale about How, or the Cossack Mamai and the Scythian Idol,* and *The Devil in Love* are performed throughout Ukraine. His short stories were published widely in newspapers and periodicals up until 1991, when he published a collection, *Temptations.* After the devastation of the publishing industry following independence in 1991, he published at his own expense the collection, *Macabresques.* Drastic paper shortages forced him back to the screen and he wrote a series of screenplays, including *The Zaporozhian Cossack Beyond the Danube, The Cossacks Are Coming,* and *Ivan the Mare.* When the government went on to wreck the film industry he turned to television where he now makes children's cartoons and hosts the TV program, *Artistic Casino.* He also works as an editor at the "Ros" film studio and teaches filmscript writing. Three marriages to the same wife have yielded just one child.

Translators

JAMES BRASFIELD is currently translating a play and selected poems by Oleh Lysheha, whom he calls "the poet's poet of Ukraine." Though Lysheha's reputation is "legendary" in Ukraine, Brasfield writes, he was forbidden from publishing his work from 1972 to 1988. "A dissident, he was expelled from Lviv State University for work published in the university literary magazine and was forced into the Soviet army where he was a manual laborer near Moscow and was soon sent into exile in Buryatia." Brasfield's translation of Lysheha's work is forthcoming in *The Literary Review*. He earned his MFA from Columbia where he studied poetry and translation with Joseph Brodsky, Derek Walcott, Daniel Halpern, Stanley Kunitz, Charles Wright, and Stanley Plumly. He served as an editorial assistant for poetry at *The Paris Review*, has published poetry in several journals, and translations in *Cutbank, International Poetry Review*, and *Talisman*. His first full-length collection of poems is under consideration at contests and presses.

PETER HO DAVIES read English at Cambridge University and received a Masters degree in Creative Writing from Boston University. His short fiction has appeared in *Agni, Antioch Review, Greensboro Review*, and *Harvard Review* and has been anthologized in *Best American Short Stories, (1995 & 1996)*. New work is forthcoming in *Story* and the *Paris Review*. His short story collection, *The Ugliest House in the World*, will be published by Houghton Mifflin next year. Born in Britain, he has been a fellow at the Fine Arts Work Center in Provincetown, Mass. and currently teaches at Emory University in Atlanta.

JHUMPA LAHIRI has published her stories in *Story Quarterly, Harvard Review*, and *New Letters*. In addition to her work on "The Tale of Holian," Ms. Lahiri has translated into English stories of the Bengali writer, Ashapurna Devi.

"The challenge in translating Natalka Bilotserkivets' poems for me lies not only in wrestling with the sound of sense transferred from one language to another," writes Ukrainian-American poet DZVINIA ORLOWSKY, "but, more importantly, in re-creating a sense of awakening, each poem culminating into one essential new voice—cautious, yet defiant, arousing and stubborn of heart." Orlowsky is a founding editor of Four Way Books and a contributing editor to *Agni* and *The Marlboro*

Review. She has published a poetry chapbook, *Burying Dolls* (Minatoby Press), and *A Handful of Bees* (Carnegie Mellon University Press, 1994).

GEORGE PACKER has published a memoir about Africa, *The Village in Waiting*, and a novel, *The Half Man.* His essays, journalism and reviews have appeared in the *New York Times, Dissent, Vogue, Doubletalk,* and elsewhere.

CHARLOTTE HOLMES directs the MFA Program at Pennsylvania State University. In 1994, she lived in Kiev while her husband, poet James Brasfield, worked there as a Fulbright scholar. Her collection, *Gifts and Other Stories,* was published in 1994 by Confluence Press. Her stories have appeared in *Antioch Review, Carolina Quarterly, Grand Street, The New Yorker,* and elsewhere.

The late VOLODYMYR HRUSZKEWYCZ was born in Ukraine, and studied literature at Wayne State University in Michigan. He has translated and published Ukrainian dissident prose and poetry. He worked as an engineering draftsman and graphic artist, and was also a photographer and printmaker.

ASSYA HUMESKY was born in Kharkiv, Ukraine in 1925; she and her family were exiled from Ukraine by Soviet authorities in 1934. In 1943, she was seized by German occupying forces and transported to Austria, where she did forced labor for two years. She emigrated to the United States in 1948, and now lives in Ann Arbor, where she is Professor of Russian and Ukrainian Language and Literature at the University of Michigan. Humesky translated *The Rainbow Bridge*, the poetry of poet/sculptor Mirtala, from Russian to Ukrainian, published in two editions: Ukrainian Writers' Association — Slovo (New York, 1976) and Ukrainsky pysmennyk (Kiev, 1992).

LISA SAPINKOPF won the 1992 *Quarterly Review of Literature* Contest, the 1991 American Translators Association Contest, the Columbia Translation Center Award, the British Comparative Literature Association Contest 2nd Prize, the Fernando Pessoa Prize, and the Robert Fitzgerald Translation Prize, and grants from the Witter Bynner and Wheatland foundations. She co-translated and edited *Clay and Star: Contemporary Bulgarian Poets* (Milkweed Editions, 1992), and her translation of Yves Bonnefoy's *Beginning and End of Snow* was published in the *Quarterly Review of Literature* Poetry Series in 1992. Her work has appeared in over fifty journals in the U.S., Canada, and Great Britain, including *American Poetry Review*, *Poetry*, *Paris Review* and *Partisan Review*. Her translation of Zabuzhko's poem, "Clytemnestra," published in *Agni*, was chosen as one of the "Best of 1994" by the *Review of Literary Magazines*.

ELIZABETH SEARLE is the author of *My Body to You*, a story collection that won the 1992 Iowa Short Fiction Prize. Her fiction has been published in *Ploughshares*, *Kenyon Review*, and *Boulevard*, as well as in other magazines and anthologies.

LLOYD SCHWARTZ is co-director of the Creative Writing Program at the University of Massachusetts, Boston, and a regular commentator on NPR's "Fresh Air." For his articles on classical music in the *Boston Phoenix*, he received the 1994 Pulitzer Prize for criticism. He edited *Elizabeth Bishop and Her Art*, and his most recent book of poems is *Goodnight, Gracie*.

A chapter from M.T. SHARIF's novel, *The Public Death of Doctor Amin*, was featured in the Fall 1995 issue of *Agni*. He has published stories in *Antioch Review* and *Best American Short Stories*.

"I have lived in several countries and cultures and have several loves and loyalties," writes CHRISTINE SOCHOCKY, the daughter of political refugees who left Ukraine in 1944. "Being an immigrant kid has, or rather, gives one rights to particular problems and neuroses. There are also particular joys." She grew up in Quebec, and settled in Pittsburgh for 25 years before returning to the city where she was raised. She resides in Beaconsfield, Quebec with her husband and two children and works as a teacher and librarian.

DEBRA SPARK edited the influential anthology, *Twenty Under Thirty* (Scribner's, 1986, 1996). She is the author of a novel, *Coconuts for the Saint* (Faber and Faber, 1995; Avon, 1996).

LARISSA SZPORLUK teaches in the Women's Studies Program at Bowling Green State University. Her first collection of poetry, *Prowler's Universe*, was published in 1996 by Graywolf Press.

MYROSIA STEFANIUK, born in Ukraine, came to the U.S. via Displaced Persons camps in Austria at the close of World War II. She has published several collections of Ukrainian poetry in translation, including *Icarus with Butterfly Wings*, poems of Vasyl Holoborodko

(Toronto: Exile Editions, 1991) and *Shifting Borders: East European Poetries of the Eighties*, poetry of Bilotserkivets, Lysheha, and Holoborodko (Fairleigh Dickinson University Press, 1993). She co-translated, with Volodymyr Hruszkewycz, *Documented Persecution, 1975–80* (Smoloskyp, 1980). Stefaniuk teaches cultural and physical geography at Wayne State University.

VIRLANA TKACZ and WANDA PHIPPS have been translating Ukrainian poetry since 1989. Their work has appeared in *Agni, Modern Poetry in Translation, Visions International, Index on Censorship*, and *Beacons*. They were awarded the Agni Translation Prize for Poetry and the National Theatre Translation Fund Award for their work on the classic verse drama, *The Forest Song*. Poet Wanda Phipps was recipient of a New York Foundation for the Arts poetry fellowship. Virlana Tkacz heads the Yara Arts Group, which is a resident company of the La Mama Experimental Theatre in New York. She has also directed shows at Brooklyn Academy of Music's Next Wave Festival in Rio de Janeiro, Kiev and Amsterdam.

JESSICA TREADWAY has published a collection of short stories called *Absent without Leave*, which received the John C. Zacharis First Book Award in 1993. She teaches at Tufts University and Emerson College.

SERHIY ZAITSEV has taught courses of Ukrainian language and culture at Pennsylvania State University and is presently an Assistant Professor of English at Chernivtsi State University, Ukraine.

Editors

ED HOGAN brings 25 years of publishing experience to this project, beginning with his founding of the literary magazine, *Aspect* (1969–80). He cofounded Zephyr Press in 1980, and was project director for Zephyr's landmark edition of *The Complete Poems of Anna Akhmatova*. For the past four years he has collaborated with Natasha Perova (Moscow) and, more recently, Arch Tait (Birmingham, U.K.) in the publication of *Glas: New Russian Writing*.

ASKOLD MELNYCZUK founded *The Agni Review*, one of America's most vital and enduring literary journals, in 1972. In recent years, he has broadened *Agni*'s mission and influence by devoting increasing attention to 20th century literature in translation with special attention to writers of Eastern Europe, Ukraine, and Russia, many of whom have been published in his journal for the first time in English translation. He has also been recognized as a poet and novelist. His poetry has appeared in over 35 magazines, including *The Village Voice, Ploughshares, Chelsea, Poetry, Grand Street, The Boston Review,* and *Index on Censorship.* Seamus Heaney called his *What is Told* (1994) "a great novel of unresentful sorrow and half-requited loss." It was named a Notable Book of the Year by the *New York Times Book Review.*

Scholar and translator MICHAEL NAYDAN has widely published translations of Russian, Ukrainian, and Romanian literature. His books include *Selected Poetry of Lina Kostenko* (Ukrainian; Garland, 1990), *Posle rossii/After Russia,* a bilingual edition of Russian poet Marina Tsvetayeva (Ardis, 1992), and *Selected Writings of Grigory Skovoroda: Philosopher and Poet.* His translations have also appeared in many journals, including *Kenyon Review, Delos, Agni Review, Nimrod, Denver Quarterly,* and the *New York Times Book Review.* He has been awarded the Pushkin Prize for Best Translation of Russian Poetry from Columbia University (1975, 1976, and 1981), and received the Eugene Kayden Meritorious Award in Translation from the University of Colorado for his translation of Ukrainian poet Attila Mohylny. He is editor of *Slavic and East European Journal,* and associate editor of *Comparative Literature Studies.*

Writer and journalist MYKOLA RIABCHUK is deputy editor of the Kiev-based journal *Vsesvit (The Universe),* and author of three books and dozens of articles published in Ukrainian, Russian, Polish, Hungarian, British, American, Latvian, and Bulgarian periodicals. Born in 1953 in the city of Lutsk, he was a technological student at the Lviv Polytechnical Institute from 1970–73, until he was expelled for "undesirable political contacts" and for publishing *Skrynia (The Chest),* a *samizdat* literary magazine. This forced him to interrupt his education for over a decade and take whatever jobs he could get. Only in 1988, during perestroika, did he graduate from the Gorky Literary Institute in Moscow. Since 1990, he has frequently lectured and participated in conferences in the U.S. He co-authored (with Zbigniew Rau) *The Re-emergence of Civil Society in Eastern Europe and the Soviet Union* (Westview Press, 1991) and (with Michael Kennedy) *Envisioning Eastern Europe* (University of Michigan Press, 1994).

OKSANA ZABUZHKO: Please see Author Notes.

eXchanges

(a journal of translation)

issue No. 7 available
September 1996

all queries concerning submissions
or subscriptions should be addressed to:
Christopher Mattison
Translation Laboratory
123 N. Linn St. Brewery Square
The University of Iowa Iowa City, IA 52242
(319) 335-2002 /2004   Fax: (319) 335-3417
email: christopher-mattison@uiowa.edu
http://www.uiowa.edu/~translab/exchanges.html

SLAVIC AND EAST EUROPEAN JOURNAL

A quarterly publication of the American Association of Teachers of Slavic and East European Languages, *SEEJ* publishes articles on Slavic and East European literatures and linguistics, on language pedagogy, and reviews of new books in these fields.

The Journal is received by all members of AATSEEL. Subscriptions may also be entered by non-members and institutions.

- Annual AATSEEL membership fees: administrators, full and associate professors, and non-academic members – $35; assistant professors, instructors, lecturers – $25; secondary school teachers – $20; sustaining members – $50; students, emeriti, unemployed – $15; joint membership (spouses: two listings, one set of publications) – $40.
- Libraries and institutions may purchase *SEEJ* for $50 per year.
- Single copies are $15.00 for libraries/$7.50 for individuals.

Subscription correspondence to:	*Submissions and other correspondence to:*
Prof. George Gutsche, Executive Secretary-Treasurer of AATSEEL Dept. of Russian and Slavic Languages University of Arizona Tuscon, AZ 85721 USA (phone: 602-621-7341) (FAX: 602-621-8885)	Prof. Michael Naydan, Editor of *SEEJ* Dept. of Slavic and East European Languages The Pennsylvania State University 211 Sparks Building University Park, PA 16802 USA (phone: 814-865-1352) (FAX: 814-865-1675) (Bitnet: MMN3@PSUADMIN) (Internet: MMN3@OAS.PSU.EDU)

HARVARD UKRAINIAN STUDIES

Vol. XVII No. 3–4

articles by

GEORGE GRABOWICZ
on Kostomarov and the Reception of Ševčenko

DAVID FRICK
on the Circulation of Information about Ivan Vyhovs'kyj

VLADIMIR OREL
on Old Slavic Graffiti of Kyiv

CLAIRE LE FEUVRE
on the Birchbark Letters of Novgorod

documents:

Simjaon Polacki's letters to Varlaam Jasyns'kyj (1664–
1670), with a commentary by PETER A. ROLLAND

a letter from Mykola Kostomarov to Pëtr A. Valuev of 23
July 1863, with a commentary by DAVID SAUNDERS

and book reviews by Daniel Kaiser, Mark von Hagen,
Hiroaki Kuromiya, Henry Abramson, and others

*Available from the Ukrainian Research Institute, 1583 Massachusetts
Avenue, Cambridge MA 02138 for $18.00 North America ($20.00
overseas); full volume (incl. No. 1–2) for $28.00 North America
($32.00 overseas).*

PELTSE and PENTAMERON

Volodymyr Dibrova

TRANSLATED BY HALYNA HRYN

First English-language publication

In these two novellas, Volodymyr Dibrova tells the story of how the Soviet system was sustained by individuals who never truly chose to support it but simply lacked the courage to oppose it. Both funny and alarming, *Peltse* portrays the formation of an average apparatchik, while *Pentameron* presents one day in the lives of five colleagues in a Soviet research institute, trapped by a system that has emasculated their ability to act decisively.

"Dibrova is the best young prose writer in Ukraine today."
— Roman Koropeckyj, UCLA

CL: ISBN 0-8101-1219-1 • $39.95
PB: ISBN 0-8101-1237-X • $14.95

RUDOLF

Marian Pankowski

TRANSLATED BY JOHN MASLEN & ELIZABETH MASLEN

First English-language publication

WRITINGS FROM AN UNBOUND EUROPE

In the 1930's, Rudolf, the son of Germans living in Poland, rebelled against the expectations of both his parents and of Polish society by leading an openly gay life in Paris. Now an old man, Rudolf tells his story to "the author," a middle-aged professor and survivor of Nazi death camps. The novel unfolds as Rudolf attempts to convince the author — and himself — that his choices were good ones.

Marian Pankowski was born in Poland in 1919, but has lived in emigration since 1945.

CL: ISBN 0-8101-1417-8 • $39.95
PB: ISBN 0-8101-1418-6 • $14.95

NORTHWESTERN UNIVERSITY PRESS

Also Available
ESTONIAN SHORT STORIES
Editors: Kajar Pruul & Darlene Reddaway
The first anthology of Estonian short prose from the 1970s and 1980s
CL: ISBN 0-8101-1240-X • $39.95
PB: ISBN 0-8101-1241-8 • $14.95

Available from your bookseller or from:
Northwestern University Press • Chicago Distribution Center
11030 South Langley Avenue, Chicago, IL 60628
(800) 621-2736 • Fax: (800) 621-8476
Postage & handling: $3.50 first book, $.75 each additional book
MasterCard & Visa Orders Accepted

Glas: New Russian Writing
Highlights from the first 13...

A Will and a Way (#13), Feb. 1997: Our second focus on women writers features Ludmilla Petrushevskaya, Dina Rubina, Larissa Miller, Maria Arbatova and others...$13.95
(U.K. prices listed below)

From Three Worlds: New Ukrainian Writing (#12): $13.95; cloth edition $21.

Captives (#11): "The Captive of the Caucasus," a brilliant story by Vladimir Makanin, and works by Georgy Vladimov, Yevgeny Fyodorov, Vassily Aksyonov and others, on the emigré, eternally a captive of his native land and Soviet past ...$13.95

Booker Winners & Others – II (#10): Our second sampling of the shortlisted authors for the Russian Booker Novel Prize features an excerpt by 1994 winner Bulat Okudzhava, and Asar Eppel, Yuri Buida, Mikhail Levitin, Alexei Slapovsky and more...$13.95

The Scared Generation (#9): Two short novels, *The Old Arbat,* by Boris Yampolsky, and Vasil Bykov's *Manhunt,* testify to the traumas that shaped the lives of the Sixties generation...$11.95

Love Russian Style (#8): A fresh look at the vagaries of the human heart, with works by Sigizmund Krziszanowsky, Ergali Ger, Sergei Task, Nina Gabrielian and others...$10.95

Booker Winners & Others (#7): Features authors short-listed for the first Russian Booker Novel Prize: Makanin, Astafiev, Yermakov, Ulitskaya and Lipkin...$9.95

Jews & Strangers (#6): "A must read for anyone who wants to understand the complicated situation of Russia's Jews" *(Forward).* Nina Sadur, Vassily Grossman, Nikolai Leskov, Evgeny Rein...$9.95

Other Available Issues: *Bulgakov and Mandelstam (#5)* • *Love and Fear (#4)* • *Women's View (#3)...* each $9.95. *Soviet Grotesque (#2)* • *Inaugural Issue (#1)...*each $8.95.

U.K. prices (each issue): £11.99 for individuals, £14.99 for institutions, post-paid. Add £6 for payments not in British pounds.

See inside front cover for addresses and subscription information. For single issues, add $2 for postage (North America orders only).